Praise for *Clearing the Hurdles*

"This book is a must read if women are going to overcome the money hurdles that can limit their growth. It helps women navigate through the myriad options and alternatives available to them and identifies many that they are not currently seeking."

—Teri Cavanagh, Senior Vice President
Director, Women Entrepreneurs' Connection
Fleet Bank

"Women setting out to organize and finance a new venture encounter all the same hurdles as men, but they often perceive the bar is set higher. This book considers all the reasons for this and offers sound advice on how female entrepreneurs can think strategically, build credibility, obtain venture capital, and realize their dreams of growth and success."

—Jack Gill, Co-founder and General Partner
Vanguard Ventures

"This is the definitive book for women who aspire to lead growing enterprises and for institutional decision-makers who recognize the power and potential of this economic segment. The authors understand the 'gut-level' decisions that an entrepreneur must make, and they combine quality research and practical recommendations to help every entrepreneur make informed choices to turn her 'biggest dreams into reality.'"

—Sharon G. Hadary, Executive Director
Center for Women's Business Research

"...absolutely first-rate, and God knows we need this, and we need it *now*! ...a dispassionate and clear-eyed look at the State of Women-Owned Businesses, a topic that's been hotly debated but poorly researched for more than two decades now. This should become the bible for anyone thinking about starting a business, anyone teaching entrepreneurship, anyone involved in economic development, anyone involved in financing young emerging companies—which means just about everyone."

—George Gendron, Entrepreneur-in-Residence at Clark University
and at the Kauffman Foundation; former Editor-in-Chief, *Inc*. Magazine

"Women entrepreneurs face many challenges during the development of their businesses. This book provides tools by which they can transform those challenges into opportunities. It provides useful information for various stages of a company's development, whether a startup enterprise or a more mature company."

—Lillian Lincoln Lambert
founder, Centennial One, Inc.

"Even in the 21st century, much of the world still systematically excludes 50% of the smartest people from full responsibility. Entrepreneurship rewards excellence and results, not gender, and this book is a wonderful gift to women who would like to respond to corporate America by saying, 'Thanks, I'll do it myself.'"

—Jim Collins, author of *Good to Great* and co-author *Built to Last*

"Savvy and inspirational, *Clearing the Hurdles* is an important book for women intent on growing new businesses. The team of talented authors provides information, insights, and advice that will educate, motivate, and challenge women aspiring to become successful entrepreneurs."

—Laura Tyson, Dean
London Business School

"With women creating new businesses at a faster rate than males, it is imperative that today's venture capitalists take an active role in mentoring and recruiting women to become venture capitalists, business owners, technologists, entrepreneurs, and government leaders. *Clearing the Hurdles* is not only a wake up call; it is a road map to start this long overdue project."

—Mark Heesen, President
National Venture Capital Association

"*Clearing the Hurdles* examines all elements behind the lack of access to capital for women entrepreneurs who want to build high growth companies. If you are a woman who has a vision for a high potential business, this book was written for you."

—Connie Duckworth, Kathy Elliott, Sharon Whiteley,
founders 8Wings Enterprises and authors of *The Old Girls Network:
Insider Advice for Women Building Businesses in a Man's World*

"*Clearing the Hurdles* debunks the myths and defines the barriers that entrepreneurs confront—a perfect roadmap for women embarking on the entrepreneurial journey."

—Kay Koplovitz, Founder, USA Networks, former Chair
National Women's Business Council

Clearing the Hurdles

Women Building
High-Growth Businesses

FT Prentice Hall
FINANCIAL TIMES

In an increasingly competitive world, it is quality
of thinking that gives an edge—an idea that opens new
doors, a technique that solves a problem, or an insight
that simply helps make sense of it all.

We work with leading authors in the various arenas
of business and finance to bring cutting-edge thinking
and best learning practice to a global market.

It is our goal to create world-class print publications
and electronic products that give readers
knowledge and understanding which can then be
applied, whether studying or at work.

To find out more about our business
products, you can visit us at www.ft-ph.com

Pearson
Education

Clearing the Hurdles

Women Building
High-Growth Businesses

Candida G. Brush
Nancy M. Carter
Elizabeth J. Gatewood
Patricia G. Greene
Myra M. Hart

FINANCIAL TIMES

An Imprint of PEARSON EDUCATION
Upper Saddle River, NJ • New York • London • San Francisco • Toronto • Sydney
Tokyo • Singapore • Hong Kong • Cape Town • Madrid
Paris • Milan • Munich • Amsterdam

www.ft-ph.com

A CIP catalog record for this book can be obtained from the Library of Congress

Editorial/Production Supervisor: *MetroVoice Publishing Services*
Executive Editor: *Jim Boyd*
Editorial Assistant: *Linda Ramagnano*
Marketing Manager: *Martin Litkowski*
Manufacturing Manager: *Alexis Heydt-Long*
Cover Design: *Nina Scuderi*
Cover Design Director: *Jerry Votta*
Series Design: *Gail Cocker-Bogusz*
Full-Service Project Manager: *Anne R. Garcia*

© 2004 Pearson Education, Inc.
Publishing as Financial Times Prentice Hall
Upper Saddle River, New Jersey 07458

The publisher offers excellent discounts on this book when ordered in quantity
for bulk purchase or special sales. For more information, contact:

**U.S. Corporate and Government Sales, 1-800-382-3419, corpsales@pearsontechgroup.com.
For sales outside of the U.S., please contact: International Sales, 1-317-581-3793,
international@pearsontechgroup.com.**

Printed in the United States of America

First Printing

ISBN 0-13-111201-5

Pearson Education Ltd.
Pearson Education Australia PTY, Limited
Pearson Education Singapore, Pte. Ltd
Pearson Education North Asia Ltd
Pearson Education Canada, Ltd.
Pearson Educación de Mexico, S.A. de C.V.
Pearson Education—Japan
Pearson Education Malaysia, Pte. Ltd

FINANCIAL TIMES PRENTICE HALL BOOKS

For more information, please go to www.ft-ph.com

Business and Technology

Sarv Devaraj and Rajiv Kohli
The IT Payoff: Measuring the Business Value of Information Technology Investments

Nicholas D. Evans
Business Agility: Strategies for Gaining Competitive Advantage through Mobile Business Solutions

Nicholas D. Evans
Business Innovation and Disruptive Technology: Harnessing the Power of Breakthrough Technology…for Competitive Advantage

Nicholas D. Evans
Consumer Gadgets: 50 Ways to Have Fun and Simplify Your Life with Today's Technology…and Tomorrow's

Faisal Hoque
The Alignment Effect: How to Get Real Business Value Out of Technology

Thomas Kern, Mary Cecelia Lacity, and Leslie P. Willcocks
Netsourcing: Renting Business Applications and Services Over a Network

Ecommerce

Dale Neef
E-procurement: From Strategy to Implementation

Economics

David Dranove
What's Your Life Worth? Health Care Rationing…Who Lives? Who Dies? Who Decides?

David R. Henderson
The Joy of Freedom: An Economist's Odyssey

Jonathan Wight
Saving Adam Smith: A Tale of Wealth, Transformation, and Virtue

Entrepreneurship

Oren Fuerst and Uri Geiger
From Concept to Wall Street: A Complete Guide to Entrepreneurship and Venture Capital

David Gladstone and Laura Gladstone
Venture Capital Handbook: An Entrepreneur's Guide to Raising Venture Capital, Revised and Updated

Erica Orloff and Kathy Levinson, Ph.D.
The 60-Second Commute: A Guide to Your 24/7 Home Office Life

Jeff Saperstein and Daniel Rouach
Creating Regional Wealth in the Innovation Economy: Models, Perspectives, and Best Practices

Management

To our parents who gave us the confidence to step across boundaries:

Barney and Juliette M. Greer

Bernie and Darleen Hoerle

Henry and Nell Vogl

Eugene and Nancy Kramer

John and Jane Maloney

To our partners in life who encourage us to soar, but also keep us grounded:

David Brush

Greg Carter

John Bates

Ken Greene

Kent Hewitt

and, to our children, heroes and heroines of the future:

Julie, Lucy, and Emily

Matt, Jason, Sonja, and Lauri

Jennifer and Nathaniel

Ken, Jr., Kevin, and Shaun

Holly, Jeanne, and Rick

ACKNOWLEDGMENTS

We thank the many women and men who supported this research project:

The women entrepreneurs and venture capitalists who provided us with their personal perspectives.

Our colleagues in academe:

Dr. Teresa Amabile (Harvard Business School)
Mr. Magnus Aronsson (ESBRI)
Dr. John Sibley Butler (University of Texas at Austin)
Dr. Jeanne Buckeye (University of St. Thomas)
Dr. Frank Hoy (University of Texas–El Paso)
Dr. James E. Post (Boston University)
Mr. Peter Russo (Boston University)
Dr. Howard Stevenson (Harvard Business School)

Professionals serving female entrepreneurs:

Denise Brousseau
Trish Costello
Sharon Hadary
Amy Millman
Andrea Silbert

Organizations that supported the research:

Babson College
Boston University
Harvard Business School
Indiana University
University of St. Thomas

Entrepreneurship and Small Business Research Institute
   ESBRI–Stockholm, Sweden
Ewing Marion Kauffman Foundation, Kansas City, MO
United States Small Business Administration Office of Advocacy

Center for Women's Business Research
National Women's Business Council
Springboard Enterprises

Manuscript Support

Grace Zimmerman, Mary Pat Hinckley, Mary Gardner & Beth Goldstein who all commented and read the manuscript pre-publication.

CONTENTS

xiii

PREFACE

*Why do we care so passionately about women and
high-growth enterprises? Because entrepreneurship is a
driving force in the growth and prosperity of the nation.
Because entrepreneurs create innovative products, provide
new jobs, and gain substantial financial rewards for themselves
and their partners in the process. And especially because,
for women, there is a significant gap between the number who
start new ventures and the number who are able to achieve
high growth and substantial success.*

Entrepreneurs as Heroes...

You know their names today, even though they made their mark 100 years
ago and more. Cornelius Vanderbilt (railroads), Andrew Carnegie (steel),
John D. Rockefeller (oil), Marshall Field (retailing), and Henry Ford
(automobiles) left an enduring legacy of innovation, market dominance,

and vast fortunes. They are among a handful of extraordinary entrepreneurs who not only achieved great wealth, but also won international celebrity. Whether you think of them as robber barons or heroes, these men who developed railroads, steel, oil, large-scale retailing, and automobiles continue to have a star quality associated with their names more than a century later.

The creation of new ventures is deeply embedded in our American heritage. The exciting part is that it is even more vibrant and widespread today than it was in the days of Rockefeller, Field, and Ford. Ever-expanding technology, support from government policy and regulations, and the redefinition of corporate America in the 1980s and 1990s made the United States a hotbed of innovation and new venture creation. Entrepreneurs, armed with promising new business concepts, lured by vast new market opportunities, and convinced of huge financial payoffs, launched millions of new ventures in the past 20 years. That they did so in an environment rich with resources—both public and private—added to the likelihood of their success. Some of the most celebrated contemporary venturers are Steve Jobs (Apple, Pixar), Bill Gates (Microsoft), Jeff Bezos (Amazon.com), Howard Shultz (Starbucks), and Michael Dell (Dell Computers).

In our hearts, we know that the kind of entrepreneurial success these men achieved is reserved for a very few. We sometimes think of them as the lucky ones, but we also recognize their focus, talents, and personal efforts. Looking only at their successes, it is easy to imagine that they hurdled over all obstacles in their race to develop new products and services, and then build new markets and industries. However, that was not really the case. Their successes were built on astute observation, practical application, and hard work. Each drew on personal resources, but when that wasn't sufficient, enlisted the help of others. Each one confronted failure more than once, but never accepted it as final.

Entrepreneurs starting new ventures today aspire to that same rarified air of success, but at the same time they recognize that these cultural icons are nothing short of heroic. The biggest winners among entrepreneurs are celebrities precisely because they are so unique in their accomplishments.

Why This Book?

Did you notice? The names on the preceding lists are all male. True, only a select few entrepreneurs become heroes—but it is also true that heroines are almost entirely absent from the list! With the notable exception of a handful of dynamos in the cosmetics (Madame C. J. Walker, Helena Rubinstein, Estee Lauder, Mary Kay Ash) and fashion industries (Coco Chanel, Liz Claiborne, Donna Karan), women have not been significant players in the world of high-stakes entrepreneurship. More recently, Carol Bartz (AutoDesk) and Meg Whitman (eBay) have become standouts in technology-based ventures.

We didn't set out to write a book. We simply wanted to find out why women, who in 2003 were majority owners of 28% of all businesses in the United States (and, if women with 50% ownership shares are counted, the total climbs to 46% of all privately owned businesses),[1] were neither reaching the highest levels of entrepreneurial success nor achieving business celebrity in numbers proportionate to their start-up activity. What factors can explain this success gap for women entrepreneurs? One of the most obvious of the hurdles that women struggle with is the acquisition of key resources—particularly financial resources—so important to growth. For example, five years ago, in the heat of the venture capital rush to fund promising new enterprises, women entrepreneurs received less than 5% of the billions of dollars invested.

Why do we care about this? We are five professors who have spent our professional careers investigating the levers of success in entrepreneurial growth (Candida Brush, Boston University; Nancy Carter, University of St. Thomas; Elizabeth Gatewood, Indiana University;

Patricia Greene, Babson College; and Myra Hart, Harvard Business School). In 1998, we decided to work together to investigate why women, who are definitely intent on climbing the ladder of entrepreneurial success, are having so much trouble getting to the top of it.

We agreed to turn our collective attention to the question of why there are so few heroines in the history of entrepreneurship. Even more important to us was the question of why contemporary women, who are starting new businesses in droves, are not highly visible among the ranks of the high-growth, high-potential entrepreneurs.

Each of us brings a different lens to the investigation. Dr. Greene is a sociologist whose work has included studies of entrepreneurship in minority communities. Dr. Brush has a long history of studying women entrepreneurs. Dr. Hart is an academic with practitioner roots. She has raised venture capital. Dr. Gatewood has served as director of business centers providing consulting and training services to entrepreneurs. She has studied motivations, attributions, and other aspects of entrepreneurial behavior. Dr. Carter has significant experience studying nascent entrepreneurs and is considered an expert in database construction and statistical methods.

The Research

We began by asking reasonable people what explanations they could offer. (Almost everyone you ask can come up with one or more plausible reasons to explain why women entrepreneurs who lead promising businesses find it so difficult to grow those businesses. Most of these have to do with women's inability to raise sufficient capital.) The answers were all some variation on one of these themes:

- **It's the women.**

  - They can't, won't, or don't seek or win outside funding because they don't aspire to high growth.

- They're not qualified or experienced.

- They're not a good business risk.

- **It's the businesses.**

  - Women choose small, locally focused businesses.

  - Women choose businesses in low-tech industries.

  - Their business concepts are not scalable.

- **It's the networks (or rather the lack thereof) that women participate in.**

  - Women aren't in the right business circles to gain access to critical management and financing resources.

  - There are no women in key decision-making roles in the financing world.

- **It's the venture capital industry**.

  - The industry is male dominated.

  - The network is closed and the decision-making models are biased against women.

These answers represent widely held beliefs about why women entrepreneurs seeking to grow their businesses find it so difficult to get the resources necessary to do so. The answers are deeply rooted in personal theories of social capital, institutional behavior, and network theory.

We used these explanations (and the theories that they represented) to frame our investigation. We conducted research to determine what was and what was not true about the entrepreneurial process. We focused on high-growth enterprises and asked what hurdles exist for entrepreneurs seeking external capital to fund their growth. Next, we wanted to understand if some of these hurdles were unique to women. We also wanted to know—if the challenges were similar—was the bar somehow set higher for women? Only then could we understand the causes and the possible remedies for women's apparent exclusion from the highest ranks of entrepreneurial success. Our body of work is referred to as the Diana Project (named after the Roman goddess of the hunt) because it focuses on women hunting for money.

The Research Methods

Together, the members of the Diana Project team have pursued several distinct but related research projects designed to explore the pathways to growth of women-owned businesses. We were particularly interested in the hurdles women encountered as they sought growth capital. We investigated the variety of oft-cited logical explanations for why women are largely unsuccessful in their hunt for venture capital money.

The research includes a detailed review of 300 articles included in the academic literature on women entrepreneurs and on venture capital to determine the state of current knowledge on the subject. The results of this research are compiled in *Women Entrepreneurs, Their Ventures, and the Venture Capital Industry: An Annotated Bibliography* (ESBRI, 2003).

Our research also includes a detailed analysis of all venture capital investments made in U.S. businesses between 1953 and 1998 to determine what proportion of the deals were made with women-led businesses. This was particularly challenging because industry data collection has not historically included any report of the sex of the founding team. Only a line-by-line review of the names of the officers in each firm receiving funding made it possible to make an educated estimate of the percentage of deals made with women entrepreneurs. (Because of the frequent use of initials only and the occasional use of unisex names, many deals had to be omitted from the tabulation. For example, from 1988 to 1998, the total sample included 8,298 investments, but in 48.1% of the companies, names could not be definitively classified by gender.)

The research next turned to the venture capital industry itself to determine the gender composition of the key decision makers in the industry. *Pratt's Guide to the Venture Capital Industry* provided a comprehensive listing of all member venture capital firms and their members by title. The guide enabled identification of all female associates, principals, and directors or partners in the industry in 1995 and 2000. A comparison of the two selected years provided insight into the retention, promotion, and mobility of these women decision makers over the five-year period. The industry survey was complemented with personal interviews with a selected group of these key female venture capitalists to understand their perceived impact on their partnerships' ability to attract and engage with women entrepreneurs.

Our next step included the identification and tracking of a select group of women entrepreneurs who were seeking growth capital in 2000. The women who submitted their business plans to Springboard Venture Forums in 2000 were ideal candidates. Although not all the plans were accepted for presentation at a Springboard event, the field of entries represented business concepts for which women were actively seeking venture funding. Follow-up phone surveys provided data on how their plans, businesses, and financing progressed from 2000 to 2002. This provided detailed information from the front lines of women entrepreneurs trying to raise growth capital.

The Findings

What was surprising in our investigation? We found that the hurdles that women must clear are just as real for men who choose entrepreneurship. Every single individual or team that decides to create a new venture must have the motivation and commitment to stick with the enterprise throughout years of challenges. Entrepreneurs must be technically capable and management savvy. They all need to build resources for the enterprise—often seeming to create something out of nothing. Successful entrepreneurs must start out with good ideas that are actually feasible and for which there is (or soon will be) a ready market. If their business concepts are not scalable, they will never be able to achieve high growth and high value status, although they might be able to successfully run smaller, local enterprises. We found that networks and the social capital to use them effectively made the process of building financial, human, and technological resources possible.

Women need all these skills and, yes, so do men. The differences we found were not in the skills required, nor in the organization-building processes. However, we found that the personal resources, the technical training, and the management experiences that women brought to their enterprises differed from their male counterparts' resources—as did the attitudes and expectations about entrepreneurial success held by both women and society as a whole.

What to Expect in This Book

This book examines the entire entrepreneurial process—from concept development, basic business planning, strategic direction, and resource acquisition and deployment, to organizational growth. It looks specifically at those enterprises that have the potential to grow beyond $1 million in revenues—led by those entrepreneurs who envision large and highly profitable organizations. It explores the hurdles entrepreneurs face in growing a new venture, recognizing that growth is—first and foremost—a personal and strategic choice. It also recognizes that once the choice for growth is exercised, resources become a top priority. This book digs deepest into the issue of resource acquisition—particularly financial resources.

Not only does our book address specific resource hurdles that must be cleared to win the race for success, it also looks at how the race for success differs for women. It does the following:

- Explores the roots and nature of misconceptions, stereotypes, and challenges women encounter in growing businesses.

- Provides critical facts for female entrepreneurs who seek money and resources to launch and grow their entrepreneurial ventures.

- Discusses the challenges encountered in building credibility and gaining access to the money, networks, and people needed to grow a young enterprise into a successful business operation.

- Offers specific prescriptions for how women can succeed in growing a business relative to their personal goals and business type.

- Provides information about various financing options and describes the venture capital process in detail.

Throughout the book, we offer specific recommendations and provide reference guides that can simplify the process of launching and growing a new venture. Our recommendations are clearly targeted at female entrepreneurs, but men will also find them useful.

Is This Book for You?

Yes, if you are in the process of creating, organizing, and growing a significant new venture. It is for everyone who aspires to join the elite list of superhero entrepreneurs. It is dedicated to those women who aspire to be the entrepreneurial heroines of the 21st century. We recognize that you must overcome all the same obstacles to success that your male colleagues face, but, in many cases, you will have to run a little faster, jump a tad higher, and, like Ginger Rogers dancing with Fred Astaire, do it while wearing high heels and moving backwards.

We started writing this book just for you—but please share it. The issues we uncovered in our research can inform men who want to take their entrepreneurial ventures to new heights. The guidelines offered here hold for all entrepreneurs—even for those who want to start new ventures of more modest proportions. Women and men who create enterprises to realize their personal dreams (without necessarily planning on changing the world) will find the book valuable.

When all is said and done, this is not a book for entrepreneurs only. It is also meant to spur those still in the managerial ranks (but dreaming the dream) into action. It can also inform providers of capital, goods, and services who benefit from the growth of entrepreneurial activity and wealth—accountants, consultants, customers, suppliers, and lawyers, to name but a few. In short, it is for everyone who wants to maximize opportunities.

Note

1. Center for Women's Business Research. 2003. *Key Facts about Women-Owned Businesses.*

1 ——————————

WOMEN BECOMING
ENTREPRENEURS

America is the land of opportunity. In the 1960s and 1970s, thanks in large part to the civil rights and feminist movements, it became a land of *equal* opportunity. Since the landmark AT&T settlement in 1973, women and minorities have made enormous progress in penetrating America's corporate ranks.[1] While great strides were made, the transformation of corporate America is still very much a work in process. Women still face very real, although often invisible, barriers known as the *glass ceiling*. Women make up the majority of managers under age 35, but they lead only 6 of the Fortune 500 corporations and comprise less than 15% of the corporate board members.[2] Both the progress and the problems are well documented. But this book is not about the glass ceiling.

No Glass Ceilings Here

This book is for women who choose another path entirely. It is for and about women entrepreneurs—women who desire to become their own

1

bosses, gain personal control, grow their business, and create independent wealth. Over the past 25 years, the ranks of women entrepreneurs grew rapidly. The many new avenues that opened in the 1960s and 1970s—to education, employment, and access to credit—gave women the tools they needed to start new businesses and they have seized the opportunities with gusto.

By 2002, women were majority owners of 6.2 million businesses and held at least a 50% share in 10.1 million businesses, or 46% of all privately held firms in the United States.[3] The Center for Women's Business Research reported that between 1997 and 2002, the number of women-owned firms increased at more than 1.5 times the national rate. Even more striking, larger businesses led by women (100 or more employees) grew 18.3%. Women launched new businesses in every industry, sector, and geographic region of the United States.

This tremendous surge of female entrepreneurship was not without its own challenges. Of course, women have far more control of their own destinies in the businesses they create and develop. But, they encounter new and unseen barriers. These are not of a hierarchical sort, so they certainly do not represent a glass ceiling. Instead women entrepreneurs report challenges in establishing partnerships—with customers, suppliers, and, most important, with financial resource providers. Women who start their own enterprises are far more likely than men to report difficulties in securing the financing that is so necessary to grow their businesses. Without financial capital, entrepreneurs are hidebound. They cannot expand their product lines, open new markets, or beef up their sales forces. They are forced to stay small and grow slowly; consequently they often miss the biggest opportunities.

These partnership barriers that women confront are often unseen hurdles. Every entrepreneur must overcome resourcing challenges in his or her quest for success, but for women, the hurdles are often higher and less apparent. This book addresses the unique challenges that growth oriented women entrepreneurs face in financing their busi-

nesses. It provides insight into why they exist, how
and how they can be overcome.

An Entrepreneurial Venture Begins

Entrepreneurship is "the pursuit of opportunity without regard to resources currently controlled."[4] It is the ability to envision new and wonderful worlds of what can be without being earthbound by what is. The vision is essential, but nothing happens until you move beyond the dream and take action. At that point, resources become critical. Although the vision should be unfettered by the resources you currently have, seldom do you have all that are needed. As an entrepreneur the most important mobilizing tasks you must undertake are the identification and engagement of the resources that will make it possible for you to turn your dream into reality.

Most entrepreneurs start out with a great idea about how to solve a problem or how they will fill a market need. They might have insight into how a business process could be improved (e-tailing vs. retailing) or they might have patented technology that will enable them to create new and useful products. Carol Latham invented and patented a filmy material that helped keep microprocessors from overheating. When she decided to package it in sheets and sell it, she created Thermagon to manufacture and market the material. Linda Kellogg launched Start-Up Resources, Inc. to provide support services (accounting, tax management, finding office space, and benefits administration) to entrepreneurs. Her bundle of business services for start-up companies made it easier for other entrepreneurs to focus attention and energy on core technology, marketing, and distribution tasks. In both cases, coming up with the idea was the easiest part for the women. Then they took the next steps to make their dreams into realities.

Of course, not every new idea becomes a business, but many do. Every year, more than 550,000 people launch new businesses in the

States. Some entrepreneurs identify growth as a strategic goal
m the outset, but most target a modest volume of business and then
stabilize when they reach manageable capacity. The outcomes depend
on the entrepreneur's personal commitment and drive, business strategy, day-to-day execution, and, of course, the business environment.[5]

Most are looking for freedom, self-expression, and a good
income.[6] Figure 1.1 depicts the distribution of entrepreneurial businesses in terms of growth. The vast majority of U.S. ventures are personal income businesses, with only a few enterprises growing to
moderate size and even fewer having truly high potential.

From the entrepreneur's point of view, launching and sustaining a
new venture means developing and introducing differentiated products,
utilizing networks effectively, and creating unique capabilities. All
these activities are vital to a venture's early success,[7] but none can be
done effectively if the key resources are missing. Even with these
resources, many start-ups will not survive. Approximately 35,000 businesses actually declare bankruptcy each year, and thousands more simply cease operations for a variety of reasons.[8]

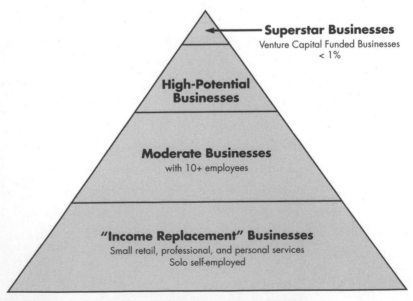

FIGURE 1.1   Pyramid of entrepreneurial businesses.

But put all thoughts of failure away. No entrepreneur would ever take the first step if she believed that failure was a possibility. This book is for entrepreneurs with very high hopes, great confidence in themselves and their businesses, and a commitment to growth. It is for those of you who truly believe that you can create the next Fortune 1000 or Inc. 500 business, introduce new goods and services, change the world, and create great value for yourselves and your partners in the process.

Venture Growth Is a Choice

For those of you with growth on your mind and optimism in your heart, you must recognize from the start that you are among a very select few. Growth is a deliberate choice that is both personal and strategic. While we recognize that most people will choose low or slow growth businesses, this book is not for them. It is for those of you who want to build significant businesses. It is also for those of you who started small but quickly embraced growth when you realized how big your opportunity really can be. Just what are those numbers?

Approximately 350,000 of the 22.9 million businesses in the United States can be classified as "gazelles," or businesses growing at more than 20% per year for at least four years.[9] The vast majority of these are self-funded at start-up, but reach out to external providers of capital (friends, family, banks, angel investors, and venture capitalists) as they grow. High-potential businesses that receive venture capital are the rarest breed. There were approximately 8,000 venture capital deals in the banner investment year of 2000, but, by 2002, this number had dropped to 2,453.[10] The few businesses that do obtain venture funding are highly innovative, scalable (usually technology-based), and in possession of unique advantages that are very hard to copy.

Growth-oriented entrepreneurs think big. Their goals include expanding their businesses in both scale and scope. Strategic choices of industry, market sector, competitive position, and technology base profoundly influence growth potential. Consider the following examples from the floral industry and their potential for growth:

Joan Larke owns Flower Power, a neighborhood flower shop that employs five people and has revenues of $100,000 a year. Her business yields a comfortable living, gives her a strong sense of satisfaction and achievement, and is easily managed. Ruth Owades launched Calyx & Corolla with an entirely different vision in mind. In 1988 with an initial investment of more than $2 million, she set up computer systems, nailed down strategic partner contracts, and launched an innovative catalog floral business that delivered flowers directly from the grower to the consumer. Revenues grew to more than $25 million and the company became a prototype for entrepreneurs hoping to cut supply-side costs while delivering greater value to customers.[11]

From the outset, Ruth Owades's aspirations clearly shaped her vision of what a floral business could be. She planned a large-scale venture and she was willing to take on all the associated challenges. She invested time and energy to develop a competitive strategy, build an organizational structure, and assemble her team. She was willing to give up some of the ownership and control to capture the needed financial resources. She maintained the primary leadership role, but shared decision making with the board in a way that Joan Larke did not.

Owades also drew deeply on her own resources, starting with her personal assets (education and experience, social contacts, personal funds) and then leveraged the resources of her management team. Together they had strength in finance, marketing, operations, human resources, and technology. She also acquired the physical resources she needed: furniture, fixtures, computers, and software. At the same time she was building the physical platform for the business, Owades was also creating the operating infrastructure: setting up policies, systems, and information flows for managing the business transactions (e.g., sales, purchasing, banking, inventory); training and supporting human resources (e.g., hiring, recruiting, work rules, benefits, etc.); and managing customer relationships. The growth process was dynamic, requiring constant invention because there was no organizational history to fall back on.

Every one of these activities requires skill and ingenuity, but their success also depends on financial resources. For most entrepreneurs, by far the biggest challenge to growth is getting the money. Few entrepreneurs—men or women—have sufficient personal assets to fund growth entirely on their own. Most "bootstrap" their businesses, working creatively and often without salary, investing their own savings and maxing out their credit cards, then turning to family and friends for informal investment, and next to banks and suppliers for credit or debt. Acquiring money to grow is daunting for even the most seasoned entrepreneurs.

Women-Led Ventures

You might anticipate that when it comes to entrepreneurship, the playing field is at last level—that men and women can choose from the same opportunity sets and that they can draw on similar skills and resources. Unfortunately, this is not yet the case.

In 1997, women-owned firms averaged $1.8 million in sales. By 2000, the U.S. average had grown to $2.4 million, but women-owned firms still lagged the national average of $12.3 million for all businesses.[12] Only 26% of women-owned firms had revenues that exceeded $1 million, whereas 39% of all firms had revenues exceeding $1 million.[13] In 2000, women employed an average of six employees per firm compared to more than nine employees for all firms.[14] Figure 1.2 reflects the distribution of men- and women-owned businesses mea-

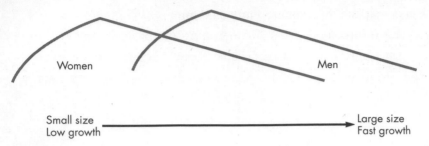

FIGURE 1.2   Distribution of men- and women-owned businesses by size and growth.

sured on the dimensions of size and growth. The figure shows that the vast majority of both women- and men-owned businesses are in the small to moderate size and revenue category with only a select few at the top end. Women-owned businesses are far more likely to be smaller and slower growing than those of their male counterparts.

Slow to Grow

Even though women are now creating new ventures at a very fast clip, most of their ventures start small and stay that way. Why? Historically, most women started businesses in traditionally female sectors—beauty parlors, flower shops, and day-care centers—while the most scalable businesses were in manufacturing, technology, construction, and financial services, fields traditionally dominated by men. Approximately 55% of women-led businesses are concentrated in services, 17% in retail, and less than 2.5% in transportation, communications and utilities, or manufacturing.[15]

Because women's businesses were clustered in service sectors with limited growth opportunities, many assumed that they preferred small, low-tech ventures and that they started them to supplement family income rather than create substantial enterprise value. However, these decisions might not have been so much a matter of choice as they were of circumstance. Women often lacked the economic power and the social and family support structure to grow their ventures. There is evidence that lack of adequate child care might have forced women to keep their businesses smaller and more manageable.

Consequent of their choice of business and industry, their more limited goals and their lack of familiarity with the systems, most women entrepreneurs did not take advantage of commercial bank loans, credit, and government programs before 1990. Networking organizations were less prominent, and social acceptance of women as high-powered entrepreneurial superstars was unheard of. Without the necessary infrastructure, most women entrepreneurs found they had a narrow range of choices. The result was a greater proportion of smaller, slow-growth business choices by women. Therefore, women have a legacy of unique obstacles to growth.

By contrast, men always had a much broader range of choices. It's assumed that men can start businesses in any sector: manufacturing, telecommunications, medicine, or food service. The opportunities for them to gain credit, find suppliers, or expand are more often available. The higher proportion of smaller, slower growing ventures led by women can thus be explained by the fact that they had farther to come.

Are There Changes in the Offing?

The boom in entrepreneurial growth throughout the 1990s included many women entrepreneurs who chose to start ventures in software, biotechnology, and financial services. Armed with MBAs, corporate experience, and technology expertise, these women sought to grow large firms in nontraditional areas. A rising number of women started firms in wholesale trade, transportation, communications, and utilities, the number now reaching 250,000 women-owned firms in these sectors.[16] Women launched new ventures in technology-driven businesses including telecommunications, medical diagnostics, and manufacturing. In addition, family and social support in the form of extensive networking organizations, child-care facilities at small business offices, and other resources made it easier for women to consider growth. It is clear that many of today's women entrepreneurs are choosing to grow their ventures. Since 1999, more than 2,500 women have applied to Springboard Venture Forums seeking angel and venture capital to fund growth.[17]

Private Equity—The Last Big Hurdle

Angel Investing

Entrepreneurs with really big ideas tap equity investors (informal investors called *angels*) and professional venture capitalists to provide additional financial support.[18] Because angels are informal investors, it is often a mystery: Who has the money? Where are they? How do you make contact? Most entrepreneurs start by reaching out to lawyers, accountants, friends, and distant contacts to identify investors who might have an interest in the business technology and its potential returns. The process requires developing a business plan and revising it countless times. Some entrepreneurs make numerous presentations to investors. Getting money from venture investors is extremely hard work, but for some, there are great rewards.

Venture Capital

Venture capitalists are to growing businesses what producers are to Broadway shows. They make the big hits possible. A recent study showed that businesses started between 1970 and 2000 that were funded by venture capital contributed more than $1.3 trillion to the U.S. economy in 2000 (more than 13% of gross domestic product) and employed more than 7.6 million people.[19] Between 1991 and 2000, investments by venture capital firms in growth businesses totaled over $234 billion. More than 33% of the initial public offerings (IPOs) of stock[20] made in the United States during the same period were venture capital funded—as were a total of more than 3,000 companies that went public between 1975 and 2000.[21] Only a very small percentage of entrepreneurs receive venture capital each year, but the impact on their businesses is extraordinary.

You might expect that, in spite of the fact that the total number of men and women who received growth capital was small, qualified women would receive funds in proportion to their entrepreneurial activity. However, this is not the case. Throughout the decade of the 1990s, women received less than 5% of all venture capital money invested. Of 1,200 companies that received venture funding in 1996, only 30 (2.5%) were women-led enterprises. During the 10-year period from 1988 to 1998, 290 (3.5%) of the total of 8,298 venture capital investments were made in women-led businesses. Even in the boom years of 1999 and 2000, women-led businesses participated in approximately 8% of venture capital deals and received less than 6% of capital invested.[22] Because growth capital is so important to expansion and development of significant enterprises, this lack of large-scale funding that venture capital money represents is a serious handicap to women-led firms. It prevents them from expanding and growing, and it limits their ability to create wealth. What is the cause of this disparity?

This mismatch between the number of women-led firms seeking investment capital and their actual receipt of the money might represent rational economic decision making or it might represent a significant market failure. This book investigates both possibilities. Either way, the reasons for the funding gap are rooted in widely held beliefs about women and their qualifications for leadership of high-growth, high-value enterprises; the businesses women choose to start; and their ability to tap into resource networks—their reputations and connections with key resource providers.

Women might be perceived as less qualified to run high-growth businesses due to their education, experience, or expertise. They might be stereotyped as less able to make tough decisions, to bring a management team together, or to manage finances. Women's businesses might be viewed as less unique and scalable and, therefore, less likely to achieve high growth.

If the suppliers of money, contacts, information, or influence doubt the commitment or the capability of the venture team, they will not provide the needed resources. Subjective opinions and especially misperceptions can raise the bar for women, making it more difficult for them to build high-potential ventures.

The Hurdle Analogy

Tenacity is a core value at our company. Maybe that's just because I've run a marathon and I'm a lousy sprinter.

—Laura Rippy, Founder, Handango

Starting a venture is a lot like competing in a track event. When you are in the starting block, every ounce of you is filled with a sense of hope, excitement, and challenge. You know that your talents and training will be tested to the limit, as will your resolution and endurance. You look to your right and your left and you see that there are fierce competitors to be reckoned with. When you look straight ahead, you see that there are also many hurdles to clear before you can claim victory. Reaching the finish line will require every bit of passion, experience, training, and skill you have.

Yes, entrepreneurs are a lot like contenders in a highly competitive race, but in many ways, they are different. Entrepreneurs chart their own course rather than following a prescribed track. Theirs is a very personal race to translate a good idea into a viable new business concept that resolves a problem or fills a market need. For most entrepreneurs, the creation of a new venture is anything but a short sprint over hurdles. It is far more likely to be a marathon that takes years. The easiest part might be getting out of the starting block. Surviving, maintaining the pace, and growing the business present far greater challenges. It might come as a surprise, but neither are there clearly stated rules that apply to all, nor is there a defined finish line for an entrepreneur at which point she can declare victory, claim the laurel wreath, and retire to the showers.

In spite of these rather obvious differences, the high hurdles race analogy captures the essence of the entrepreneurial challenges that women face when growing their new businesses. In truth, women with high aspirations for their ventures face challenges remarkably like the men in the next lanes. For women, however, the hurdles are often higher and closer together. Throughout this book, we will identify the obstacles you are likely to encounter and we will make recommendations for clearing them with ease (or getting around them, if that makes more sense). Remember that there are no hard and fast rules in the entrepreneurial game.

Each chapter considers the hurdle faced by women entrepreneurs, presents examples, and explores the roots of the perceptions. We suggest what might go right or wrong and provide suggestions for what you can do to minimize the impact of these hurdles. We provide both explanations and recommendations primarily for female entrepreneurs, and secondarily for equity investors and other entrepreneurial partners.

The Plan for this Book

This book provides a look at the financing gap that apparently keeps qualified women-led firms seeking growth capital from getting the money they need. In it, we set out to discover precisely what the critical perceptions about women and their entrepreneurial leadership qualifications are. We look at what is and is not true—both generally and specifically—and we make recommendations about how women entrepreneurs can overcome these hurdles. We investigate the strategic choices that women entrepreneurs make to determine the impact of these choices on scalability and growth potential. Finally, we examine how well women are connected to key resource providers—how they get heard and seen and how credible they are with those decision makers.

In Chapter 2, we begin with a discussion of the pathways to growth, showing that not all women aspire to grow, and detailing the challenges encountered in this process. We discuss the nature of the personal and strategic hurdles growth oriented women encounter and explore the reasons why these exist. In Chapter 3 we present an overview of the process of financing growth and the alternatives available. The range of aspirations and commitment to growth are covered in Chapter 4, and the influences of human capital components are considered in Chapter 5. Chapter 6 explores the financial savvy and risk propensity of women. The effects of strategic choice of industry sector and business potential on growth are discussed in Chapter 7. Chapter 8 presents a discussion of networks and social capital, and Chapter 9 examines how women build powerful management teams. Chapter 10 investigates the network connections (and disconnections) that women have with venture capitalists and offer suggestions about why there are gaps and how those can be closed. We conclude with a look at the future for women and growth ventures.

By identifying hurdles and suggesting strategies for overcoming these, we hope to contribute to new wealth and reward for all the players. However, our work goes much further than this. In our study of women entrepreneurs and their quest for growth capital, we learned that the obstacles confronting women in their quest for growth are pervasive throughout our society. The widely held beliefs about women, their businesses, and ability to create weath influence decision making in corporate, non profit, and entrepreneurial settings. A better understanding of what the hurdles are and what misconceptions they include can provide guidance to women in any profession. It is important to note that this study is directed at the financing strategies of women entrepreneurs in the United States, but our research extends to other countries, where we consistently found the challenges to be even greater and the persistence of these beliefs might be even stronger.

Notes

1. The Equal Pay Act (1963), the Civil Rights Act of 1964 (Title VII), the Equal Education Opportunity Act (Title IX), the Equal Opportunity Act of 1972, the Equal Credit Act of 1975, and the landmark EEOC–AT&T agreement had important ramifications for women's (and minorities') access to education, career opportunities, and credit. Corporate affirmative action policies instituted in the 1970s encouraged the recruitment and development of women and minorities into all types of industry sectors, occupations, and positions. Professional schools, including medical, law, and business institutions, also began actively recruiting women.

2. Catalyst Web site. www.catalystwomen.org/press_room/press_releases/WBD _03_PR.pdf

3. Center for Women's Business Research. 2003. *Key Facts about Women-Owned Businesses.*

4. Stevenson, H. 1983. *A Perspective on Entrepreneurship* (Harvard Business School Teaching Note 9-384-131).

5. Carter, N. M., Gartner, W. B., & Reynolds, P. D. 1996. Exploring start-up sequences. *Journal of Business Venturing.*11:3, 151–166; Kirchhoff, B. 1994. *Entrepreneurship and Dynamic Capitalism.* Westport, CT: Praeger.

6. More than 60 percent of U.S. businesses are clustered in the retailing, professional and business services segments and have less than 5 employees. More than 75 percent have fewer than 10 employees. Similarly, more than 40 percent of all firms produce less than $500,000 in revenues. Approximately 80% (18.4 million of the 22.9 million businesses in the U.S.) are sole proprietorships, not corporations or partnerships. The majority of these are self-employed individuals who do not have any employees. *Women in Business, 2001.* Office of Economic Research of the U.S. Small Business Administration, Office of Advocacy, Washington, DC: U.S. Government Printing Office; *Small Business Economic Indicators for 2002.* A reference guide to the latest data on small business activity, including state and industry data. Office of Economic Research of the U.S. Small Business Administration, Office of Advocacy, Washington DC: U.S. Government Printing Office.

7. Brush, C. G., Greene, P. G., & Hart, M. M. 2001. From initial idea to unique advantage: The entrepreneurial challenge of constructing a resource base. *Academy of Management Executive.* 15:1, 64–80.

8. *Small Business Economic Indicators for 2002.* Washington, DC: U.S. Government Printing Office, Office of Advocacy.

9. Inc. 2001, *The State of Small Business*, 28–29.

10. National Venture Capital Association Web site. 2003. *Industry Statistics. www.nvca.org*

11. Salmon, W. J., & Wylie, D. Calyx & Corolla. Harvard Business School. Case #592035, 11/01/91.

12. Center for Women's Business Research. 2001. *Removing the Boundaries.*

13. Ibid.

14. Ibid.

15. *Women in Business, 2001*. Washington, DC: U.S. Government Printing Office, Office of Advocacy.

16. Ibid.

17. *www.springboardenterprises.org/about/default.asp*.

18. *Venture capital* is the financial capital supplied to young and innovative ventures by private investors who risk their money and receive potential rewards if the new venture succeeds in growing rapidly and becoming profitable. Private investors are referred to as angels, whereas institutional venture capitalists invest and manage money supplied by individual or institutional investors in different companies.

19. National Venture Capital Association Web site. 2001. DRI-WEFA report. *www.NVCA.org* (formerly Wharton Econometric Forecasting Associates).

20. An IPO is a sale or distribution of a venture's stock to the public for the first time.

21. National Venture Capital Association Web site: *www.NVCA.org*.

22. CWBR Venture Capital Study. 2001.

2

WOMEN ENTREPRENEURS: PATHWAYS AND CHALLENGES

Chances are that you, your mother, your best friend, or the woman next door is an entrepreneur. In fact, one out of every 11 women in the United States is an entrepreneur with a 50% or greater ownership stake,[1] and the number is rising at a rapid rate.

More than 550,000 entrepreneurs start new ventures every year. Moving from a good idea to the creation of a real enterprise is a major accomplishment. Nurturing the young organization through its infancy is exhilarating, but managing continuing growth and sustaining a high level of engagement require constant attention and unwavering dedication. If you plan to grow a large-scale business, you need a clear strategy, a sound management team, great execution skills, persistence, and money. As we noted in Chapter 1, the rate and trajectory of growth varies dramatically from one business to another. Some enterprises reach capacity quickly and stabilize, others grow slowly and incrementally, whereas still others grow at lightning speed. These variations in the rate and size of business growth are influenced by three major factors: the entrepreneur (aspirations, goals, and capabilities), strategic choice (industry and venture concept), and the resources available. Of course, all of these must fit together with the right synergy for success to be a possibility.

The Entrepreneur

Aspirations and Goals

Entrepreneurs begin with a set of personal aspirations and ambitions that are then translated into their visions of success for the business venture. These motivations for starting a business vary widely. For instance, some entrepreneurs start a business because they want to work independently, make key business decisions, and take control of their work lives. Still other entrepreneurs are focused on creating a particular work environment. Some are driven by the need to solve a particular business or social problem, or to translate an innovative technology into a commercial product. Some do not place a high value on monetary returns as long as the business yields sufficient income to support their families. Others want to build large organizations and claim the financial rewards that come with leading such an entity. Some define success as building and leading a high-growth, high-value venture, whereas still others envision a lifestyle business that provides steady income, predictable hours, and a satisfying environment.

The personal motives for starting a new venture have a direct bearing on the choice of business and its growth and profitability goals. For instance, if you are a horticulturist having personal goals of beauty creation and personal expression, and your financial goals are focused on providing a good family income, you might start a landscaping business that specializes in waterscapes and fountains. If, on the other hand, you developed a patented technology that enhances plant growth or disease resistance your business goals will be to run a rapidly growing venture that can bring the product to market, support its widespread distribution, and reward you and your investors for the efforts and risks undertaken.

Personal motivation and business growth goals are also closely related. Those with big dreams of making the Inc. 500 or the Forbes 400 see themselves as leading a global company. To achieve that end, they are likely to pursue a fast-paced growth strategy with every intention of building a big business. Those with more modest dreams might choose incremental growth—a path that is less frenetic for the entrepreneur and poses less risk to the business.

Capabilities

In addition to their personal goals and aspirations, entrepreneurs start with a set of personal aptitudes and attitudes, and then add skills learned through formal education and on-the-job experience. This combination of natural talent and learned skills comprises *human capital*. Each entrepreneur has a unique bundle of this human capital. Some have high energy, clear focus, and an optimistic point of view. Many have a college education, and others bring advanced professional degrees to their ventures. Still others gain valuable expertise through specialized training. Most learn through directly related industry experience. The package of capabilities that the entrepreneur (or her entrepreneurial team) brings to the table provides the foundation of the new venture.[2] These capabilities might include functional expertise in marketing, accounting, and operations, as well as skills in fund-raising, people management, and negotiation. The combination of relevant business talents, skills, and experience that you and your team represent can make a significant difference in how the business grows.

Of course, to have any significant value, the capabilities must be well matched to the needs of the business. (Entrepreneurs can and do start businesses in industries in which they are not experienced, but this increases the risk and limits ability to raise capital.) If you have a decade of marketing and sales experience in the fast-food industry, but you want to start a construction business, then all your industry-specific experience will be irrelevant to this new venture. If you have spent years in audit accounting working with books and numbers, then choose to launch a temporary personnel business, you might lack the requisite skills in human resource management for such a venture. There are several ways to assure that you have the full complement of skills: Gain experience in your industry of choice and consider starting a new venture with one or more partners whose experience complements yours. If growth is your goal, the composite of human capital possessed by the team needs to be strong and relevant to the business.

Strategic Choices

The Venture Concept

The venture concept is what your business does, how it delivers value to customers and clients. It starts from an idea—"Wouldn't it be great if I could solve the problem of…"—followed by the next logical step—"That could happen if…." When you take your thinking to the next level and come to the conclusion, "I could make that happen by organizing a business that supplies…" you are zeroing in on the actual business concept. The solution to the problem that your new venture delivers will define the activities of the organization.

Sustainability is largely dependent on what is unique about your business concept. Do you have a distinct competitive advantage over potential competitors because you have a patent, a secret recipe, the prime location, or close connections to key customers and suppliers? If you do not have some way of distinguishing your business from other players in the marketplace, it will be very difficult to survive, let alone grow and prosper.

Some companies are based on innovative technologies. Amazon.com is a retailer that took advantage of the Internet platform to reach very large markets. It holds relatively little inventory and has orders dispatched directly from the supplier to the end user. Although a local boutique selling "wearable art" is also a retailer, it stands in stark contrast to Amazon.com. Its growth is constrained by both its unique product (limited supply) and its local distribution.

There are several key decisions about your concept that will determine your business's potential for growth. Is it a potentially big idea? How large is the demand for the product or service? Is your approach innovative? Is it scalable? Can it be delivered in larger and larger quantities without increasing the complexity and costs at the same rate? Will you continue to be able to satisfy growing numbers of clients or customers without reducing the quality or service levels? Can your concept withstand competition well? Strong competitors or available substitutes can put enormous pressures on a young company in terms of price, quality, and service differentiation. What other limiting factors do you foresee? An innovative business with strong demand, supply, and delivery capability has a better chance at growth than one without these characteristics.

Industry

Potential for business growth is also directly influenced by choice of industry. It is important to look beyond your own business concept and identify what is going on in your industry sector. For example, when eBay was founded, Internet shopping had just arrived and hundreds of thousands of people were jumping on the Web to find out what was new. eBay rode the wave of Internet success—riding the tide of the underlying sectoral growth. Of course, it became a winner by differentiating itself and offering an innovative service. Its auction-based format made it a facilitator of retail transactions rather than actually being a retailer. As its user base increased, its value to all users increased exponentially. Hence the growth of the Internet sector contributed to the ability of eBay to acquire resources and grow.

Resources

Whatever your business vision, you will need the resources to realize it. Resources provide the fuel to convert business concept to reality. They make it possible to translate an idea into tangible goods and services and to deliver them to the marketplace. Resources include the entrepreneur's personal reserves of human, financial, and social capital. The financial capital—money from self, family, and friends; credit from vendors, banks, commercial lending organizations, and private individuals; and equity investments from angels or venture capitalists—often provides the means to engage additional human, physical, and technological resources. The entrepreneur's social capital—her network of personal and business contacts—provides the currency that enables her to reach and engage key resource partners.

It is not only who you know, but also who recognizes and values you. The people with whom you interact are all important contacts when it comes to assembling the critical resources for the business. Your network of contacts together with your skills and expertise help you acquire and develop the human, physical, financial, and technological resources necessary for the developing organization.

When Donna Dubinsky and Jeff Hawkins started Handspring to create a new generation of personal hand-held computing devices, the two had a wealth of technology experience in a not new industry. Because they had been very successful with Palm Computing, a company they had founded six years earlier, they had well-established contacts with suppliers, manufacturers, distributors, and investors. They also had substantial personal wealth that they could use to fund the business. They invested their own capital in the initial research, development, and business planning stages, but soon sought outside financial resources to build the business.[3] They used their contacts

**with key technology investors and leveraged prior relation-
ships to make deals with suppliers, identify potential management team members, and develop distribution
channels. In other words, they used their starting bundles
of human and social resources to acquire all the other
resources they needed to build the venture.**

At Handspring, personal capabilities and strong network connections were the starting points in building the inventory of resources
needed to start and build a business. Their personal resources were used
to develop the venture concept and acquire more resources. Unlike
Handspring, most new businesses are launched on a shoestring. Facilities are bare bones, computers might be leased, and employees might be
working at below-market rates. In the end, entrepreneurs must find a
way to add those resources that are critical to the business. For example,
a software company needs computers, technical equipment, and skilled
programmers. A snack chip business needs a large warehouse and
equipment that can bake, flavor, and package the chips. No matter what
the business, it will need specific resources to move forward.

Figure 2.1 graphically shows the relationship among the entrepreneur,
strategic choices (venture concept and industry), resources, and growth.

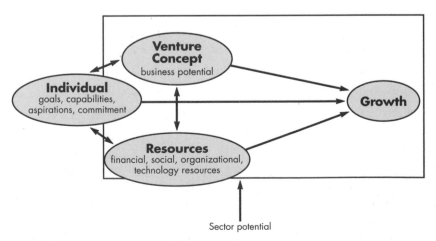

FIGURE 2.1   Factors influencing growth.

Certainly some entrepreneurs have more "choice" in their approach to growth. For example, if you have substantial cash reserves, a Ph.D. in engineering, or experience in start-up, you already have substantial resources and you might be able to attract many more, so your big dreams might be within your grasp. On the other hand, if you have less experience, lack substantial personal start-up cash, or face high industry barriers (e.g., regulatory requirements or a labor shortage), you will have to take a very strategic approach to resource acquisition. Given a concept with its associated business and sector potential, the combination of your personal goals and individual capabilities, along with the resources you acquire and develop, will suggest your pathways to growth.

Hurdles to Overcome

No matter which strategy you choose, seldom does an entrepreneur have everything it takes for a smooth, uneventful launch. There are always challenges no matter what growth pathway you follow.

For instance, when Lisa Sharples and her husband Cliff and their friend Jamie O'Neill quit their jobs at Trilogy software to start Gardening.com, they were armed with technical expertise and education.[4] But, they were not gardeners and they possessed little knowledge of the $40 billion industry. So the team set up focus groups, did interviews with suppliers, and learned about the variety of seeds and plants, as well as the nature of customers.

Richard Worth, founder and CEO of Frookies, which makes cookies sweetened from fruit juice rather than sugar faced a different challenge. He was unable to get shelf space in a market dominated by big players. Even though

he had a great product, unless he could gain assess to customers, the business would not survive.[5]

But, as any entrepreneur will tell you, growing a venture is even more challenging. Everyone has a story about how she went to several banks to get a loan, how she couldn't find a skilled employee, or how she faced delays in getting registrations or permits. Others recount difficulties in getting access to distributors, learning informal rules of an industry, or just plain finding sources of money. Growing swiftly or slowly might make a difference in the point at which you reach the hurdle, or how high it is, but chances are if you are growing your business, you'll encounter these challenges.

Our research identified seven major hurdles that are to related to the entrepreneur, strategic choices, and resources available. Getting past these hurdles is essential if you plan to claim success.

Motives, Aspirations, and Commitment

The challenge of managing a business requires a significant commitment of time and energy. It is often easy to know the time and personal commitment required when you take a job with an existing organization, but when a venture is newly founded, it is very hard to anticipate how much effort will be needed. First-time entrepreneurs can be surprised by the hours of work and effort needed to launch and grow a business. At the same time, a misfit between your personal aspirations and the commitment required can interfere with the growth of the venture. Do you have a clear idea of your motives for entrepreneurship? Do your aspirations match your commitment and the growth needs of the new venture?

Human Capital

Human capital includes the full range of personal attributes, skills, and experience of the entrepreneur. This is the single most important factor relating to venture success, and there must be a fit between your background and the venture. Even though you might have experience and education that is related to the type of business, activities, or the industry, there is always a learning curve for the entrepreneur in transferring these skills to a new business and growing it. Some skills will transfer and some will not. Some skills are right for start-up, and others are right for growth. Do you have the right combination of experience, capabilities, and expertise to grow your venture? If not, can you develop the required experience? Can you find a partner or partners with the right experience?

Financial Knowledge and Business Savvy

Financial savvy and money management skills are necessary for growing any business because these enterprises are typically cash poor and must conserve cash to survive. There is a big difference between working in a business that has established financial practices and policies and creating these. Even entrepreneurs experienced in accounting and finance encounter difficulties when setting up or expanding financial systems, making budgeting or investment decisions, and negotiating transactions. Do you have the right financial and money management skills to grow your venture? If not, how can you either develop these or find a reliable partner to provide them?

Growth Orientation and Strategies

The initial choice of venture concept, business sector, and industry influence the growth options. The nature of the product or service and the extent to which it is novel, new, simple, or localized influence the possibilities for growth. Whether the industry is expanding rapidly with minimal competition, or is mature and highly competitive, affects choices for how to grow. Have you chosen a concept that provides room for growth? Given your choice, what is the best strategy to achieve that growth? Does the strategy you have chosen fit with both the marketplace and your personal skill sets?

Social Capital and Social Networks

Access to networks of contacts leading to money and business finance is critical for any business. When entrepreneurs grow businesses, they make use of contacts from organizations, social relationships, or membership groups. These networks and relationships are the keys to gaining information, finding employees, and often getting money. Developing these relationships and finding the right contacts for the business can take time and can be difficult. Do you have the right mix of contacts to attract financial resources, employees, and other resource providers to expand your business? If not, what steps do you need to take to build the social network you need? How will you start and how long will it take? What contacts do you already have that can help you build the network connections you need?

Building a Management Team

Identifying and building a qualified management team and keeping that team motivated through the tough times are among the hardest, yet most important jobs of the entrepreneur. Although a business can be started by an individual, if it is to grow in any way, it will eventually need people to fill the various functional roles of marketing, finance, operations, strategy, and human resource management. For a fast-growing company, an experienced management team needs to be brought together early in the process. Finding qualified team members can be a significant challenge. Do you have a strategy for building a top management team?

Funding Connections

Money, capital, and deal making are not very well understood by most entrepreneurs. Identifying sources of funding, getting into the network, and persuading people to fund your business is a significant challenge. Is equity capital (angel or venture capital) appropriate for your firm?

You might have thought about these questions before. Having the right answers and the ability to deliver on them are major challenges for all entrepreneurs. These challenges are the hurdles entrepreneurs face in their race for success. Somehow, though, the hurdles are higher for women. Women have to work harder, race faster, and persist longer in their efforts to grow a large-scale business. Where do these higher hurdles come from?

Higher Hurdles for Women

We believe it comes down to a collision of beliefs about entrepreneurs in general and specific perceptions and expectations about women's roles and capabilities. Entrepreneurs are portrayed as risk-taking, independent, aggressive, highly innovative, and financially motivated heroes of industry. Even though little research supports this heroic stereotype, these qualities are rooted in stories about successful male entrepreneurs, from which popular stereotypes have arisen.[6] This characterization is pervasive in movies, the media, and even stories about success. Our American culture celebrates the innovative individual risk taker who creates a fabulous new product, sells it widely, and accumulates enormous wealth.

For example, if you ask any group of people to name an entrepreneur, chances are Paul Allen, Michael Dell, or Sam Walton will be among the first names mentioned. Of course, the reality is that these individuals would not have succeeded without a team of managers, persistent hard work, commitment, high aspirations, and careful acquisition and management of resources. However, for most, believing in the image of the flamboyant heroic entrepreneur is easier.

If you press, asking why they didn't think of any women entrepreneurs, you will probably get answers like, "Women don't have the 'qualities' necessary to be a successful, fast-growing entrepreneur." Or people likely will offer other seemingly reasonable explanations that women "are risky investments," they are "less ambitious," or they "don't have experience and the financial savvy." Others might say, "Women should stay home and take care of their children," suggesting a different expectation for women's roles in the household and entrepreneurship than for men. These perceptions might not be explicitly articulated, visible, or even true, but they are obstacles to gaining resources and growth. There is a contradiction in perceptions about the expectations for women's roles and beliefs about successful entrepreneurs. Take for instance the story of Mary Anne Baxter.

Mary Anne Baxter owned a snack food company, producing cereals, dried fruit products, and granola bars.[7] Her products were 100% organic, vitamin-enhanced, and included a range of healthy new ingredients (kashi, soy, barley, and herbs). She distributed her products in top-line gourmet markets, and sold by mail order through her Web page. Prior to founding her business, she was an elementary school teacher in a suburb of Philadelphia. When her children were 8 and 12 she decided it was time to do something different. After taking several entrepreneurship courses and workshops and seeking the advice of accountants, lawyers, and a local university professor, she launched her business. The manufacture of her products was subcontracted, but she organized all the advertising, packaging, distribution, product development, and testing operations, in-house, working with a paid staff of fifteen. One of her employees was a home economist and nutrition specialist who developed products and tested recipes. Five years later, she had $1 million in sales and the business showed a 19% gross profit. She decided to step up the growth of the thriving venture. After researching venture capital firms on the Web, she mailed her business plan to 20 different venture capital firms that specialized in foods. A month later, she had no replies, so she followed up with

phone calls. Only one venture capitalist agreed to meet with her, but, because he was leaving town, he asked that she join him in his limo to the airport.

Joe Smith started the conversation with a very simple request: "So dear, tell me about this little business of yours." She gave him samples, which he tasted and liked, and then she proceeded with her pitch, consisting of professional overhead transparencies enclosed in a binder. Smith asked a few questions: "How is it you are running a business with just an elementary education degree? Who keeps the books, you or your husband?" and "Who babysits for your children?" Baxter was surprised by the questions but answered them carefully as the limo motored toward the airport. When they arrived, Smith said, "Thanks for the snacks, good luck with your business, dear." And that was all she heard from Joe Smith. (The characters, business, and certain facts are disguised but the story is true.)

In this story, it's apparent that Joe Smith held certain strong preconceptions about Baxter, and had certain expectations for how she or a woman with a family should behave. At the same time, he underestimated her capabilities, which influenced his evaluation and ultimate decision. Smith's questions reflect some of the perceptions or misperceptions women entrepreneurs might encounter. The effect of these expectations increases the height of the bar women must leap to be successful. For instance, Baxter would have to work harder to convince Joe Smith she was financially savvy, even though she had already started and grown a $1 million business. Where do these perceptions and expectations come from? They are embedded in the history of entrepreneurship and women's roles in society.

Why Are the Hurdles Higher?

Throughout economic history, government statistics, books, research, and media attention focused primarily on men. Names like John D. Rockefeller, Henry Ford, and Bill Gates capture the spirit of entrepreneurship in the United States and help define the characteristics that are associated with potential success: risk taking, independence, and rational and instrumental pursuit of economic opportunities.[8] Until the early 1990s, what we knew about venture creation came purely from our knowledge of the experiences of male entrepreneurs and their businesses.[9] Not surprisingly, the characteristics and expected behaviors for entrepreneurs were "male" in nature.

At the same time, women historically were socialized to pursue careers such as teaching, retailing, or service provision, rather than independent entrepreneurship. This led to women's greater participation in some economic sectors such as health care, education, and retailing, rather than finance, manufacturing, and technology. The result was occupational segregation and wage disparity by gender.

For example, even today more than 90% of billing clerks, bookkeepers, audit clerks, dental hygienists, and secretaries are female. More than 90% of all airline pilots, electricians, mechanical engineers, construction employees, and plumbers are male.[10] Coincident with these occupational facts, family and cultural norms and traditional female role expectations still reinforce the perception that women are ill suited for enterprise creation and development.

Gender perceptions are formed early in life. Studies show that most people have clear views on female or male leadership styles, skills, and abilities. These perceptions are rooted in the social and environmental messages children receive as they grow up. Parents, teachers, peers, family friends, media, textbooks, and institutions influence how we act, communicate, think, and learn. Children carry these messages, and what they learn from their own observations and experiences, into their workplaces.[11] This often leads to stereotypes and expectations about how women and men should act, what roles they should assume, and how they should perform.[12] These perceptions can be held by either men or women.

There are two approaches to how stereotypes develop: One suggests that they are biologically based and the other addresses social construction or cognitive behavior. Although there is no agreement on which approach is most influential, it is likely that both have some effect on the development of gender perceptions. Biological views follow Darwin's theory of natural selection, and argue that characteristics and behaviors are the result of biological differences. Referred to as *sociobiology*,[13] this argument focuses on biological factors such as hormones, physical attributes, the reproductive system, and brain functionality to explain sex differences in behavior. Some argue the connector between the left and right hemispheres is larger in men than women, which causes them to be left-brain dominant, whereas women use both sides equally.[14] Because this connector is thought to influence behaviors, a dominant left brain results in more logical, rational, and linear approaches, whereas a dominant right brain is related to artistic, intuitive, and emotional behavior.

An alternative view argues that cognitive factors influence gender perceptions, and that these are socially constructed. This theory assumes that a child is influenced by cultural forces that shape behavior based on an individual's sex. In this view, gender stereotypes are socially constructed. For instance, how parents describe behavior, clothing, or toys as male or female can elicit certain types of stereotypical perceptions and behavior. If a parent says to a young boy, "You can't do the dishes, this is a girl's job," or to a young girl, "You can't do carpentry, this is boy's work," that child will see certain household tasks as being feminine or masculine. Gender roles are generated through an ongoing process of teaching and modeling what children learn.[15]

Perceptions about women in general, and women entrepreneurs in particular, are derived from five major sources: parents, peers, education, media, and work experience.[16] The differential affects of these five factors have led to socially constructed perceptions and expectations held by both men and women that effectively raise the bar for women in their race for success.[17]

Parents

Parents have a strong impact on gender roles through what they say and the examples they set. In particular, they influence the appropriateness of certain careers and business opportunities. If parents infer that boys are better at managing money, negotiating, or taking chances, and girls are better off being compliant, nurturing, and domestic, these inferences might suggest traditional gender roles. Over time, boys will feel more capable with money, negotiation, and risk taking, and girls will feel less capable in these areas. In some families, the mother stays at home, cares for the family, and carries out homemaker duties. In other families, the father might assume a greater responsibility for the family and children. However, even in two-parent households, when both parents work, the mother generally takes on the responsibility for child care, cleaning, and arranging for housekeeping, whereas the father is more likely to fix or build.[18]

Think about your own childhood. Did your parents have clearly defined household roles? Were girls the cooks and household caretakers, and boys worked outside, did home repairs, and painted? The extent to which traditional work and household roles are reinforced has an impact on how men and women perceive their career opportunities and the possibilities for entrepreneurship or growing a venture.

Peers

Social networks develop at an early age. Over time, frequency of interactions can lead to mutuality and trust. The friendships that evolve between boys and girls are influenced by social context, activities, and school norms. For example, activities such as competitive sports teach competition, develop loyalty toward an organization, and build relationships through their team play. Girls' friendships are more conversation based, with thoughts and feelings, whereas for boys, friendships are more activity based. When relationships are gender segregated, girls and boys are less likely to reach out and build networks with the other sex. Alternatively, boys' networks tend to be more transactional, ordered, status oriented, and competitive, whereas for girls they are more affinitive, inclusive, and communication based.[19] When early social networks are sex segregated, women might later encounter difficulties in understanding the language, ground rules for, and values in business networks.

In the business world, effective utilization of personal networks is important to gaining information, access to capital, and access to technology. Therefore it is important to be able to establish ties across diverse networks.[20] Young boys and girls who had predominantly single-sex network relationships might have difficulty building cross-sex relationships. Perceptions about the expectations and goals of such relationships might be gendered depending on their early social experiences. For example, for the young boy whose network was based on years of hockey, gamesmanship, competition, and winning would be salient. Similarly, for the young girl whose network was based on the orchestra or glee club, affiliation, congruence, and cooperation would be more important. Thus, early experiences in peer networks and relationships influence later participation in formal and informal networks, as well as set up expectations for who participates, how they communicate, and norms for behaviors.

Education

Most of our younger years are spent in school. Our ultimate career choices and approaches are heavily influenced by teacher–student interactions and the content of classes. Similarly, the content of textbooks has an impact on perceptions of success, as does the incidence of either male or female role models in textbooks or class examples. In the classroom setting, the extent to which boys and girls are encouraged to participate in class discussions also has important consequences. Boys generally receive more consistent responses to their work, such as praise and encouragement, yet they break the rules, and interrupt more often even if they don't know the answer. On the other hand, girls receive less praise and might be less likely to raise their hands unless they know the answer. The encouragement or lack of encouragement can be a subtle barrier for young girls in pursuing math- or science-related topics.

The extent to which girls are encouraged to study math, science, or engineering as careers is also important. When girls are discouraged from these areas, they are less confident about pursuit of studies, careers, and jobs. If science textbooks feature only male inventors and scientists in the pictures and stories, the perception is created that only boys can be scientists, and successful female role models are missing.[21] Although these educational influences are increasingly gender neutral, with regards to encouragement for women to study law, business, and medicine, girls are still less often encouraged to study hard sciences such as physics or engineering. In sum, our educational experiences directly influence the expectations for qualifications of entrepreneurs, and the types of skills they should bring to their ventures.

Media

The constant and compelling presence of the media influences our perceptions about successful entrepreneurs and role models. From early childhood, games, television programs, movies, newspapers, and magazines influence what and how we think about careers. If we consider that the average child watches 22 hours of television a week, the roles and activities of women in advertising, movies, and weekly programs has a significant influence on their perceptions.[22] The extent to which women are in positions of decision making, have professional occupations, and manage equally with their male counterparts influences both boys and girls in terms of their aspirations and views of what is acceptable or not for a career or boss. Similarly, if you flip through the average business magazine, it's a good bet that less than 20% of the pictures and stories feature women managers, executives, or entrepreneurs. The same is true for media and academic articles—in the 1990s, women were featured in less than 10% of all these.[23] The influence of the media affects the way women are perceived and expectations for their success in business.

Work Experience

Work experiences of both men and women influence perceptions of gender roles. Work rules that are inflexible, including norms for hours worked per day, amount of notice for travel trips, expected number of travel days per year, and international relocation might more often be associated with traditional male-developed company cultures. This type of experience can influence a man's expectations for how women-led businesses should be structured and operate. Some women working in an environment where expectations are for 16-hour days or 230 days of travel per year might feel unsuited for these settings. Further, the extent to which a company has a critical mass of women in management positions impacts the culture, policies, and values of the work environment, and of course the work experience that women and men take into business or entrepreneurship.

When it comes to women in leadership positions, women are less often in positions of authority. Today few women hold senior executive positions in Fortune 500 companies. For this reason, men might not work in companies where they see women in charge, making decisions, or leading the organization. This can create the perception that women are less capable of leading a fast-growth company, building a management team, or growing the venture. The work experience and type of company culture from which men and women move to either venture capital investing or entrepreneurship has a major impact on their expectations and perceptions for venture-funded businesses.

From these five general factors—parents, peers, education, media, and work experience—conflicting expectations for women and their roles emerges. More often than not, women are socialized to pursue education and careers that are less financially oriented, to have lower aspirations, seek lower level jobs, or create businesses in service sectors. In addition, expectations for a primary role in family responsibilities continue. By contrast, the behaviors associated with successful entrepreneurship are encouraged in men, and celebrated by the media. The expectations for entrepreneurial success can be opposite the qualities and behaviors associated with women, which creates a contradiction when we think about women leading growing ventures.

Winning the Race for Success

The persistence of these perceptions and expectations about entrepreneurial success and women's roles raises the bar women must clear in their race for growth. Higher hurdles slow women's ability to develop products, inhibit their chances of hiring capable employees, and limit money invested in a business. They affect the ability of women to innovate and expand a venture, and cause women to work harder and longer to locate, gain a meeting with, or convince investors, lawyers, or accountants that their business has high potential. Importantly, it also means investors might be missing good opportunities for investment, and that unique business ideas might not be rapidly and widely diffused. By knowing more about the hurdles, women entrepreneurs can take stock of their situation and craft a better strategy to clear them in their race for success.

The rest of this book should help growth-oriented women entrepreneurs specifically, and women in business generally, realize their full potential by understanding and dealing with the hurdles encountered. The next chapter focuses on resource acquisition. It tells the story of two women entrepreneurs starting an innovative growth venture. It explains their start-up process, early financing activities, and quest for money. This sets the stage for a deeper exploration of the hurdles. In each chapter, we provide examples of one major hurdle and explain why the bar is higher. We include stories and lessons from women entrepreneurs, and offer specific steps women can take to get over the bar, improving their chances of success in growing a venture.

Notes

1. Center for Women's Business Research. 2003. *Key Facts about Women-Owned Businesses.*

2. Brush, C. G., Greene, P. G., & Hart, M. M. 2001. From initial idea to unique advantage: The entrepreneurial challenge of constructing a resource base, *Academy of Management Executive.* 15:1, 64–80.

3. Ibid.

4. Welles, E. O. 1999, August. The perfect Internet business. *Inc.,* 71–78.

5. Longsworth, E. 1991. *Anatomy of a Start-Up: Why Some New Businesses Succeed and Others Fail.* Boston, MA: Goldhirsch Group.

6. Bird, B. J. 1989. *Entrepreneurial Behavior.* New York: Scott Foresman.

7. The name and company are disguised.

8. Collins, O. E., & Moore, D. G. 1964. *The Enterprising Man.* East Lansing, MI: MSU Business Studies; McClelland, D. 1961. *The Achieving Society.* Princeton, NJ: Van Nostrand; Hebert, R. F. & Link, A. N. 1982. *The Entrepreneur: Mainstream Views and Radical Critiques.* New York: Praeger.

9. Brush, C. G. 1992. Research on women business owners: Past trends, a new perspective and future directions. *Entrepreneurship Theory and Practice.* 16:4, 5–30.

10. Blau, F., Ferber, M., & Winkler, A. 2002. *The Economics of Women, Men, and Work.* Upper Saddle River, NJ: Prentice Hall.

11. Bem, S. 1993. *The Lenses of Gender.* New Haven, CT: Yale University Press; Hauser, A., & Zaslow, E. 2002. Gender roles: From childhood to professional life, in Smith, D. M. *Women at Work: Leadership for the Next Century.* Upper Saddle River, NJ: Prentice Hall.

12. Stereotypes occur as a result of attributing the supposed characteristic of a whole group to all its individual members. Stereotyping assumes and emphasizes the uniformity within a group and then exaggerates differences between groups. A stereotype may also ascribe characteristics to the group that are more

positive or negative than other groups, or that are patently untrue. *www.oise .utoronto.ca/projects/inclusive/HTML-versions/defn.html*

13. Blau, F. D., Ferber, M. A., & Winkler, A. E. 2002. *The Economics of Women, Men, and Work* (4th ed.). Upper Saddle River, NJ: Prentice Hall.

14. Hauser, A., & Zaslow, E. 2002. Gender roles: From childhood to professional life, in Smith, D. M. *Women at Work: Leadership for the Next Century.* Upper Saddle River, NJ: Prentice Hall.

15. Bandura, A., & Wallers, R. H. 1963. *Social Learning and Personality Development.* New York: Holt Rinhart and Winston.

16. For a more extensive discussion of gender roles, see Smith, D. M. 2002. *Women at Work: Leadership for the Next Century.* Upper Saddle River, NJ: Prentice Hall.

17. Powell, G. 1993. *Women & Men in Management.* Newbury Park, CA: Sage.

18. Smith, D. M. 2002., op. cit.

19. Gilligan, C. 1982. *In a Different Voice.* Cambridge, MA: Harvard University Press.

20. Aldrich, H. 1989. Networking among women entrepreneurs, in Hagan, O., Rivchun, C., & Sexton, D. L. (Eds.). *Women-Owned Businesses.* New York: Praeger.

21. American Association of University Women, 1995.

22. Smith, D. M. 2002., op. cit.

23. Baker, T., Aldrich, H., & Liou, N. 1997. Invisible entrepreneurs: The neglect of women business owners by mass media and scholarly journals in the USA. *Entrepreneurship and Regional Development.* 9:3, 221–239.

3

FUNDING SOURCES
FOR BUSINESSES
ON THE "GROW"

There are many ways to fund a young and growing business. You know many of them, but there are some rather ingenious alternatives that creative entrepreneurs have used. In this chapter, we provide a brief overview of informal sources of capital (self, family, friends, suppliers, and customers). We also consider private and commercial debt and equity investments, whether by angel investors or venture capitalists. Private equity is a very important source of capital for those entrepreneurs who have great expectations—not because of the number of enterprises it supports (less than 1% of all start-ups get venture capital)—but because it is such a powerful force driving the growth of the largest and most successful ventures.

Robin Chase and Antje Danielson's search for resources to fund their new Zipcar start-up illustrates how to launch a business on a shoestring and then how to attract and engage equity investors.[1]

Robin Chase and Antje Danielson met on the playground of a Cambridge elementary school. Both were parents of kindergartners. They were also well-trained professionals with dreams of building businesses of their own. Chase, a mother of three, had forged a successful career in consulting, financial services, and publishing after completing her MBA at the Massachusetts Institute of Technology (MIT). Danielson, a Ph.D. trained in Germany and employed at Harvard University, was married to a doctoral student and was the mother of one son.

Their friendship grew as the two women discussed possibilities for new ventures they might start. Danielson had seen a car-sharing concept in Europe that she thought had great potential in the U.S. market. Robin Chase agreed and, in September 1999, she began doing research and writing a business plan for a Boston-based version of the concept. Over a year passed from their first discussions to the closing of the first round of financing. During that time, the two founders talked to friends, advisors, business mentors, angel investor groups, and venture capitalists about Zipcar, refined the concept and gathered the resources they needed to build the business. They contracted with technical consultants to develop the operating and billing technology.

The two launched the company with "sweat equity" (their own investment of hard work and personal funds). They worked out of their own homes, took no salaries, and kept full-time staff to a minimum by outsourcing work to consultants, co-opted free services, then cobbled together a series of loans from friends using a bridge note that would convert to equity at the Series A price with an interest premium. They leased the cars for their fleet, thereby minimizing the up-front investment they had to make in the business.

They eventually tapped out their own funds and exhausted the resources available from their closest contacts. The company was not a likely candidate for bank debt because it owned few tangible assets that could serve as collateral. The founders were well aware that their business venture would be unlikely to reach its full potential without a substantial equity investment. Consequently, Robin Chase devoted as much time and energy to raising capital as she did to building the new business organization, finding customers, and setting up operation during the first year. She minimized capital commitments and took on personal debt to ensure the company's operation during the fund-raising process.

Chase and Danielson were typical entrepreneurs in many ways. They shared a burning desire to create a business of their own. Each had independently investigated several business ideas and, if she found that a proposal was not sufficiently promising, rejected it. When the two women came on a concept that made sense to both of them, they went into action. They were aggressive and creative in building the Zipcar business organization with very limited resources. They called on experts in their own network for free advice and assistance and followed up on every lead. They asked friends and relatives to supply services and didn't hesitate to follow up with a request for business loans as well. A former classmate of Chase's provided the first large investment ($50,000) in the form of a loan.

Where Chase and Danielson definitely differed from most entrepreneurs was in their decision to grow the business rapidly and to fund that growth with angel investments and venture capital.

Robin Chase and Antje Danielson brought significant personal resources to their new venture that enabled them to get the business started on their own. In addition to their vision, their energy and commitment, and their financial contributions, they brought advanced degrees, professional work experience, some industry knowledge, and important network contacts within the Boston business community. Chase had established a strong reputation as a business manager that provided the team with credibility and contacts. Danielson was an academic, but her expertise in energy conservation and her research relationship with Ford Motor Company translated to strong credibility within the context of the automotive industry. The pair divided the tasks of start-up along the lines of their respective expertise. Chase refined the business concept, researched the market, and wrote the plan, and Danielson focused on building relationships in the car industry.

Money and the Start-Up Process

The vast majority of businesses in the United States are launched on the founder's own dime. Entrepreneurs draw on their personal savings and provide lots of free labor to get the ball rolling. These early investments are frequently used to conduct research, lease space and office equipment, create brochures and buy ads, stock inventory, or hire employees. In a 2002 survey of women business owners, 55% reported that they needed less than $25,000 to start up their businesses and only 6.5% reported needing more than $100,000.[2]

When personal accounts are exhausted, most entrepreneurs continue to build their ventures by using credit card debt. They also turn to family and friends seeking gifts, loans, and investments. Sometimes these exchanges are treated as "arm's length" transactions, with the entrepreneur and the investor or creditor drawing up documents that call for repayment on specified terms. If it is an investment rather than a loan, the documents might represent the transfer of some portion of the ownership of the business. The fact that these businesses started with limited resources does not mean that they do not have great potential. Of the entrepreneurs who were included in the 2003 Inc. 500,[3] 61% reported that they started their businesses with less than $50,000. At the close of 2002, these 500 private companies had aggregate revenue of $14.4 billion, with the median company revenue reported at $10.8 million.

When a new business begins to gain momentum, it might also generate excess cash. Many entrepreneurs depend on these internally generated funds as the primary source of investment capital for continued growth. Although you could argue that this is the most prudent way to operate, taking this conservative approach poses its own set of risks. A slow growth strategy could give competitors an opportunity to establish brand leadership or claim the best locations. It could cost the company its best chance at success.

If more cash is required than either the founders or the business can generate, entrepreneurs often seek debt financing. When we speak about debt, you might think immediately of banks, but there are several less formal sources of debt capital. For example, you could stretch out the time you take to pay creditors, thereby making your suppliers a source of short-term financing. Or you might organize a business in which customers pay in advance. Magazine subscriptions, club dues, retainers for personal services, and deposits for custom orders are all examples of how you can get money from customers before you have to deliver anything.

Banks and other lending institutions are important sources of debt capital. In a recent survey of 607 independent business owners, 37% of the men and 33% of the women reported that they had sought bank financing within the last 12 months.[4] Of course, banks expect the loan applicant to provide collateral, sign personal guarantees, or show

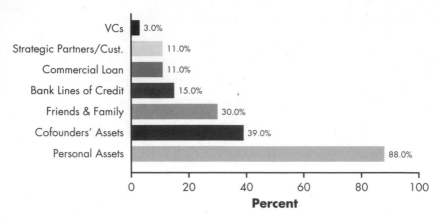

FIGURE 3.1   Sources of capital. Adapted from *Inc.*, October 2002.

strong evidence of positive cash flow over time. These requirements make it very difficult for early-stage ventures (especially those with no hard assets) to use conventional bank debt. However, once the business has an established track record with a reasonably secure and predictable source of revenues, commercial bank debt is an option. Figure 3.1 illustrates the primary sources of start-up capital as reported by entrepreneurs in 2002.[5]

Growth Capital versus Start-Up Funds

A Strategic Approach

All financing decisions are really strategic choices. The choices about where, when, and how much money to raise are based not only on the needs of the business, but also on the entrepreneur's attitudes toward ownership, control, and risk. Whatever the reasons behind them, they are strategic decisions that affect the size of the business and the time it takes to reach profitability.

Almost all new businesses—whether ultimately large or small—start out self-funded. For example, like Chase and Danielson, founding teams usually put up all the seed capital, invest their own labor, and take on personal debt (credit card, home equity loans, or informal or formal loans from family and friends). These early investments enable them to build the business foundation and to demonstrate the viability of the concept and their own capabilities in executing. Although the founders have some financial exposure, at this stage, the risk is limited to those who are personally involved in or connected to the enterprise.

Although the majority of entrepreneurs rely on funds generated by the business to achieve growth, as the business becomes more complex and the financial needs increase, the founding team might find it has exhausted its own resources. Internal funding might be insufficient to grow the business. If that is the case, outside funding becomes an important alternative.

To go beyond the circle of investors who know and love you well (and who often are investing in you rather than in the business itself), you must establish concrete evidence of the business's success and of its potential for the future. Whether you are seeking debt or equity capital, you need to be able to demonstrate that not only is the business concept viable, but also that you have the managerial competence to run it.

When you have exhausted your initial capital, you might choose to raise money from outside investors, rather than creditors. If this is an option you want to pursue, you are most likely to be able to tap into your own circle of friends and business associates first. Investments from these sources are usually relatively small ($500–$10,000). However, if your business has larger capital needs, angel funding (private investments from wealthy individuals who are not personal friends, but are often entrepreneurs themselves) is another reasonable alternative. Angel investments might be as low as $10,000, but are more likely to be in the range of $50,000 to $250,000. Only a very small number of start-ups will actually seek institutional venture capital to fund their business growth and development and less than 10% of those are likely to be seriously considered for investment. Early-stage venture capital investments usually range from $500,000 to $3 million.

The decisions about where, when, and how much capital to raise will have substantial impact on what projects a business can undertake, how quickly it can get products to market, how much it can advertise, and how well it can support customers. These decisions will also determine who has a claim on the assets of the company or shares in the ownership and governance of the business. The choice of investment partners, the terms of the deal, and the timing of the decisions will not only enable growth; they will also determine the flexibility and governance of the firm. The decisions are never just about the money. The following sections cover the various financing options in more detail.

Bootstrap Financing

Building a business through the use of one's own resources and those generated internally by the business is referred to as *bootstrapping*—a term that means picking up oneself by one's own bootstraps. The dictionary definition: *"**Bootstrap**: to help oneself without the aid of others; to use one's own resources"*[6]

In entrepreneurial ventures, bootstrapping translates to finding creative ways of getting resources for the business that free the management team from the need to raise external funds—either from equity investors or institutional lenders.[7] Some typical bootstrapping techniques are shown in Table 3.1.[8]

TABLE 3.1   Bootstrapping Techniques

Cash Generation	Cash Substitutes	Cash Conservation
Use of personal credit card	Bartering for goods and services	Withholding or reducing entrepreneur's salary
Loans and investments from family and friends	Borrowing or leasing equipment	Hiring employees at below-market wages
Collecting early (billing quickly and limiting accounts receivable)		Paying late (slowing down payments to suppliers)
		Reducing quality on nonessential items; using lower cost substitutes
		Minimizing inventory

Most bootstrap entrepreneurs reinvest cash from the business operation in the development of business systems, the expansion of the goods and services offered, or the addition of new locations. A 1996 study of U.S. entrepreneurs indicated that 71% of business owners used internally generated funds to support growth, 22% used commercial bank loans, and 25% used credit cards. Furthermore, 21% continued to draw on personal or family resources, 12% used leasing arrangements, 11% worked with vendor credit, and 9% used personal loans.[9] This growth through a creative combination of personal investment, debt, and internally generated funds focuses management attention on cash flow.

A bootstrapping strategy requires both patience and ingenuity. It enables entrepreneurs to retain tighter personal control over their businesses, but it can also slow the rate at which their ventures develop new products, add locations, or enter new markets. Because bootstrapping takes time, this approach to financing might put the enterprise at risk of being overtaken by competitors with greater resources and faster time to market.

Chase and Danielson began by investing their own funds in the business. When the business plan was completed, they tested its viability with trusted advisors. After several iterations, they identified a list of prospects and used their network to get meetings with potential advisors and investors. They began establishing relationships with suppliers and negotiating to finance their fleet of automobiles through leasing arrangements. They also began to build a board of directors and to gain attention from the press. To conserve capital, they took no salary for the first year and they enlisted staff members who were willing to work at discounted rates or to accept deferred compensation. Chase was able to secure a loan of $50,000 from a former Sloan School classmate, another female entrepreneur who had built a very successful company.

Credit

Most entrepreneurs use a combination of savings, personal debt, and "minimizing" techniques such as foregone or delayed payments of salary and benefit packages and the use of alternative office space, equipment, and staff support during the start-up phase of their businesses. Credit cards and bank loans can provide additional financing options. The most common sources of credit during the earliest stages of the business are personal credit cards. (In fact, most entrepreneurs use more than one personal credit card to maximize their purchasing power.)[10] Businesses that have been operating successfully for two to three years find bank financing more accessible because they have a demonstrated track record, predictable cash flow, and, in many cases, more tangible assets that can serve as collateral.

> **Robin Chase learned to stretch the company's limited cash by stretching payables while accelerating the collection of receivables. She set up the technology to support a billing system that enabled Zipcar to bill customers' credit cards immediately upon their return of a car, thus eliminating any of the normal delays associated with a traditional billing and collection cycle.**

> **Although their initial funding came from private loans, Zipcar's founders knew that they would need commercial credit to build the necessary infrastructure and grow their business. They were confident that they could secure it once they began to establish a track record. They also structured the deal so that a major portion of the private debt they raised would be converted to equity if and when the company closed a round of equity financing.**

Institutional Debt

Debt financing is available from many sources, including banks, other commercial lending institutions, leasing companies, and suppliers. Most loan agreements call for regular repayments of the principal plus interest, whether set at a specified rate or adjusted according to a formula. Credit cards are often an entrepreneur's easiest source of credit for the business. Although convenient for meeting short-term financial needs, credit card debt is an expensive form of financing, usually bearing higher rates of interest and shorter repayment cycles than commercial credit. Many entrepreneurs raise funds for the business by taking out personal bank loans and pledging assets such as their homes.

Commercial loans secured with business collateral provide another alternative. Short-term loans from a bank might be unsecured if needed for less than 90 days. The team might instead seek a line of credit to be drawn down only when needed—particularly to meet short-term capital requirements. Longer-term loans from commercial banks or lending institutions must be negotiated carefully. The terms include the amount of funding available, how interest rates will be determined, the repayment formula, restrictions on use, and business operating covenants. One major disadvantage of debt is the fact that payments are due on a regular basis, whether or not the business is generating revenue. Furthermore, lenders can call their loans if the terms of the agreement are not met or if economic times change. Doing so is almost certain to precipitate a business crisis and could force a struggling venture to shut down or seriously curtail its operations.

Since the early 1990s, many banks have aggressively sought out new business with women entrepreneurs. Wells Fargo & Co. and Fleet Bank are two notable examples of banks with loan funds dedicated to women business owners.[11] Most banks became much more responsive to the needs of women business owners in the early 1990s and—whether or not they have funds specifically dedicated to women-owned businesses—have made the process of securing commercial bank credit accessible to women on the same terms available to men.[12]

> **Chase and Danielson made use of business credit in their start-up phase. They structured debt agreements with private lenders and secured lease agreements for the fleet of cars they needed. They also sought venture capital and approached banks for commercial loans.**

Equity

Outsiders who purchase equity in a new business have an ownership share in the venture. These investors expect to receive a substantial share of the wealth created by the enterprise (profits or proceeds of a sale) and many expect to play a meaningful role in the governance of the company. Early-stage equity investments made by the founders include personal financial investments, including cash and foregone compensation, concept development and business planning, and the sweat equity involved in operating the business. As long as they are the sole investors, the entrepreneurs own the entire business, but as they bring in partners who provide additional financial capital or managerial expertise, they exchange shares of ownership for the resources that these partners contribute. The good news about equity is that if there are no profits generated by the business, there is generally no repayment of funds required of the company. (Preferred stock might require interest payments, but these are usually deferred for an extended period of time or until a liquidity event takes place.) Unlike bankers or other holders of debt instruments, equity investors don't have their hand out every month. The bad news is that equity investors are partners for as long as the business continues, or until their shares are transferred or liquidated and, if they are directors of the company, they can force reorganization, including the replacement of the president and CEO.

Typical examples of equity holders include the founding team, private investors (family, friends, and business angels), small business investment companies (SBICs, which are similar to venture capital partnerships, but which can leverage invested capital with debt), private venture capital partnerships, partnerships affiliated with financial corporations, investment banks, corporate venturing programs, and direct investments from banks or financial corporations.

Sources of Equity Capital

The kind of private equity investment that might be most suitable for a young venture varies according to the age, stage of development, and capital needs of the business. Investments by family, friends, and angel investors are frequently used to fund the early stages of a company's development—when the capital required is less than $1 million and the proof of concept is still underway. Although there are some venture funds and SBICs that target early-stage companies and provide seed investments, most prefer to become involved when the capital needs are higher (over $1 million) and the company's product and market are more fully developed.

When venture capitalists invest in a young company, they often agree to participate in subsequent rounds of financing—provided the company meets its benchmarks successfully and is able to attract other reputable investors. Table 3.2, adapted from *Pratt's Guide to Venture Capital*, illustrates at what stage of development and at what level of capital needs different private equity investors are most interested and appropriate.

TABLE 3.2   Equity Financing Sources by Stage of Development

Round	Description	Amounts	Source
Seed	Prove concept	$25K–500K	Friends & family Angels Early-stage venture capitalists
Start-Up	Complete development Initial marketing	$500K–3MM	Angels Early-stage venture capitalists
First	Full scale mfg. & sales	$1.5–5MM	Venture capitalists
Second	WC for initial expansion	$3–10MM	Venture capitalists Private placement
Third	Expansion capital	$5–30MM	Venture capitalists Private placement
Bridge	Funds to allow company to reach IPO within year	$3–20MM	Mezzanine firms Investment bankers Private placement Venture capitalists

Note. FROM *Pratt's Guide to Venture Capital Sources.* 2001.[13]

Angel Investing

Angel investors are individuals who invest their own money in promising new ventures. The term *angel* was originally used to describe the investors who backed Broadway musicals, but is now more widely applied to private investors in new ventures of all types. Business angels are usually successful business executives and entrepreneurs who want to invest in the next generation of promising new ventures. They differ from the circle of family and friends who invest because their interest is an "arm's length" transaction. Most angels invest in early-stage or seed funding for businesses that will later seek venture capital.

Because of the level of risk they assume, angels are required by law to meet certain baseline requirements that assure they are either accredited or sophisticated investors. Regulation D (Rules Governing the Limited Offer and Sale of Securities Without Registration Under the Securities Act of 1933) defines an *accredited investor* as someone who meets at least one of the following criteria: net worth of $1 million, annual income for past two years of $200,000, or joint income with spouse of $300,000 for past two years. A *sophisticated investor* is defined as one who has the educational, professional, and investment background sufficient to make reasonable investment decisions about the specific company.[14]

Although many private investors have organized into investing groups (e.g., Band of Angels, Walnut Ventures, HubAngels, Tech Coast Angels, Colorado Capital Alliance, 8 Wings, Seraph Capital), most angels choose to invest on an individual basis. Angels usually focus on businesses within their own geographic area and are most likely to invest in industries and technologies that are related to their own expertise.

Like venture capitalists, angels expect a higher than average return on capital (approximately 10–15 points above the S & P 500 return on equity) and they anticipate a liquidity event (a public or private sale of the company) within five to seven years of the investment. They provide capital in much smaller allocations than do venture capitalists (generally in the $50,000–$250,000 range) and are often more interested in hands-on involvement in the organization. The investments through this informal source of funding are smaller on a deal-by-deal basis than are venture capital investments, but in the aggregate, angels invest substantially more in the entrepreneurial economy than do venture capitalists. (For example, in 1997, venture capitalists invested approximately $16 billion in new ventures, whereas angels were estimated to have invested close to $20 billion.)[15]

A major challenge for entrepreneurs lies in the identification and engagement of business angels in the enterprise. Most networks are local and the most fruitful connections are those with individuals who have experience in an industry or technology similar to that of the new venture. There are many organizations—both local and national—that sponsor networking events intended to bring angels and entrepreneurs together. For example, the MIT Enterprise Forum operates 24 chapters worldwide that serve both entrepreneurs and resource providers. Springboard Enterprises is a national not-for-profit organization dedicated to facilitating women's access to the equity markets through regional venture forums that bring entrepreneurs, venture capitalists, and angels together. The University of New Hampshire hosts the Angel Capital Electronic (ACE) Network, which is an electronic matching service for angel investors and entrepreneurs. The Small Business Administration provides a wide range of financing references on its Web page, *www.sba.gov.*

Although finding and engaging angel investors is a challenge for anyone, women entrepreneurs have experienced particular difficulty. They are less likely to have prior entrepreneurial experience or to have achieved a high level of managerial responsibility in a corporate setting. As a result, they are unlikely to participate in networks with high-net-worth individuals who are potential angel investors. If they do establish contacts, they need to build a strong case for their capability and commitment to carry out the new business successfully, often without the benefit of established reputation or the trust engendered by longstanding relationships. Table 3.3 summarizes how angel investors connect and make deals with entrepreneurs (particularly women entrepreneurs).

TABLE 3.3   Framework for Angel Investing

| Topic | Supply | | Demand |
	Angel Investing	Public Investing	Women Entrepreneurs
Locating potential investments	Informal word of mouth, friends	Many sources (e.g., investment periodicals, brokers, trade publications)	Relationship development through social capital
Available information	Limited historical information, often in new markets with limited information	Public information about historical performance and markets	Market information search through social capital and applied human capital
Investment terms	Extensive negotiation regarding price, type of security, terms	Price set by market	Extensive and sophisticated financial acumen to allow for negotiation
Liquidity	Illiquid—usually locked in for several years	Liquid—can see at will	Financial resources to allow for flexibility

TABLE 3.3   Framework for Angel Investing (Continued)

	Supply		Demand
Topic	Angel Investing	Public Investing	Women Entrepreneurs
Involvement with investors	Frequent reporting, advising, board membership	None	Organizational capital regarding systems and culture
Portfolio characteristics	Limited diversification (in early years might only be 1–4 investments) in private equity	Broad diversification is easily and quickly achieved	Venture performance to sustain firm attractiveness

Note. ADAPTED FROM *Business Angels.* KEELEY, COOPER, BLOOMER (1998)

During the first year of Zipcar's operation, Robin Chase managed to negotiate a series of bridge loans (short term funding to be repaid when more permanent equity financing was in place), leasing agreements for 19 cars, and an equity investment of $1.3 million. When the equity investment closed in November 2000, Chase paid off the company's $360,000 in loans and converted the remaining portion of the early financing to equity. She planned to use the remainder to pay off accounts payable and to build the Boston market, generate positive cash flow, and prove the Zipcar concept. Throughout the first year, she and Danielson had conserved cash by working without salary, subcontracting out specific projects rather than hiring permanent staff, and working out of their homes instead of renting office space. They presented their plan to former business associates, business school professors, private investors, and venture forums (Springboard 2000). They listened to the feedback and constantly revised the plan. The equity financing they secured included funding from one Boston-based community venture fund and several individual angels. The funding was committed in September 2000, but the deal did not close and the cash exchange hands until November—nearly 14 months after Chase and Danielson first committed to create the new venture.

Government-Supported Investments

Unlike equity investors who expect to own part of the new business, special equity investments are grants from programs created to stimulate small business start-ups or technological innovation. The funds typically support initial product or technology development and the granting agency does not share in ownership of the business. Federally sponsored special equity programs include the Small Business Innovation Research (SBIR) Program and Small Business Technology Transfer (STTR) Program. At the state level, such grants might come from programs managing employee pension funds, or from state high-technology development programs. Detailed information about how to secure assistance under these programs is available at *www.sba.gov/sbir/*.

Hybrids: Government-Supported Venture Capital

In 1958, Congress paved the way for the infusion of substantially more money into the venture capital pipeline. The Small Business Investment Act provided the means for SBICs, private companies licensed by the Small Business Administration, to increase the venture capital available for new companies. The act enabled SBICs to leverage the capital they had raised (by a factor of two to three times) through the use of debentures guaranteed by the Small Business Administration. SBICs must raise a minimum of $5 million ($10 million if they intend to use participating securities) with a minimum of 30% ($1.5–3 million) raised from sources unaffiliated with management. Each SBIC is eligible to add to the capital raised by selling debentures that are guaranteed by the Small Business Administration. (SBICs can increase funds raised from investors up to 300% of funds, but the total fund size is capped at $108.8 million.) SBIC funds are much smaller than many of the established venture firms and are more likely to be interested in seed and early-stage investments. Throughout the 1960s and 1970s,

SBICs accounted for up to one third of all venture financing, but by 1990, the percentage had fallen to only 5%.

Venture Capital

If entrepreneurial firms are the engines of the U.S. economy, then venture capital is the high-octane fuel that powers many of the most promising among them. It is, of course, a source of funding limited to a small and select group of entrepreneurs but, because venture capital has figured so prominently in the success of U.S. companies, it is considered by many to be the premier financial resource for entrepreneurs. More than 33% of the companies that went public (made an IPO of their stock) between 1991 and 2000 were able to achieve critical mass rapidly because they were funded by venture capital.

Not only do venture-backed companies have a greater likelihood of being sold—either privately or as publicly traded companies—but, they also consistently outperform other ventures. For example, the venture-capital-funded public companies had approximately twice the sales and paid nearly three times the federal taxes (per $1,000 of assets) as did the average non-venture-backed public company.[16] They also led in research and development investment (three times that of non-venture-funded companies) and exports. With results like these, it's natural to ask, "What is the magic associated with venture capital?"

Venture capital is money provided by professional investors to promising young firms in exchange for an ownership stake in the business. (The term *private equity* is sometimes used interchangeably with venture capital, but actually includes all equity investments including angel investments and professionally organized funds that are dedicated to mergers, acquisitions, turnarounds, and leveraged buyouts.) Venture capital is that form of private equity invested in the early and expansion stages of a new company's growth. Although the terms and conditions vary from one deal to the next, funds are generally invested with a long-term perspective and deep commitment to managerial assistance and oversight. Ventures capitalists who fund early-growth-stage businesses generally expect to invest in subsequent rounds and to harvest their gains in three to seven years. The investments enable entrepreneurial firms to complete product development, launch production, carry out a marketing campaign, hire key staff members, and undertake geographic expansion at a much faster pace and on a larger scale than those that are bootstrapped.

Venture capitalists today serve as professional intermediaries between large numbers of investors—both individual and institutional—and new enterprises that are hungry for growth and development capital.

Venture firms might take a corporate form as they did at the inception of the industry in 1946, but most are organized as limited partnerships (see Figure 3.2). These two forms of venture capital firms predominate in the venture marketplace, but affiliates or subsidiaries of banks, insurance companies, and large corporations (particularly those in technology-driven businesses) also create and manage venture funds. Corporate venture funds frequently seek out and finance new ventures in technologies related to their core business to create new opportunities or partners that fit with the corporation's long-term strategic goals.

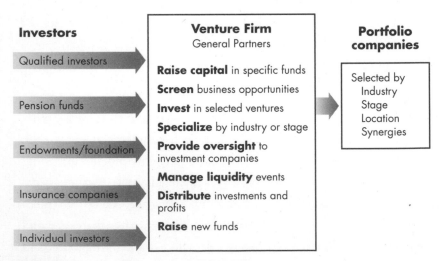

FIGURE 3.2   The Flow of venture capital.

The general partners (or managing directors) of a venture fund raise money from investors who commit discrete amounts of capital to be invested in a specific fund. Investments in the fund are generally made in "units" with $5 million to $20 million being the norm in recent years. (This high entrance price precludes most individuals from investing directly in venture capital funds, although some alternative vehicles have been developed to allow smaller investors to pool their capital.) The amount of money that each investor commits to the fund is drawn down or *called* during the early years of the fund's life—either at specified rates (e.g., one third each year for the first three years) or as individual investments are made. The general partners' goal is to invest the funds during the first three years and then manage the growth, financing, and exit strategies of their portfolio companies throughout the remainder of the fund's life.

Investments in venture capital funds are very illiquid. The funds are committed for the duration of the fund life and there is no formal secondary (or resale) market for the limited partners' positions. Returns are distributed to the limited partners when the entrepreneurial firms achieve liquidity either through public or private sale. All remaining holdings, whether they are liquid or not, are distributed at the end date of the fund. Because most funds are fully committed within the first three to four years, partners often raise second or "follow on" funds before the first fund is fully distributed and before its performance can be accurately measured. Because of the high risk associated with new start-ups, venture capital is not for the faint of heart.

Venture capital professionals serve as general partners and those who provide the funds are limited partners. (Their role in the investment is passive and their liability is limited to the funds invested.) The size of venture capital firms varies, depending on the number and size of funds under management as well as the complexity of the investment portfolio. A venture firm often manages several different funds, each with a different mix of general and limited partners.

Many funds are focused on particular industries (software, tele-communications, health care), or stage of development (seed, expansion, mezzanine). This specialization enables the general partners to be very focused, usually drawing on the expertise and experience of the partnership to define the scope of their investment portfolio. It also helps entrepreneurs determine which venture firms are most likely to be interested in a particular deal. For example, Boston-based Grey-lock's Web page identifies the firm's primary interests as early-stage investments in communications and enterprise information technology businesses. Highland Venture Partners shares an interest in communications and information technology businesses, and also actively invests in health care deals. The Silicon Valley partnership, Kleiner Perkins, Calufield & Byers has a portfolio heavily concentrated in the broadband, enterprise software and services, Internet infrastructure, and medical devices industries. Axxon Capital looks at opportunities in high-growth technology, wireless communication, and new media businesses, and is particularly interested in investing in women- and minority-led enterprises. Although not geographically limited, most venture capital firms prefer to invest in entrepreneurial teams in their own region so that they can leverage their business connections and be more directly involved in the business oversight.

Once they have secured the commitments to the fund from their limited partners, venture capitalists conduct searches for promising business opportunities, scrutinizing industry prospects, business concepts, and management teams. The general partners might be supported by a team of professional associates and principals who prescreen deals or assist in the due diligence process, but the investment decision making is done by the general partners working as a team. In addition to identifying and selecting particular deals, the general partners are responsible for diversifying the risk associated with investing in a start-up by building a portfolio of companies.

Venture capital represents a relatively high risk to investors, but with commensurately high returns. The 5- and 10-year annual returns for venture investments reported at the close of 2001 were 35.9% and 26.4%, respectively (Thomson Financial Venture Economics, NVCA 6/10/02). Such high rewards are a powerful inducement to participate in venture-capital-funded deals. In fact, more than $200 billion of venture capital was raised and invested between 1991 and 2000. A 2001 DRI-WEFA (formerly Wharton Econometric Forecasting Associates)[17] study indicated that venture-backed firms created between 1970 and 2000 contributed more than $1.3 trillion to the U.S. economy in 2000 (more than 13% of GDP). These firms employed more than 7.6 million people.

Because venture-funded enterprises are so highly visible in the marketplace (e.g., Digital Equipment, FedEx, Apple Computer, Microsoft, Yahoo!, Netscape, and eBay) and because their payoffs are so highly touted, many people believe that venture capital investment is a widespread phenomenon. However, the opposite is true. Of the more than 500,000 new firms created annually,[18] less than 1% participate in venture capital funding. As an example, in 2000, the $107 billion invested by venture capitalists went to just 8,208 companies, of which approximately 25% were first-time investments in young companies. Most investments represented follow-on (second or third round) rather than initial investment dollars.[19] In 2001 and 2002, the number of investments fell to 4,691 and 3,028, respectively, and the percentage of early-stage or first-time investments fell to 22%.[20]

Venture capital is not absolutely essential to the growth and financial success of promising firms, but it can reduce the time and the risks associated with growing a vibrant enterprise. Venture capitalists provide large amounts of money to support the growth of promising companies and they also provide oversight and network connections of significant value to the young firms. On average, only 2,201 companies were funded annually between 1991 and 2000. Those enterprises were screened carefully and judged by their venture capital investors to have substantial promise of high returns within an acceptable time horizon. Because they were able to secure venture capital investment, these enterprises had distinct competitive resource advantages in the race for success. They were among the most likely to get to market with new and useful goods and services, to create jobs, to spur the economy, and to provide high returns to their owners and investors. More details about the history and organization of the U.S. venture capital industry, as well as a description of the process of raising venture money, are included in Chapter 10.

Although the fund-raising bar was high for these two women entrepreneurs, Robin Chase and Antje Danielson were able to clear the financing hurdles—one by one—with their focus, persistence, and creative application of their own resources. They were highly motivated to create a large-scale enterprise that could be tested in Boston, then rolled out nationally to those metropolitan areas that had dense populations and a good public transportation infrastructure. By doing so, they were flying in the face of conventional wisdom—that women are only interested in small, local business enterprises that provide a good income and increased control of their work environment. They demonstrated commitment through their full-time, professional pursuit of the opportunity for over a year before securing equity funding—crafting, then recrafting the business plan—based on both informal and formal feedback. Both brought substantial relevant human capital to the venture, including business leadership, financial skills, and a knowledge of transportation and energy issues. They also conducted research on similar business operations in Europe to understand both operating and financial issues. They tapped an extensive network of professional contacts to gain advice, contacts, and contract labor—demonstrating in the process that women can be good "networkers" and build effective management teams. They developed a competent team that was willing to work on the fly. They were willing to assume the risk associated with debt capital and, over time, they were able to launch the Boston-area Zipcar, then extend it to Washington, DC and New York City. In 2003, with the concept proven and the competitive markets heating up, Chase raised an additional $4 million to continue Zipcar's growth.

Although Chase and Danielson were successful in clearing the hurdles they faced in starting and growing Zipcar, many women never get out of the starting blocks. The remainder of this book focuses on specific hurdles that women have to overcome to succeed in financing their entrepreneurial dreams. We will identify important challenges, discuss the underlying perceptions and realities, and offer strategies for clearing each bar on the way to entrepreneurial success.

Notes

1. The details of the founding and funding of Zipcar are taken from Hart and Carter, *Zipcar*, Harvard Business School Case 9-802-085, Harvard Business School Publishing, 9-02.
2. Center for Women's Business Research, 2002. *Women Business Owners of Color: New Accomplishments, Continuing Challenges.*
3. The 500 fastest growing privately held companies that have been in business at least five years and had at least $200,000 in revenues in 1998.
4. National Foundation for Women Business Owners, 1998. *Capital, Credit, and Financing: An Update Comparing Women and Men Business Owners' Sources and Uses of Capital.*
5. Mochari, I., October, 2002. The Numbers Game. *Inc.*
6. *Webster's Encyclopedic Dictionary of the English Language.* 1989. Avenel, NJ: Gramercy Books. p. 171.
7. Van Osnabrugge, M., & Robinson, R. J. 2000. *Angel Investing: Matching Start-Up Funds with Start-Up Companies.* San Francisco: Jossey-Bass.
8. Winborg, J. 2000. *Financing Small Businesses.* Halmstad, Sweden: SIRE Halmstad University.
9. National Foundation for Women Business Owners. 1996. *Capital, Credit, and Financing: Comparing Women and Men Business Owners' Sources and Uses of Capital.*
10. Ibid.
11. Wells Fargo has committed to lending $20 billion to women business owners over a 10-year period. Fleet Bank established the Women Entrepreneur's Connection in 1998, building on the early work of Bank Boston.
12. Ibid.
13. Pratt's Guide to Venture Capital Sources, 2001. Wellesley Hills, MA: Venture Economics, Inc.
14. Keeley, R., Cooper, J., & Bloomer, G. 1998. *Business Angels: A Guide to Private Investing.* Boulder, CO: Colorado Capital Alliance.

15. Ibid.

16. DRI-WEFA, a Global Insight Company: Economic Impact of Venture Capital. 2002. Summary accessed July 21, 2003, at *www.nvca.org/nvca06_25_02.html*.

17. Ibid.

18. Small Business Association, SBA.gov Web site. Average annual number new businesses 2000–2002 = 556,000.

19. National Venture Capital Association Web site, NVCA.org. Industry statistics.

20. Ibid.

4

MOTIVES, ASPIRATIONS, AND COMMITMENT

*Even as a young girl, I always saw myself sitting in a
large skyscraper office, running the company I founded.
It never occurred to me that others would think
this was an unusual goal.*

—Sophomore at Boston University, 1995

Dreams of entrepreneurship are woven throughout the fabric of American life. Liz Claiborne, Jenny Craig, and Oprah Winfrey allowed themselves to dream "big" and then, through hard work, careful planning, and brilliant execution, they made those dreams come true. You might have a similar vision and, if you are reading this book, you are probably already well on the way to making it a reality. If so, you are among the entrepreneurial elite. Many people think long and hard about starting their own businesses, but only a few will take action, and even fewer will pursue growth.

Why? Because, exciting as it sounds, starting a new venture is daunting. It requires imagination, courage, and commitment from you. Whether you choose to create an independent movie production company, sign on as a restaurant franchisee, acquire a local print shop, or launch the next Internet colossus, you will face enormous challenges before you can claim the rewards that are calling to you. If it is so challenging, why do people do it? Why have you chosen to be an entrepreneur?

Your answer depends on your underlying motives. You might be seeking wealth and fame, or you might be looking for an avenue to express your creative genius. Perhaps you want to deliver an extraordinary product or service that will enable others to live more comfortable lives or you hope to find the personal satisfaction that comes from creating something useful and enduring. For many people, entrepreneurship represents their best opportunity for personal independence or work flexibility. No matter what your primary drivers are, the economic rewards are likely to be important, whether your goal is to become the next Internet billionaire or simply to provide a better living for your family.[1] Power, achievement, personal comfort, and self-actualization are among the energizers that spur entrepreneurs to action. Sometimes, just satisfying a personal need is sufficient motivation. For example:

When Marla Malcom was unable to locate cosmetic products she preferred, she started her own company. She bought and refurbished two cosmetic boutiques in Washington, DC to launch Bluemercury, Inc., a retail distributor of high-end and hard-to-find beauty products. Three years later, she added a mail order catalog and launched an online store, achieving revenues of $8 million.[2] Her business philosophy? "(Offer) super-cheap, reliable products and serve the customer."

Just how high you set the goal for yourself depends on your level of personal aspirations. Those aspirations will determine what kind of new venture you choose to start. For example, achieving financial comfort might be one of your goals. If financial comfort means home ownership, a full pantry, college education funds, and a secure retirement, you are likely to choose a business that can meet those expectations. If, on the other hand, your view of financial comfort includes multiple homes, luxury cars, exotic vacations, designer jewelry, and yachts, you might be interested in starting an entirely different type of business— one that has boundless opportunities for growth and profit.

Anita Roddick, founder of the Body Shop, started small, but quickly saw an opportunity to expand her natural cosmetics business worldwide. In her words, "if you have a company with an itsy bitsy vision, you have an itsy bitsy company."[3]

Many women business owners are highly motivated by personal comfort and self-actualization goals and, as a result, their financial aspirations for the business are relatively low. They tend to start local retail and service businesses that allow them to work at something interesting, but maintain flexibility so that they can spend substantial time with (and sometimes give priority to) family. On the other hand, large-scale businesses are extremely demanding, requiring full-time attention, high levels of energy, and significant leadership and deal-making skills. Because these behaviors are inconsistent with the motives and aspirations generally attributed to women, there is widespread belief that few, if any, women are suited to running a high-growth, high-potential new venture. This chapter investigates motives, aspirations, and commitment of female entrepreneurs and maps these to the demands of high-growth businesses. It concludes with tips for overcoming possible concerns about your entrepreneurial motivation, goals, and commitment.

The Entrepreneurial Choice

What you choose to do with your life is motivated by a unique bundle of wants and needs—some of which might seem inconsistent with one another, and many of which might compete for priority at different times in your life. Your motives are largely shaped by your personal characteristics (talents, interests), your deeply held beliefs, your family influences and social role models, and of course, the cultural context. The decision to become an entrepreneur is never as simple as "wanting the money" or "seeking fame" or "building a better world." The act of starting a business is usually the result of a combination of personal motives or drives that you try to satisfy through the business.[4] Your commitment to the enterprise is determined by the priorities you set among the many competing motivators you have.

After starting your new venture, the decisions about how fast and how big to grow it depend in large measure on how the American dream plays out in your head. The hopes you have for your business are a reflection of your personal aspirations. Aspirations are conscious goals, strong desires, and ambitions.[5] They are often the embodiment of how you satisfy your motives. Everyone has widely varying levels of aspiration for the different projects, tasks, activities, or jobs they undertake and these assume distinct quantity and quality characteristics.[6] Aspirations influence how high you set a bar for yourself and influence what you seek from each activity. Your motive for power, achievement, or meaning will vary widely whether you are engaged in a marketing project, golf game, or church volunteer effort. In other words, motives are why you start your business and aspirations are how you choose to do it.

Aspirations are influenced by many things. Social context—your friends' and family's support—as well as cultural role expectations play a large part in shaping your role and hopes for your company. Your level of self-confidence affects the way you collect and interpret information about growth. At the same time your perception of risks and benefits determine your estimates of future size and scope of the company.[7]

Whatever your aspirations and hopes for your business, you will need to make a personal commitment to the venture to succeed. Starting and growing a new venture requires time, energy, belief, and effort. It is often very difficult to estimate exactly how much of each will be required, but it is certain to be substantial. In a fledgling business, it's hard to know what systems and policies are needed, how to find employees, or how many meetings will be needed to contract with a supplier. As the business grows, the unknowns increase. New competition, technologies, and stakeholders emerge, and needs for money, employees, and other resources increase.

The level of commitment is a personal choice that both men and women entrepreneurs make, and this is usually related to your motives and aspirations. In the United States, we often hear that anything is possible. An aspiration to lead a billion-dollar company can be anyone's dream if they are willing to work for it. However, if you also want to be the best first-grade room Mom at the same time, it might be harder to grow a company that big no matter what your commitment is. Either way, we would think all entrepreneurs have an equal chance at making their dreams a reality. Yet, sometimes it's just assumed that women will choose family as their primary commitment. Consider the following examples:

After she made a presentation to a group of investors, Christine Warren, CEO of IT Profiler, a technology human resources firm, was approached by a male participant who asked if she had any children. She said she had a 4-year-old and a 1-year-old. "So, you're done?" he asked. Warren recalls thinking, "Are you really asking me that?"[8]

A few conference participants were sitting down to lunch following a series of presentations by women entrepreneurs

at the first Springboard Forum at Oracle Computing. A reporter was just finishing up her interview with a venture capitalist at a nearby table. She asked, "What do you think of this event?" The gray-haired, tanned man leaned back and said, "It's just terrific. But, I would never invest in a women-led business. Don't get me wrong, women are great for running day care centers and have done a lot for customer service, but as an investor, you can't take a chance that they might leave to get married or pregnant."

It's a given that growing a venture requires a grand vision for the company, as well as commitment of significant time and energy that can interfere with family and personal life. Is it also true that women don't really want to lead fast-growth companies? Are they misguided if they aspire to do so? Are women less willing to make the commitment to develop and grow a venture? Or do they persist and stick with their venture throughout growth transitions?

This is where women with big dreams and plans for fast growth are challenged. For them, the entrepreneurial bar is higher than for men, because there is a gender-based stereotype. It is the preconception that women do not have a singular focus on the business, nor do they have the commitment to see it through if other priorities emerge. The investors in the preceding stories had a perception about what the role and commitment of a successful entrepreneur was. This view contrasted with their beliefs about women and expectations for their roles in the family. Why are women perceived less credibly? Where do these perceptions and expectations come from?

Motives for Entrepreneurship

Like their male counterparts, drivers for women to be entrepreneurs include a desire for achievement, independence, to make money, and to be their own boss. The fact is that no single motivation for entrepreneurship for either men or women has been identified. Both groups are motivated by a desire for independence or achievement.[9]

> **Valerie Marks of Sockeye Networks started her business because she wanted the challenge of starting a company from scratch.**[10]

> **Kevin Brewer founded Creative Visions Integrated Marketing concepts because he was artistic, passionate, and didn't want to be bossed around.**[11]

Besides these popular motives for start-up, women also state other reasons for entrepreneurship like providing family income, having a flexible schedule, solving social problems, and doing meaningful work.[12] Motives are the underlying reasons you choose a particular pathway for your business, but the impetus to take action is usually triggered by an event — the last child enters first grade, the plant downsizes and you get fired, management contract buyout, failure to get a deserved promotion, or a friend has a great idea and she calls you to collaborate.

These Catalysts are referred to as pushes or pulls: Some people are pushed to entrepreneurial start-up and others are pulled into it.[13] For women, being pulled to entrepreneurship can be a result of life-stage changes. Maybe the children have graduated from school and you now have time (and energy and dollars) to devote to an idea you have always wanted to pursue. Perhaps a new educational program became available in the region and you learned more about how to scale your business. You might be pulled into venture creation through friends who need start-up partners, or maybe you have a hobby that can be expanded into a business. On the other hand, you might be pushed to entrepreneurship by company downsizing, a feeling of frustration about lack of career promotion in a company, or a family situation change.

No matter what triggers your decision to act on these, motives influence the aspirations for the business. Generally, there is a difference between women and men in how they explain their aspirations. Women tend to express a broader variety of aspirations and it is not uncommon for women to articulate a social purpose to their business.[14] In contrast, when men articulate aspirations for their business, they are usually more focused and economically specific.

Women's Aspirations Contrast with Entrepreneurial Reality

The rub comes when you map these generalized tendencies on to the reality of the entrepreneurial environment. The dominant view of entrepreneurship—especially high-growth, high-potential ventures— focuses on wealth creation, changing the world with a new innovation or technology, and gaining recognition as the new American hero. To achieve this, an articulation of goals that express size, scope, leadership, importance, and economic results are the expected norm. Following years of research on men, we have a pretty good understanding of a very tiny subset of men who probably subordinated their personal goals and actually put all their attention into growing a business for which they had very high expectations. Those men who shared diverse motivations and broad aspirations were often considered less capable. Men seeking entrepreneurial success more often express focused aspirations that fit the norms and perceptions of entrepreneurial success quite well.

In contrast, women often have a broader array of motives and aspirations for their business and they say so. Because women might express more holistic aspirations encompassing social and economic purposes, they might appear to have competing aspirations, or they come across as diffused and fragmented rather than focused in their approach. At the same time, there is an assumption that fast-growth ventures require huge amounts of capital and energy, which requires the minimization or ignoring of personal and family goals. Because women often express their personal and family goals, this creates a perception that they are not well suited to run high-growth businesses. This is not to say that men don't have strong personal and family goals—indeed they do—but men more often realize that when seeking growth, it's important to focus on the economic objectives of the company because investors are looking for economic returns.

Even though we know that there is no single motive for business creation and that there are many ways to reach success, it appears that women are being judged differently in two ways. First, because women historically were clustered in service-type businesses with fewer employees and lower revenues, it's assumed that they choose these because they are flexible and permit family or social focus over economic goals. This is a limitation because the women founding construction, wholesale, or manufacturing firms have to work harder to overcome this perception.

Second, because women express multiple aspirations, they are often judged on the means by which they hope to achieve their success, rather than whether they get there or not. Men and women have different expressions of goals, and the sheer difference in articulation by women creates a hurdle. The goals and aspirations they express don't match the norm for behaviors associated with growing a business. We know from the evidence shown in earlier chapters that women can grow their businesses just as competently and successfully as men. However, when they express aspirations that are broader and more holistic, they might appear less credible.

Therefore to judge all women based on a narrow economic expression of aspirations and to assume they are less ambitious is limiting to the subset of those women who, like their male counterparts, do have big dreams. On top of this, there are expectations for family roles that confound this challenge.

Family Role Expectations

In nearly every society, it was traditional for men to work outside the house while women cared for households and families. It was a woman's "role" to maintain the household and care for dependents. Over the past 30 years, women have entered the workforce to help support families all over the world. In Europe and the United States, nearly 40% of women work outside the home, and contribute as much as half of household income.[15] Bureau of Labor statistics from 2000 show that 81% of women between 25 and 54 work full time, and more than 70% of married couples with children over 6 years of age both work. Even though vast changes have occurred and men are now cooks and house husbands, in many ways the expectation and role for women to assume responsibility for organizing household and dependent care is still very prevalent.

Those women who choose not to work full time might go to school, do volunteer work, or care full time for their children, all of which are their personal choices. It is also true that many men choose not to work full time as well, for a similar variety of reasons. Yet, more often than not, the activities of nonworking women are generalized to working women and women entrepreneurs far more frequently than for men. For instance, when a woman entrepreneur explains that she is planning to travel to seek new customers, she might have to explain why she is leaving her children in day care. This unfairly places differential expectations on women's behavior, especially when they choose to found a new venture or grow a high-potential business. The bar is again higher because the commitment of a woman growing her business might seem less because she acknowledges her family and personal responsibilities. At the same time, if she is not minding her children, some might have an emotional reaction because they feel she is abandoning her children. Either way, it lessens a woman entrepreneur's credibility to run a growing venture.

This is really a double standard. Seldom is the same test put to men. How often are male entrepreneurs asked about the impact of working long hours on their family? Or whether significant travel to set up sales offices will be a problem? If a male entrepreneur spends 60 or 70 hours a week working to grow his business, how often do we make the attribution that he is a bad father? At the same time, if he acknowledged personal or family goals while seeking growth, he would be more often perceived as a good father, having a balanced life. The contradiction in expectations about family roles raises the bar for women who aspire to grow a business by challenging their behavior and actions.

Women's Self-Expression Leads to Perceptions

In addition to broad aspirations and family expectations, women's self-expression contributes to their lack of credibility in growing a business. Countless books and articles are written about styles of communication and self-expression, and what and how women communicate about everything from business to personal relationships. However, self-expression and communication are factors influencing the perception of women's aspirations and commitment. Simply stated, women communicate differently than men.[16]

The work of Deborah Tannen as well as other linguists and social scientists shows that women use different communication styles, habits, and patterns. For example, a language tendency for women to downplay their certainty whereas men downplay their doubts can make women come across as less confident. Women might "qualify" their comments by saying things like, "I'm not entirely sure about my projections for growth," or "I'm not going to pretend that I know for sure what the market will do." Although these comments might reflect the reality, they can be interpreted that women are less confident about their business aspirations or have not done their homework thoroughly.

Similarly, women are less likely to brag about their achievements, sometimes keeping quiet or sharing the credit. For instance, men are quick to nominate their companies for local competitions, or to self-nominate to be part of Inc.'s fastest growing companies list. Although there are women on the list, it is never one-third of the nominees. The same is true with the Ernst and Young Entrepreneurs of the Year, where there might be a woman in the finals, the proportion of nominees is generally dominated by men. Instead, women have their own contests, such as the National Association of Women's Business Owners (NAWBO) or other local Woman Entrepreneur of the Year awards. Either way, the legitimacy of aspiring women-led ventures might be diminished either because of small numbers on these lists of achievers or the perception that the rules for separate contests are less rigorous.

Another example is that women use conversation for interaction whereas men use conversation for information. It is not unusual for women to mix talk about their personal lives and families in with business conversation, whereas men will more often add talk about sports, politics, or business news.[17] For women entrepreneurs, seeking to grow their ventures, mention of children or families can leave the impression that they are not fully committed to the growth of the venture.

In a third example, women are more likely to bring up issues, problems, or concerns so these can be discussed and rapport can be built. In contrast, men bring up problems when they want solutions.[18] For women entrepreneurs, if they are unsure of how to bring on new employees or how to launch new technology, they might introduce this as a topic of discussion so that everyone involved is on board and committed to the new idea. On the other hand, men might only bring up issues when they want them solved so they can move on to the next issue. This difference can create the impression that women question their aspirations and ability to lead a growth-oriented venture.

Truths and Realities

The aspirations of women business owners are indeed rooted in their motives for start-up. However, the reality is that their motives are as varied as those of their male counterparts. For instance:

> **Richard Keener and Leif Blodee had just retired after 30 years of corporate experience in manufacturing when they decided to launch a company making and selling stylish, expensive office chairs with craftsman-like quality.**[19]

> **Sharon Childers, founder of the Asheville Comedy Club and Deli, started her business with her husband in order to be "self reliant in these turbulent financial and economic times."**[20]

> **Frank Deford was a writer with 27 years experience. He was at a point where he felt he was writing the same story one too many times. After a vacation and some soul searching, he decided to launch a new newspaper—a sports daily for the United States called *The National*.**[21]

> **Verna Kuyper was "pushed" to start her company. After suffering extreme financial difficulties, she decided to use her artistic talents to run Maui Goose of Hawaii, Ltd., a direct mail flora and gift business.**[22]

These examples suggest the reasons for launching ventures are complex and varied for both men and women. It's just not reasonable to generalize certain motives for start-up to all women. The same applies when we consider the group of women who seek growth. In our survey of Springboard Forum participants we found that personal goals varied widely as we note in Table 4.1. The top reasons given were learning and personal achievement, and flexibility and economic reasons were relatively less important.

This variation in aspirations is also found among nascent or new entrepreneurs, and there are variations between men and women. Our analysis of more than 800 nascent entrepreneurs showed that 24% of men report wanting to have a business as large as possible, whereas only 15% of women report the same. When we compared younger women and men 18 to 24, we found that there were few differences in aspirations for size, but among those aged 25 to 34—an age more likely to have an MBA education—we found that 33% of the men wanted large ventures and only 22% of the women in this age bracket preferred the same.[23]

TABLE 4.1   **Personal Goals in Start-Up Initiative**

Learning and personal growth	4.43
Personal achievement	4.29
Independence	4.25
Test and implement my own ideas	4.11
Satisfying work relationships	4.10
Meet economic needs	4.01
Money and wealth	3.63
Flexibility in work and family	3.46
Personal recognition	3.15
Status and prestige	2.72

Note. RESPONSE ON A SCALE OF 1 TO 5. MULTIPLE ANSWERS ALLOWED.

When it comes to commitment to a venture, certainly many women choose not to go for it all and prefer to run ventures part time to manage work and family commitments. Some entrepreneurs want to keep the business small so they can also manage their other life, that of the family and home. They feel they need to stay flexible and believe that growing a company larger will take too much of their already limited time and energy. Although some women choose slow growth or to table their careers, this generalization does not apply to all. Certainly role models, family situation, and expectations about gender roles influence how people perceive women entrepreneurs, but to expect that all women will not want to devote the time and energy to a venture holds them back.

On the flip side, family changes might have a positive benefit. Children (or elder dependents) entering a woman's life might either cause her to constrain growth, or cause her to seek it even more strongly to provide more for her new family. Similarly, dependents leaving home can cause aspirations to fluctuate either way. Some will see the departures as an opportunity to further grow their business as they experience new flexibility. Others will see the departures as an opportunity to scale back their business. Less financial income will be needed and they desire increased non-business-related activities.

This issue of time and commitment is one of great importance, particularly to women. Time is a resource equal for everyone.[24] We all have 24 hours in a day so we start from the same point. What we do with our time varies considerably, not only by gender, but also by types of human capital such as education, income, and employment status.[25] A recent time-use study was included in the Panel Study of Entrepreneurial Dynamics (PSED) and helped illustrate how people in the process of trying to start a business used their time. The people included in this research charted what they did each day and divided their activities into categories that included sleeping, personal care, eating, paid work, household work, infant and child care, care of older family members, personal time with their spouse, and leisure activities such as reading, TV, sports, and recreation. Among those launching a new business, 35% of the average workday was spent on personal time, much of it sleeping (both men and women).[26] Men spent 15% of the day on free-time activities, whereas women spend 12%. These are not drastic differences.

The major difference in the allocation of time between men and women was between time spent in work for hire (contracted) and time spent in unpaid work (committed). Men had more contracted time than women (30% compared with 26%), whereas women had more committed time than men (13% compared with 8%). Most of this difference represents women doing more unpaid work in the household. Notably, there was very little difference in the time men and women spent work-ing on their new businesses. Men reported that 9% of their time working was spent on their entrepreneurial ventures; women spent almost the same at 8%.[27] There was little difference in time commitment to the efforts in trying to start the new business. However, there might be a greater potential cost in what has to be given up to find that time.

Moving Beyond the Expectations

I know I face more skepticism. But, that's all right for as soon as I start the presentation, I have everything to gain. There is more pressure but often more reward as well.

—Jerusha Stewart, I Spiritus Soul Spa[28]

Being a female and fund seeker is a curse and a blessing. On the one hand, you're likely to stand out. On the other hand, they're going to comment on your hair, nails, dress, and some-times everything but your plan.[29]

How can women overcome these expectations? As we noted earlier, part of overcoming higher hurdles is understanding the entrepreneurial environment. If you hope to grow a large business quickly, you should expect investors and resource providers to react if you present broad statements of your aspirations and goals. Their primary interest is gain-ing a return on their investment, payment for goods and services, or reas-surance that you are committed to delivering on your growth promise.

This is not to say you shouldn't have them. In fact, it's better if you do. Businesses that express a social purpose can be at least as profitable if not more profitable if they have both social and economic missions.[30]

However, you do have to be aware of the standard that is being applied to you and to men as well.

Then, focus on your vision—there is no single right or wrong way, or prescription for what a venture aspiration should be. This is true for both men and women. Your aspirations for the business in terms of scope and size are very much related to your vision for the future of the business. Whatever it is, the vision should be clear and easily communicated, in words, pictures, diagrams, or all of these. A business vision should articulate scope, size, and functions of the company. Because business vision is shaped by your personal values, it will reflect what is important to you. For example:

We plan to be a global market leader in developing products that enhance self-esteem for the handicapped, by developing an organization that highly values employees and customers.

This statement reflects the market, the products, and the goal (global leader), as well as the strategic approach (values employees and customers). A goal of market leadership implies growth, wide distribution, and rising sales within a niche market. With this, aspirations are grand and would require a big personal commitment.

Another example suggests a different approach:

My restaurant will offer high-quality authentic Greek food prepared in an innovative fashion.

By contrast, this vision statement focuses on the quality and innovation, rather than growth. This vision statement implies minimal or no growth, but a strong emphasis on creativity.

No matter what your aspirations, a clear articulation is needed. This requires self-introspection, and carefully thinking through what the business might be into the future and what your role will be. Because expectations about aspirations tend to focus more on economic factors and most businesses are started to build wealth, business goals should reflect this. Typically, these goals are market share, date of breakeven, when the business will turn cash flow positive, and other profitability measures.

At the same time, if you have broad aspirations, how should you manage these? Like men, women entrepreneurs make trade-offs. Some find ways to share growth activities with partners or teammates. Others seek family help. Still others choose to grow more gradually and incrementally to protect personal time. For entrepreneurs with families, these choices can be emotionally difficult, but there are a variety of solutions. Some choose to integrate family into work life by including day care centers or flex time, whereas others elect to grow the venture more slowly, taking necessary time off for family needs. Importantly, the commitment of an entrepreneur varies over the life cycle of the venture. In the beginning, it might mean 80-hour weeks and no vacations. As the venture develops, the founder might have a management team that can take over many roles and free up the founder's personal time.

Although there are certainly women who have lower aspirations and commitment to their ventures, there are those who have big ambitions and are willing to give it their all. Either way, you should begin with a careful assessment of your personal goals, and your hopes for your company's future size and scope. Think about how you see yourself contributing to the business—will you be the president? CEO? Or will you assume a lesser role in start-up and operations? Then, evaluate the requisite commitment. How many hours per week will your role require? Will these hours be during the day? Night? Weekend? All of these? You can talk to people in similar roles who have started similar businesses to get an idea of the potential company demands. Then of course, you need to consider what trade-offs might be involved for personal time, recreation, family, or a spouse's job or business. Aspirations and commitment do interact. For instance, high aspirations for growth and expansion usually require high commitment; on the other hand, if you have low commitment and high aspirations, this is a recipe for failure (see Figure 4.1).

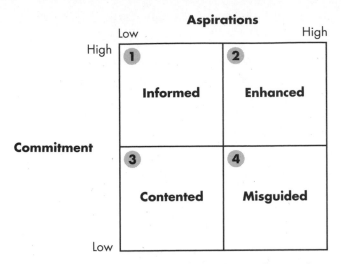

FIGURE 4.1 Aspirations and Commitment Interactions

1. *Informed entrepreneurs* make careful aspiration choices, and might not choose to run the next eBay. However, they are committed to building a solid venture, and make the appropriate time and energy commitment for the venture. The balance between the personal goals, vision, and the work required is an informed approach.

2. *Enhanced entrepreneurs* have both lofty aspirations and are prepared to make a significant commitment. They see themselves leading fast-growth, high-potential companies, and are willing to sacrifice personal time, putting in extra energy to the venture. Typically, they have high self-confidence.

3. *Contented entrepreneurs* don't feel the pressure to have a high-flying venture, or to do anything that they don't want to. They have a balanced set of priorities for aspirations and commitment, and they like to be in control.

4. *Misguided entrepreneurs* have a mismatched set of aspirations and commitment. Either they have not properly assessed the commitment needed by doing their homework, or they just don't want to put the time into the venture to make it work, instead

"wishing" it will work rather than working for it. These entre-preneurs would benefit from listening to advisors and being more willing to make changes in their entrepreneurial plans to achieve a better fit between commitment and aspirations.

Besides personal assessment, women entrepreneurs need to be emotionally prepared to move forward despite the nay-sayers. Critics will suggest that women can't or shouldn't have the aspirations they do, or make the commitment they do. How should women deal with this? Find out how other women in similar circumstances handle this. Personal advisors and experts can be helpful to overcoming this perception.

Finally, women should "brag" about their ventures. The benefits of the publicity can facilitate future growth. The evidence suggests that women might not be as active in this regard. As noted earlier, every year the Inc. 100 list of fastest growing companies has only a minority of women-led firms. This is not because Inc. does not want to include women on the list, but the list is comprised of those companies volun-tarily submitting information to be considered. In any given year, the number of women entrepreneurs on the list is less than 15%. For women having midsized businesses, don't rely on organizations to find and nominate you—it's perfectly legitimate to self-nominate and reap the benefits of recognition for a successful entrepreneurial endeavor.

Summary

Perceptions that women have lower aspirations and commitment are rooted in three factors: motives, role expectations, and self-expression. The assumption that all women's motives for start-up and growth derive solely from a family–work balance is just not true for all. Women have widely varying motives, just like men. When compared to men, some women might have slightly lower aspirations for business size, and might not have dreams as grand. Again, like men, there is a rising number of women who seek growth and leadership in large companies. On the other hand, women are still spending more time in unpaid household activities, and have less free time, which might not only take time away from the growth and success of the venture, but also create a perception that a woman is less committed, whether or not this is the case.

In summary, the net effect of aspirations and commitment shows that we can't put women into a single category when referring to their aspirations and commitment. The generalization of these expectations to all women, and the indication that women are still putting more time into household and family activities, does make the hurdle higher, no matter what their aspirations and intended business commitment. However, aspirations and commitment are only a small part of the key ingredients for success. The experience and education of women entrepreneurs is the foundation on which the business is founded. Do women have what it takes in terms of experience and academic studies? The next chapter explores these questions in detail.

Notes

1. See Vesper, K. 1990. *New Venture Strategies*. Englewood Cliffs, NJ: Prentice Hall; Cooper, A. C., & Gimeno-Gascon, J. 1992. The process of founding and new firm performance, in Sexton D., & Kasarda J. (Eds.). *The State of the Art of Entrepreneurship*, Boston: PWS Kent, 301–340.

2. Stuart, A. 2002. Beauty and the best. *Inc. Tech* 2000, No. 2, 53.

3. Roddick, A. 1991. *Body and Soul*. New York: Crown, p. 223.

4. See Vesper, K. 1990. *New Venture Strategies*. Englewood Cliffs, NJ: Prentice Hall; Brush, C. G. 1992. Research on women business owners: Past trends, a new perspective and future directions. *Entrepreneurship Theory and Practice*. 16:4, 5–30.

5. Bird, B. J. 1989. *Entrepreneurial Behavior*. Glenview, IL: Scott Foresman.

6. McClelland, D. 1985. *Human Motivation*. New York: Holt Rinehart & Winston.

7. Lau, C. M., & Busenitz, L. 2001. Growth intentions of entrepreneurs in a transitional economy: The People's Republic of China. *Entrepreneurship Theory and Practice*. 26:1, 5–20.

8. Hopkins, J. 2001, August 14. *A woman's work is rarely funded*. www.usatoday.com/money/covers/2001-08-15-bcovwed.htm.

9. Vesper, K. 1990. *New Venture Strategies*. Englewood Cliffs, NJ: Prentice Hall.

10. Graves, H. 2003, January. Women to watch. *Women's Business Boston*, 5.

11. Torres, N. L. 2003, August. Biz 101: Best of both worlds. *Entrepreneur Magazine*, 100.

12. Brush, C. G. 1992. Research on women business owners: Past trends, a new perspective and future directions. *Entrepreneurship Theory and Practice*. 16:4, 5–30; Bird, B. J., & Brush, C. G. 2002. A gendered perspective on organizational creation. *Entrepreneurship Theory and Practice*. 26:3, 41–65.

13. Shapero, A., & Sokol, L. 1982. The social dimensions of entrepreneurship, in Kent, C., Sexton, D., & Vesper, K. (Eds). *The Encyclopedia of Entrepreneurship*. New York: Prentice Hall, 72–90.

14. Bird, B. J., & Brush, C. G. 2002. A gendered perspective on organizational creation. *Entrepreneurship Theory and Practice*. 26:3, 41–65.

15. Ducheneaut, B. 1997. *Women Entrepreneurs in SMEs*. Paris: OECD.

16. Tannen, D. 1991. *You Just Don't Understand Me*. New York: Ballantine.

17. Smith, D. 2000. *Women at Work: Leadership for the Next Century*. Upper Saddle River, NJ: Prentice Hall.

18. Ibid.

19. Longsworth, E. (Ed). 1991. *Anatomy of a Start-Up: Why Some Businesses Succeed and Others Fail*. Boston: Goldhirsch Group.

20. Katz, M. 2002, September–October. *ABWA Entrepreneurs Are Making Fun Their Business,* ABWA Newsletter, Vol. 1, 18.

21. Longsworth, op. cit.

22. Katz, op. cit., 19.

23. Carter, N. M., & Brush, C. G. 2004. Gender, in Gartner, W. B., Shaver, K. G., Carter, N. M., & Reynolds, P. D. (Eds.). *The handbook of entrepreneurial dynamics*. Thousand Oaks, CA: Sage, forthcoming.

24. Fleming, R., & Spellerberg, A. 1999. Using time and use data: History of time use surveys and uses of time use data, Statistics New Zealand, Te Tari Tatu, Wellington, New Zealand, catalogue number 04.021.0098.

25. Owen, M., & Greene, P. G. 2004. Time use, in Gartner, W. B., Shaver, K. G., Carter, N. M., & Reynolds, P. D. (Eds.). *The handbook of entrepreneurial dynamics*. Thousand Oaks, CA: Sage, forthcoming.

26. Panel Study of Entrepreneurial Dynamics.

27. Owen & Greene. 2003.

28. Sherman, A. P. 2002. The opposite sex, women in search of money still face a man's world. *www.entrepreneur.com/article/0,4621,302235,00.html*.

29. Ibid.

30. *www.bsr.org/BSRResources/IssueBriefDetail.cfm?DocumentID=48809*.

5

WOMEN AND HUMAN CAPITAL

Bet on the jockey, not on the horse.

*I'd rather have an A team and a B idea than the
other way around.*

Ask any investor what the single most important factor is in determining whether or not to invest in a business and he or she will say, "People, people, and people." In fact, bankers, private investors, venture capitalists, and other resource providers rely more heavily on the people than they do on the business ideas.[1] As you think about your dreams of success, how do you know if you have the "right stuff"? What is the right stuff needed to gain money and other resources to grow your business?

We talked about your motives, aspirations, and commitment to your venture in Chapter 4, but achieved attributes are also an important consideration in business start-up and growth. This includes your education, work experience, acquired skills, and developed capabilities which are all components of human capital. Human capital is based on the idea that people acquire individual resources like education, training, and different types of work experiences to increase or enhance their productivity. As an entrepreneur, this means that your human capital serves as the basis for obtaining or creating other types of resources, like money, technology, and management talent. Your college degrees, your industry expertise, and your accomplishments give you credibility in the eyes of resource providers. In this chapter, we explore the individual qualities resource providers look for, examine challenges women face, and consider ways in which you can enhance your personal experience, education, and skills.

What Do Resource Providers Look For?

Growing a business requires good execution. Some people are better at doing this than others, just like some are better at innovating than others. Because resource providers, whether they are bankers, suppliers, investors, or family members, are betting on the success of the business, the assessment of the people running it becomes central to any investment decision. An individual's qualities inspire confidence that the growth plan can and will be executed, leading to returns for the investors, loan payback for the banker, or payables to the supplier.

Because individual qualities assume such central importance in the decision, nearly all investors have created some sort of calculus by which they evaluate the lead entrepreneur and the team. For example, they might ask:[2]

- Does the entrepreneur have a track record?

- Does the entrepreneur exhibit leadership?

- Is the entrepreneur capable and focused?

- Does the entrepreneur have high technology, operational, or marketing expertise?

• Is the entrepreneur competent?

• Does the entrepreneur have relevant experience?

As you can see, the calculus for assessing the lead entrepreneur appears on the surface to be very objective. Therefore, it would seem that if you want to grow your business, having the education, industry experience, and general management expertise, would certainly meet the standards. Unfortunately, there is a widely held perception that women lack the right human capital to lead high-growth start-ups. Consider the following case.

Maria O'Connell had an MBA from a top business school and a BA in economics when she developed her plan for a start-up sports accessory company. She also had 11 years experience in the athletic footwear and apparel business. Her management responsibilities included marketing, advertising, international sales, and marketing. She also served as president and CEO of the company, leading it through substantial changes. Although she was able to launch her start-up in a related sportswear accessories business, two years later O'Connell's initial investors asked her to step down. She had been unable to convince venture capitalists that she could lead the company's growth and expansion successfully. Potential investors did not give her credit for having the right human capital to lead the business's growth.

O'Connell's case illustrates how, even though she was highly qualified in both managerial experience and technical knowledge, she was still perceived as having less potential to succeed and therefore being a higher risk. The determination of what is the right mix of human capital is often based on the investors' experience with other successful entrepreneurs and what they hear from others in the industry. Investors build models in their minds of the profile for a successful entrepreneur based on founders in their portfolios who achieved high returns. Many times the right mix is somewhat subjective. Why is this the case?

First, these mind models quickly become the prototype for future investments. In today's technology-driven world, it's often expected that entrepreneurs desiring growth should have an advanced technical degree and solid business training, especially in strategic management, marketing, and finance, if they want to sail through the funding process. Their résumés should include upper level management experience, significant industry expertise, and previous start-up involvement. This adds up to a superstar, or ideal-type entrepreneur. Of course it is rare that all of these qualities are found in a single individual, which is why most high-growth ventures are founded by teams of individuals that collectively offer the full scope of qualifications (we will address this in Chapter 9). However, the quest for the ideal type, or superstar entrepreneur, persists, especially when the economy is slow or the risk of the money invested is higher.

Second, success is widely attributed to the traits of the entrepreneur. Ask your friends, business associates, or parents what the qualities of a successful entrepreneur are and no doubt they will say "creative, innovative, independent, competitive, and risk seeking." If you ask entrepreneurs why they succeeded, they will often suggest these same personality traits were key. However, the reality is that these stereotypes are based on conjecture about distinctive personality traits that are fundamental to entrepreneurship. Surprisingly, there is little direct evidence showing that specific traits predict start-up success.[3]

Third, there are cognitive biases that influence the decisions of resource providers. The belief that an entrepreneur can succeed, inspires confidence, seems credible, or resonates true is less often objectively determined. Instead, these conclusions are influenced by things like overconfidence, memory biases (we remember good things more easily), confirmation biases (where we consider data supporting our view and pay less attention to data refuting it), and self-fulfilling prophecies (where we act in accordance with our prior beliefs).[4] These biases cause resource providers to process information incorrectly and lead to errors in decisions.[5] For example, overconfidence might lead a resource provider to overestimate the possibility that a favored outcome will occur, and overestimating one's knowledge might cause a decision to be based on incomplete information. There is evidence that investors are significantly overconfident in their investment decision making, which tends to reduce the information they will seek about prospective investment.

Therefore, the decision for resource investment, particularly money, is based on objective qualities that are colored by subjective influences of the search for ideal type, expectations for heroic traits, and cognitive biases. The result is that more than 95% of all ventures receiving investment capital over recent decades were led by White men. This means that the human capital composite of the right mix is based almost completely on a single narrow group of individuals. Men have the right mix but women don't seem to fit the model.

Assumptions about Women Entrepreneurs

For women, there is a perception that they just don't have what it takes. Where does this perception come from? It's based on two primary assumptions:

- Women don't have the right educational training.

- Women don't have sufficient or appropriate professional experience.

In other words, there is an underlying perception that women just don't have the know-how, the body of knowledge, the skills, or the capabilities to lead a venture of substantial size. In part, messages about appropriate know-how derive from early education, and often this is gender specific.

Traditionally women were encouraged to study liberal arts and education and then enter occupations that served others: nursing, teaching, retailing, and services. Although opportunities for women to pursue engineering, management, medicine, and science have improved dramatically since the 1980s, for the most part, there are few role models of women scientists, surgeons, and engineering leaders for decision makers to use as standards for comparative evaluation.

The focus on male models of success was reinforced by the content of management training courses. For example, before 1995 fewer than 10% of all business school teaching cases featured a woman leader or entrepreneur as the protagonist.[6] This fact is startling, given that approximately 48% of all undergraduates and 35% of all MBAs are women.[7] During the last six years, Harvard Business School, the largest provider of case teaching materials, has added more than 100 new cases featuring women as successful managers and entrepreneurs. As these materials are diffused throughout the business education network, models of success will become more diverse and more gender neutral. Major business schools are aggressively recruiting women to their classrooms and at least one school, George Washington University, has tested an entire curriculum on women's entrepreneurship.

Exposure to women as chief decision makers in all organizations remains limited so both men and women generalize that women will work in corporations, but are unlikely to lead or found them. Because the preponderance of success stories feature men as the leaders, women are perceived as less likely to be in leadership positions or to succeed as leaders when they serve in those roles. The intense media attention on women who do succeed (Carly Fiorina, Meg Whitman, Katherine Graham) only reinforces what a newsworthy (and thus unusual) situation it is to find a woman in a position of leadership. In the eyes of the public and, by extension, in the eyes of investors, women business owners are seen as unlikely to have adequate managerial proficiencies. The combined effect of educational career socialization, focus on male role models, and limited exposure to women as chief decision makers influences the perceptions of women entrepreneurs in terms of education, experience, and qualification to run a high-growth firm.

Sorting Fact from Fiction

There's a profile in the venture world of what a successful entrepreneur looks like . . . It's someone who's aggressive, very competitive, and hard-driving. A lot of those are typical male characteristics. A woman may have those qualities, but the way she demonstrates them may be very different.
So what you'll hear from VCs is "She doesn't have the characteristics we're looking for in a CEO."[8]
—Jennifer Gill Roberts, a general partner at Sevin Rosen Funds

What are the facts? Is it true that women are less qualified to lead high-growth firms? A quick review of the history of women in the workplace will help us answer this question. Over the last four decades, women joined the labor force in droves. In 1960 the labor force participation rate for women was 37.6%. By 1997 that rate rose to 60.5%. Over the same time period, the percentage of women in the labor force with college degrees more than doubled. Since 1975 the number of women in executive and professional occupations also almost doubled.[9] The proportion of women in the labor force is expected to grow from 45% of the total labor force in 1988 to a projected 48% for 2010.[10]

Education

Most people assume that women who are highly educated (have a graduate degree) majored in English or the humanities. The reality is quite different, however.[11] Although women are not enrolled in the same proportion as men in MBA and engineering programs, the AACSB, the accrediting body for higher education, reports that the number of women receiving MBAs has been steadily increasing over the last three years. Additionally, a rising number of undergraduate women are now majoring in business. Likewise, the majority of law and medical students are now female. The fact is that some women entrepreneurs in the United States have attained education levels very similar to that of men.

The statistics for women studying engineering tell a different story. In 1997 women accounted for only 19% of engineering graduate students, and in 1998, almost 20% of the engineering undergraduates. In 1999, only 10.6% of employed engineers (individuals gaining industry experience that might eventually be applied in a new technology venture) were female.[12] However, the more general numbers mask the fact that there is a broader degree of participation by women in related fields at both the associate and undergraduate levels. Furthermore, 37% of undergraduates in the physical sciences were women, as were 33% of those in the earth, atmospheric, and ocean sciences; 45.8% in mathematics, and 27.6% in computer science.[13] These are women earning degrees with high potential value in the entrepreneurial arena.

Tech-minded teachers worry that programming is to this generation what math was to their mothers—a boys' club preventing girls from getting a foothold in the technological world.[14]

When it comes to technological education, there is reason to be concerned about the training of teenage and even younger girls. Teachers of computer courses feel they face significant challenges when trying to recruit girls for their courses. The difficulties faced are compared to the more familiar challenges of getting and keeping girls in science and math courses over the years because these traditionally have been viewed as male arenas. The challenge persists. An advanced placement computer science examination given in Los Angeles in 2001 attracted more than 19,000 boys, but only 2,400 girls took the exam.

Why is a technical education important? Because this type of human capital is considered essential for developing the intellectual property needed to launch an innovative and scalable new venture. Innovation, however, is not just about coming up with the idea for a new product, the classic building a better mousetrap. It might be an entirely new product (a radical innovation), an improved product (incremental innovation), or some other form of novelty—new markets, new processes to build or deliver the products, and new partnerships to improve efficiency and quality.[15] The knowledge or expertise to develop innovations might come from various sources, but the result is a unique combination of human capital.

Innovation, in the form of intellectual property, is essential when launching a growth venture. Historically, women appear to lag in one of the most obvious and visible forms of intellectual property—the filing of patents. From 1793 until 1840, only about 20 patents were issued to women. However, this number might vastly underestimate women's real power for invention. Married women in the United States were not legally entitled to own property until the mid-19th century. Therefore, patents for inventions created by women often were registered under their husband's or father's name. Inventions such as drip coffee, Scotchguard, bulletproof vests, and disposable diapers were all invented by women.[16] There is an encouraging trend showing the share of patents issued to women rose from 2.6% in 1977 to 10.3% in 1998. One current estimate is that 20% of all inventors are female and this number is projected to rise to approximately 50% over the next decade.[17]

Although the formal components of human capital are important, not all business ideas come from the entrepreneur's work experience or education. Ideas also emerge from a hobby, avocation, or the home. A survey of Inc. 100 founders shows that although 43% of the entrepreneurs founded their businesses based on an idea they gained from previous work experience, at least 16% based their venture concept on a hobby. Somehow a need was identified and the individual was able to translate that into a potential business idea. What they do with that idea helps to determine whether or not they have a business opportunity, one that solves a problem for which there is demand (and that people will pay for), or merely an intriguing idea. Human capital, particularly business knowledge, then becomes a very important factor in making the critical distinction between an exciting idea and a genuine business opportunity.

Technology is not the only area important to business creation and growth that has gender issues. While a high percentage of teenage girls expect to attend graduate school, only a small minority expect to have a "business"-related career. Among the reasons young women cited for not pursuing a business career were their perceptions that it would be constraining, risky, and cutthroat, and they preferred careers that offered an environment in which they could be individuals, ethical, and doing good things for the community.[18] Of those girls expecting to enter business, entrepreneurship was the most popular choice.

Although women entrepreneurs in the United States are generally well educated, they are not a homogeneous group and education potentially impacts them differently. The differences involving race and ethnicity are striking. Higher education is associated with the probability of a White woman being involved in a start-up process, but the impact is almost twice as strong for African-American women.[19] At the same time there is no significant influence among Hispanic women. The Center for Women's Business Research reported that 33% of the respondents of a study of Latina business owners had at least a bachelor's degree with an additional 35% having attended some college or even holding a two-year degree.[20]

Considering the existing data about educational level, type, and skills of women entrepreneurs, it's hard to make the generalization that all women lack the relevant depth and breadth of education needed to run a high-tech business.

Experience

There are no internal limits today. There are some
practical ones, like getting more business experience, doing

*more networking, and going back to business school
to get more education.*
— A successful woman entrepreneur

Work experience is the second major component of human capital. There are three basic components of experience that are believed to be important in determining success:

• Industry experience

• General business experience

• Start-up experience

Resource providers look for these three types of experience in their evaluation of growth-stage ventures.

Relevant experience in the industry provides opportunity to develop the know-how, the contacts, and a sense of the norms and business practices that are used in the industry of choice. General business experience gives an entrepreneur the chance to make decisions affecting the whole business or gain expertise in specific areas (e.g., marketing, finance, operations). Either way, experience in running something in a hands-on way is important. It is extremely important to note that general business experience is not limited to the for-profit arena but can also be gained from participation in volunteer organizations, schools, and so forth. Finally, start-up experience can provide lessons for what to do or not do, as well as give an entrepreneur the opportunity to build a team, raise money, and acquire resources.

The challenge for women acquiring resources, especially money, is based at least in part on the facts: Women are less likely to gain human capital through experience in higher levels of executive or technical management. On average, 25% of all managers in Fortune 200 companies are female with some companies reporting rates as low as only 7% female managers. In 1998 only 11% of the total board seats in Fortune 500 companies were held by women, and less than 4% of the highest ranking positions in these companies (Chairman, Vice-Chair, CEO, President, COO, SEVP, and EVP).[21]

Women are, however, moving into higher positions in corporate America in increasing numbers. Approximately 15.7% of Fortune 500 corporate officers are women.[22] Yet 393 of the Fortune 500 companies have no women among their top five executives. Of those that do, only six on this elite list boast female CEOs: Hewlett Packard (Carly Fiorina), Golden West Financial (Marion Sandler), Mirant (Marce Fuller), Lucent (Pat Russo), Avon (Andrea Jung), and Xerox (Anne Mulcahy). Only three of these executives have women reporting to them as the next group of highest paid executives. This suggests that the chances of a woman gaining corporate experience running a very large company are still extremely small.[23]

The good news is that there are indicators that women are now gaining work experience in environments that should be valued by resource providers. Of firms that went public in 1988 no women served on any of the top management teams. By 1993, 27% of 535 companies that went public had women in top management ranks. More recently, 43% of the companies that went public in 1999 had women in senior management posts.[24] For the woman on these management teams, the experience and recognition is invaluable.

In general, start-up experience in an entrepreneurial venture is considered to be very important, not only for the individual entrepreneur, but also for the management team. The understanding of how to work well together is almost as important as the knowledge of business cycles, shortcuts, substitutions, benchmarking, and meeting deadlines. To better understand these teams, we examined the characteristics of women who were applicants to a series of venture capital forums introduced in January 2000—Springboard 2000. The first three of these events attracted more than 900 applicants, all of whom desired to grow large businesses. The average team size of the ventures described by the Springboard applicants was two or three people, and 53% of those team members were women. These teams had an average of 39 years of industry experience per venture, with half of the team members averaging 12 years of industry experience relevant to their latest entrepreneurial endeavor. More than 40% of the ventures had team members with previous start-up experience. Indeed, almost one quarter of the teams reported starting four or more previous ventures (see Figure 5.1).

As expected women applying for equity capital through the Springboard program reported significant human capital in terms of personal and team education levels. These were highly focused and ambitious women who had decided to search for equity capital investments for their businesses. In fact, only 6% of the women applying had less than a bachelor's degree. One third of the women applying to the program had bachelor's degrees and an additional 49% held graduate degrees. Whereas 18% of the graduate degrees were MBAs, 31% of the Springboard applicants had graduate degrees in science or technology.

From these data about industry, general business, and start-up experience of women, we see that again it is unfair to generalize. Indeed, there are many areas where women have made great strides, and in fact would meet the human capital qualifications for some ventures. Even though it's appealing to believe special traits discriminate between success and nonsuccess, or entrepreneurs and nonentrepreneurs, the fact is that the "right stuff" is different for every business, and it's something you can learn on your road to success.[25]

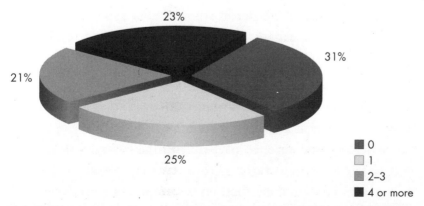

FIGURE 5.1   **Number of previous businesses started by venture teams.**

Overcoming the Hurdle

Katherine (Kay) Hammer was 34 years old and the mother of two children when she decided to reinvent herself as an entrepreneur in 1980. At the time, Hammer had a BA in English and a Ph.D in linguistics. She was an associate professor in linguistics at Washington State University (WSU), but after her husband, a literature professor, left her and their children to pursue acting in New York, she decided that the rolling wheat fields would not deliver the gold or the sparkle in her life. As a single parent, her salary as an academic seemed to be barely enough to sustain her family. She decided to leave WSU, recalling, "I felt like I was either going to get tenure at Washington State and get poorer every year I taught and feel like a victim, or I was going to have to figure out something different to do. Software seemed to be where there is money and mobility."

At WSU she had used computers in her classes to teach sophomore literature, and classes in syntactic theory and psycholinguistics. Noam Chomsky's writings about the possibility of universal rules of language suggested a business idea to her. As in linguistics, computer programming had similar rules about the order of words and/or symbols and how they create meaning. She decided to apply the techniques learned in linguistics to problems in system software.

To prepare, she joined the University of Texas at Austin for a sabbatical year as a visiting scholar at the Center of Cognitive Science and enrolled part-time in the computer science department to work on natural language processing: giving commands and instructions to computers in English rather than computer code. After the year, she stayed in

Texas and joined Texas Instruments (TI) where she managed a group that developed tools for English-language interfaces, NaturalLink. She worked long hours, then would go home to feed her kids and be back at work later in the evening. However, despite strong interest in the marketplace, TI would not agree to sell NaturalLink in anything but its proprietary PC platform. Hammer felt that her hard work was not being put to its best use. By 1984, Hammer decided to move on to MCC, a consortium of the world's leading computer, semiconductor, and electronics manufacturers, and users and producers of information technology, where she worked on a program for computer-aided chip design.

She soon became aware of the huge amount of time and money large companies spent writing data conversion programs. With a colleague, Tina Timmerman, Hammer decided they could use the same techniques that they had used with natural language interfaces to develop a software product to automate the generation of data conversion programs. Working from home on weekends on their own PCs, they soon realized the venture required more resources than they personally had. They applied for funding from MCC for their project. Despite the skeptics, seven firms agreed to sponsor the project, even though they were not overly enthusiastic about the concept, and one of them even openly predicted failure.

Hammer's persistence, technical skills, and "dare the naysayers" attitude led to successful development of the prototype of the product. In two years, Hammer and three others had developed tens of thousands of lines of code: half in Lisp and half in the C programming language. Both at TI

and at MCC, Hammer had been involved in the development of products that she thought were perfect for the customers, but the organizations showed lack of enthusiasm
for them and would either kill them or shelve them. She
was not going to let that happen to this project. She was
willing to reinvent herself, again![26] In fall 1991, Hammer
attracted an initial investment of $250,000 from Admiral
Inman, a business angel. Following 200% growth in the
next five years, a West Coast venture capital firm, VC1,
also invested $1.25 million.

Hammer's story is not unusual. She used her academic experience
and education in literature and language as a basis for developing new
capabilities in computer programming. This knowledge and experience
inspired the idea for her new venture. Her human capital formed the
basis for the venture idea, and the seed for the unique technology providing market differentiation. Importantly, she was willing to learn, to
improve her human capital, and in her words, to "reinvent herself."

Unlike Kay Hammer, most women do not have a Ph.D., a background in computer science, and the backing of Texas Instruments. The
big question here is this: How can women who want to lead high-
growth businesses address questions about their human capital?

Assessing Your Education and Experience

In the first place, consider the link between your educational background and your business. For instance, someone with only a high
school education might be less likely to found a technology-based
company than someone who has some type of technological education
or training. Although formal education and clearly related technical
experience provide the most common ways to gain education, there are
many other ways to develop this knowledge. Take the example of Ann
Price, founder of Motek, a provider of supply-chain executive systems.

Price attended one year of high school before joining the workforce and was self-taught in the area of technology. Yet, she was able to build a company that successfully competes in a technology market space. She gained the knowledge necessary to launch her venture through means other than formal education. After years of consistent growth in profits, Motek was named to the Deloitte Touché Fast 50 list three times, she won a Smithsonian award for innovation and boasted a Fortune 50 client list.

Education can come from a variety of sources including volunteer activities, workshops, courses, and self–study, and it works together with experience. Consider the example of Gina Jacoby.

Gina Jacoby was just 25 when she opened her first Merle Norman Cosmetics Studio franchise in Van Nuys, California. Becoming a franchisee at such a young age was daunting, but thanks to her previous experience as a consultant and her training, the franchisor had complete confidence in her ability. While starting up, Jacoby took business classes through a local economic development center to improve her business skills.[27]

Like education, the three forms of experience—industry, venture start-up, and general business—directly influence growth patterns. Most entrepreneurs start businesses based on what they already know, drawing heavily either from their previous occupation or their avocations. This is not surprising, because if you know the industry, it is likely you can identify new opportunities or ways to solve problems. Having this type of experience makes it easier for you to navigate the distribution channels, understand customers, analyze competitors, and build a solid network.

Although industry experience is central, start-up experience is another form of knowledge. You can transfer your previous start-up learning to a new industry or business concept. If you have already started one venture, you might be considered a serial entrepreneur. Serial entrepreneurs sometimes create businesses in the same industry and sometimes in different industries. Donna Dubinsky founded Palm Computing, which manufactured a hand-held computing device, then later launched another company making the same product, Handspring. On the other hand, Nolan Bushnell is famous for founding more than 20 companies ranging from Atari video games to Chuck E. Cheese's Pizza Time Theaters. In both cases, the experience of starting ventures, building teams, acquiring resources, and developing networks directly facilitated the ability to launch a second venture successfully.

Then there is general business experience. To what extent do you have general business experience? This might be general management oriented, where you would make decisions affecting the whole organization and learn how different functions (e.g., marketing, operations, finance) are related and work together. Or it might be more functionally based, where you use this as a foundation to build your business. For example:

Charlotte Bogardus founded Gazelle Systems to help restaurant operators increase sales by linking critical customer information to marketing, site selection, and menu development through a patented point-of-sale process that collects data and appends customer demographic information. Prior to start-up, Bogardus served in executive marketing positions in national and regional food service companies like Starbucks and Legal Seafoods, and previously had her own hospitality marketing firm.[28]

In this case, it's clear that Bogardus's marketing experience related well to Gazelle's customer group (restaurants) and her hospitality experience helped her understand their needs. General business experience can be obtained in many ways. For instance, if you are chair of the finance committee for your church, you might be responsible for a capital building campaign that would help you to understand equipment and building contracting. Or, perhaps you have general administrative experience from work in a business. This experience might help you to understand how the business obtains customers, conducts operations, and pays its bills.

Ideally, you would have all three types of experience—industry experience, venture start-up experience, and general business and functional experience—but the reality is that most entrepreneurs have one or two types of experience when they launch their ventures. Of course, there are examples of entrepreneurs who start businesses with minimal industry, functional, or general business experience. A good example is two founders of a fashion accessory business.

> **Marcia was a nurse, looking to break out of the health care industry, and Martin was an artist who hoped to use his artistic talents to design fashion items. They carefully explored several options in the fashion industry, and following significant research, they decided to create high-end specialty fashion accessories made of unique wools, velvets, and silks. Over the years, they expanded their product line to include a variety of scarves, capes, and other accessories. Neither one of them had previous experience in the industry, in business management, or in another start-up, and as a result, it took lots of on-the-job learning and persistence for them to build their business.**

Besides influencing the type of business and the start-up process, human capital directly influences your growth potential. For instance, if you start a small firm designed to provide a comfortable living, chances are that you will need sufficient industry experience and general management expertise to manage a small number of employees. On the other hand, to create much larger, growth-oriented businesses, entrepreneurial human capital is reported to be the single most important factor that investors consider.

Finally, it's important to remember how an investor (whether it is a venture capitalist or a family member) evaluates human capital in assessing the risk of a potential investment. In essence, it requires a clear-eyed inventory of human capital assets and a careful matching of those resources to the needs of the entrepreneurial opportunity and organization. If the entrepreneur's human capital does not fit all of the major management aspects of the venture, how can the entrepreneur compensate for any deficits?

Enhancing Your Human Capital

We suggest five areas in which you might enhance your human capital: school, training, work experience, advisors, and affiliation with associations.

School

More than 600 colleges and universities offer entrepreneurship courses and programs, and an increasing number are offering concentrations and majors, both at the undergraduate and graduate level. Although some would argue that entrepreneurship can't be taught in business schools, the fact is that there is great value in writing a business plan and gaining skills and tools from multiple disciplines or functional areas.

Training

There is a plethora of excellent training programs sponsored by the Small Business Administration, women's associations, networking groups, and women's business centers. These range from a half-day to a full semester. You should do serious due diligence on the programs to make an informed choice. Training programs are often excellent for developing lifestyle businesses, but they often lack trainers with expertise in equity investment funding or fast-growth strategies. In fact, on more than one occasion we have heard local trainers address introductory entrepreneurship students with references to "vulture capitalists" and warnings to beware of equity providers or you will lose your company. Although these references might be accurate in certain situations, they also set the stage for limiting opportunity scaling at very critical early stages. If you seek high growth, you want a program that focuses on writing a professional business plan, building and attracting a top management team, learning financing options, negotiation, and possibly networking with investors. This type of program is a distinct contrast to a program that offers business feasibility analysis or basic cash flow management. Many areas now have entrepreneurship resource centers or programs specifically targeted for women entrepreneurs that focus on topics where they frequently have lower levels of human capital (e.g., finances).

Work Experience

Barnett Helzberg, author of *What I Learned Before I Sold to Warren Buffett,* is fond of advising students and young entrepreneurs to "learn on somebody else's nickel (or sometimes it's a dime)." You can gain industry experience, management opportunities, and start-up exposure in almost any size business. Large businesses offer an opportunity to participate in an industry and observe (if not make) strategic decisions. Some large companies might provide opportunities to engage in corporate venturing, where you can work on developing a new business within the company or one connected to the parent firm. On the other hand, new or small businesses might offer the chance for deeper learning experiences within the industry and more involved strategic decision making.

Summary

It's fair to say that perceptions that women lack the requisite human capital to run high-growth ventures are not realistic. Women have achieved near equality in undergraduate business education, medical schools, and law schools, with substantial gains in MBA education as well. Likewise, women with extensive managerial and executive expertise are no longer the exception. Our research shows that among high-growth women entrepreneurs, their experience and education is equal or better to their male counterparts running high-potential ventures. Although there certainly is variation in women's composite industry, functional and technical backgrounds, as well as educational degrees, the statistics don't suggest that women are in any way substandard or inadequate compared to their male counterparts. The reality is that each entrepreneur, male or female, needs to be assessed for "fit" to the particular venture, its strategy, and the product or market opportunity void it seeks to fill. A right combination of human capital is "right" for the venture not because the woman entrepreneur needs to meet a certain standard. The same is true for women executives, managers of nonprofits, or those in public administration. This perception thus has minimal basis for limiting women's opportunities to acquire money for growth.

There are only two areas where women's human capital development might be slower than expected; in terms of industry experience, they are still the exception and minority at the most senior corporate executive level, such as CEOs and board members of Fortune 500 firms, and with regard to the percentage of women graduating with engineering degrees. However, when we consider the composite of experience and education, women should be confident in their capabilities. One woman entrepreneur stated that confidence in your human capital is based not only on what you have done, but what you can do, your potential.

The next chapter considers the composite of human capital for the venture and women's ability to build a management team. Are women less capable of bringing people together to run a venture?

Notes

1. Mason, C., & Harrison, R. 1999. Venture capital: Rationale, aims and scope. *Venture Capital.* 1:1, 1–46.

2. Bhide, A. 2000. *The Origin and Evolution of New Businesses.* New York: Oxford University Press; Shepherd, D. A., & Douglas, E. 1999. *Attracting Equity Investors.* Thousand Oaks, CA: Sage Publications; Zider, R. 1998. How venture capital works. *Harvard Business Review,* #98611.

3. Shaver, K. G. & Scott, L. 1991. Person, process and choice: The psychology of new venture creation. *Entrepreneurship Theory & Practice.* 16:2, 23–47; Cooper, A. C. & Jimeno-Gascon, F. J. 1992. Entrepreneurs, processes of founding and new firm performance, in Sexton, D. L. & Kasarda, J. (Eds.). *The State of the Art of Entrepreneurship.* Boston: PWS Kent.

4. Bhide, op. cit.; Zacharakis, A., & Shepherd, D. 2001. The nature of information overconfidence on venture capitalists' decision-making. *Journal of Business Venturing.* 16:4, 311–332.

5. Zacharakis & Shepherd, op. cit.; Khaneman, D., & Tversky, A. 1982. The psychology of preferences. *Scientific America.* 246: 160–173.

6. Recent efforts by the largest producer of business school cases to correct this deficiency has resulted in focused attention on cases about women entrepreneurs and their businesses, and resulted in a special catalog featuring these: *http://harvardbusinessonline.hbsp.harvard.edu/.*

7. *www.aacsb.org/.*

8. Osborne, D. M. 2000, September 1. *A Network of Her Own. www.inc.com/articles/start_biz/20125-print.html.*

9. Employment Policy Foundation. 2003, February 24. Media advisory: Equal pay day observances may not capture significant progress by women. *www.epf.org/media/newsreleases.*

10. U.S. Department of Commerce. Winter 2001-02. *Occupational Outlook Quarterly.*

11. Employment Policy Foundation. op. cit.

12. Society of Women Engineers based on statistics from the National Science Foundation and the Bureau of the Census. *www.swe.org.*

13. National Science Foundation. *www.nsf.gov/sbe/srs/nsf00327/frames.htm.*

14. *New York Times.* 2003, January 12.

15. Schumpeter, J. 1984. The theory of economic development, (reprint of 1934 version) Cambridge, MA: Harvard University Press.

16. *www.inventivewomen.com.*

17. *http://inventors.about.com/library/inventors/blwomeninventors.htm.*

18. Teen girl's interest in business raises concern. 2003, January. *Women's Business.* 5:4, 15.

19. For detailed information on the Panel Study of Entrepreneurial Dynamics see Reynolds, P. D., Carter, N. M., Gartner, W. B., Greene, P. G., & Cox, L. 2002. *The Entrepreneur Next Door: Executive Report of the Panel Study of Entrepreneurial Dynamic*s. Kansas City, MO: Ewing Marion Kauffman Foundaton.

20. National Foundation for Women's Business Owners, 2000.

21. Catalyst, *The 1998 Census of Women Corporate Officers and Top Earners of the Fortune 500.*

22. 2002 Catalyst Census of Women Corporate Officers and Top Earners.

23. Jones, D. 2002. Few women hold top executive jobs, *USA Today.*

24. Welbourne, T. 2001. *Wall Street Likes Its Women: An Examination of Women in the Top Management Teams of Initial Public Offerings.* Working paper. University of Michigan. Summary in: Gutner, T. 2001. Do Top Women Execs = Stronger IPOs? *www.BusinessWeekOnline.com.* February 5, 2001.

25. Cooper & Gimeno-Gascon, op. cit.

26. Mishra, S. 1999. *ETI: For Managing Data Inconsistency.* Personal Entrepreneurial Strategy.

27. Be your own boss. 2003, November. *Entrepreneur Magazine*, 106.

28. *www.gaz.com/management.*

6

FINANCIAL KNOWLEDGE AND BUSINESS SAVVY

*Financial capital does not ensure a new venture's success,
but lack of funding can sound the death knell for even
the most brilliant business concept.*

New ventures are typically long on ideas and short on cash. By now, you already know that entrepreneurs must invest not only their own energy, but also their own cash in their start-ups. Of course, you would be very unusual if you could continue to fund the business out of your own pocket indefinitely. In fact, in 1997, 92% of all women business owners reported using some outside suppliers of capital including family, friends, commercial banks and thrifts, finance companies, brokerage and leasing arrangements, and government loans.[1]

When rapid growth is a part of your plan, you are likely to need financial partners to fund the expansion stages. You will have to identify potential creditors and investors, and then pique their interest in the business concept. Your own investments of seed money and sweat equity will provide evidence of both your confidence in the venture and your commitment to making it work. Next, you will have to demonstrate to potential partners that you have a sound financial strategy for growth and the management capability to make success a reality. Of course, all the while that you are raising funds, you will also have to tend to the business operations and manage cash flow very carefully.

Prior experience in money management can provide you an extremely useful toolkit of skills for both securing and managing financial assets. Experience is also invaluable in managing relationships with the partners who provide the cash. Besides building critical skills, credible business experience serves to reassure investors of your competence. If you lack this experience, you will need to enlist the help of partners and advisors to fill in the gaps.

Why? Because, if you lack personal financial resources to make a meaningful initial investment or if you are unable to inspire confidence among potential investors as you expand, you will be severely challenged in growing your business successfully. This chapter addresses the fundamental question, "How well are women entrepreneurs faring in the entrepreneurial fund-raising process?" The answer is, "Not as well as they should be." Here we examine key issues that traditionally have raised the bar for women entrepreneurs.

Challenges Built into the System

Building sufficient cash reserves to launch a business and managing subsequent fund raising are challenges for every entrepreneur, but they are particularly daunting tasks for women. Women often come up short of cash at start-up and, when they are ready to grow their businesses, they find that many would-be partners are not convinced that women have the necessary financial skills and management savvy. These assumptions are based on several different, but closely related, stereotypes about women, money, and financial management capabilities. They fall into three general categories:

1. Women do not invest sufficient capital in their own businesses. Either:

   a) They can't.

   b) They won't.

2. Women lack fundamental business skills and experience:

   a) They do not have strong math skills.

   b) They have little or no relevant financial experience.

3. Women are bad business risks because:

   a) They are risk averse.

   b) They can't make tough decisions.

Whether or not they are true, these assumptions create significant barriers to success for women entrepreneurs who want to build large enterprises. If true, they might reflect fundamental problems in the educational and employment infrastructures rather than problems with women's capabilities and commitment. The following sections explore these widely held beliefs about women's investment in, commitment to, and capability to run substantial businesses of their own.

Do Women Underinvest in Their Businesses?

Personal savings and family assistance fund the launch of nearly all start-ups. The founders' current income, cash reserves, credit card capacity, and "mortgagable" assets account for most of the early stage capital in the United States.[2] Other forms of non-cash entrepreneurial investments include assignment of patent rights (and any associated licensing revenue) to the company and foregoing salary.

There is a perception that women entrepreneurs do not invest sufficient start-up capital in their enterprises. If there is any truth to that, the important question is "Why?" Do women lack a fundamental understanding of what it takes to launch the business? Do women invest less because they lack confidence in their businesses or the size of the opportunities? Do they have reservations about their ability to see the venture through hard times? Is their level of investment simply a function of their personal financial circumstances?

Our research indicates that women invest in their enterprises at a lower rate than men do, not because they do not believe in their ventures, but because they simply do not have the same level of financial resources available. In spite of improving conditions, a wage gap has persisted for more than 30 years. Professional women currently earn approximately 73% of what their male counterparts are paid for the same work at commensurate levels of responsibility.[3] This gap means that on average, in 2000, women working full time received $9,984 less in gross earnings than did men.[4] In 2001, median weekly earnings of full-time female college graduates were 72.5% that of male college graduates and women with master's degrees earned 72.2% of what their male counterparts did.[5] A particularly large gender disparity was reported between male and female executives. For example, in 1999, only 5% of women executives were then earning $80,000 or more, but 23% of male executives were in the $80,000 bracket.[6]

This well-documented earnings gap between working men and women is exacerbated by several other important factors.

- Women in business and financial industries tend to move up the managerial ladder at a slower pace, so they stay in lower paying positions much longer.

- Women often choose "female" industries (health care, education, nonprofit) in which compensation is lower across the board.

- Very few women are serial entrepreneurs. Consequently, they are not in a position to stake their new ventures with the rich rewards that might come from selling an enterprise.

- Many women choose entrepreneurship after having been out of the paid workforce for several years, tending to the needs of a young family.

As a result of some or all of these factors, women continue to lag in building the substantial cash reserves necessary to stake a young venture. The wage gap is closing but it continues to be a challenge for women, even after they exit the paid workforce to become entrepreneurs.

A lower level of personal investment is only one of many reasons that investors question whether women entrepreneurs are truly committed to their business. People often conclude that women start new businesses not because they are pulled toward a great opportunity, but because they are responding to personal life changes; for example, their children are now all in school or they have recently experienced divorce or widowhood. These circumstances reinforce the belief that women entrepreneurs are reactive rather than proactive in envisioning and building new ventures. The net effect is that women are viewed as being less driven by the concept and, consequently, less serious about their commitment to the enterprise. We know that the caregiving responsibilities of parenthood fall more heavily on women's shoulders. If a woman has been out of the paid workforce for several years while raising children, she bears negative consequences in the entrepreneurial world: Not only does she have reduced cash reserves to invest, but also her business skills might be somewhat rusty, and she might be out of touch with important business networks.

That's the bad news. However, there is also considerable good news. More women are on career paths with high earnings potential today than ever before.[7] They have yet to close the earnings gap completely, but their increasing capacity to create wealth allows them greater opportunities to accumulate resources for a business start-up.

Furthermore, most women have learned that they need help to create and build their businesses. They are assembling multi-talented entrepreneurial teams that bring a broad base of resources—including initial financial investment money.

Outside sources of financing for early-stage businesses are also becoming more accessible. Financing through government-sponsored lending programs such as the 7(a) General Business Loan Guaranty program, the Certified Development Company (504) loan program, and the Microloan program provided funds to more than 76,000 U.S. companies in fiscal year 2003.[8] These loan programs, readily available credit cards, and equal opportunity lending have improved women's options dramatically over the past 30 years and have brought early-stage financing within closer reach for women entrepreneurs.

These programs have the added benefit of giving women entrepreneurs experience in understanding and meeting loan requirements, negotiating terms, and operating under covenants. In 1998, women who achieved high growth in their businesses had an average of 4.2 different sources of capital, including business earnings, personal and business credit cards, private sources, and bank loans.[9]

Women have made extraordinary progress, but they still have much to learn. In spite of narrowing the debt-financing gap over the past decade, women continue to rely too heavily on personal credit cards, which carry a higher rate of interest, to finance their businesses.[10] Women business owners, even those who declared high-growth goals from the start, still lag men in their willingness to seek bank financing for their enterprises. In 2000, women-owned businesses claimed only 21% of the total SBA loans,[11] which generally provide much better terms than do personal credit cards.

In 1998, only 52% of women business owners had some form of bank credit, whereas 59% of men business owners did so[12] and those women who did seek commercial credit did not aim as high. Only 34% of those women had secured credit commitments of $50,000 or more, as compared to 58% of their male counterparts.[13] However, when women choose to seek debt capital, there appears to be no systematic gender bias. Instead, the owner's age, the size of the firm, credit history, and the ability to provide collateral and guarantees are much more reliable predictors of success in securing loans than is gender.[14]

The personal financial resources that entrepreneurs invest really "stake" the business. They not only provide the funds to rent space, get a computer and software, file a patent application, or get on a plane to meet with potential customers and suppliers; they also provide an important buffer against revenue fluctuations in times when the business meets bumps in the road. Your entrepreneurial investment helps the business get some breathing space while it builds a solid operating record and establishes a credit history. It also signals to outside investors that you have "skin in the game," that your own resources are on the line to sustain the enterprise. Your level of investment determines how long the business can function on its own, how much research and development can be completed, and how much space can be leased or inventory purchased before outside investors or bankers must be brought into the deal.

Of course, the more fully developed your business is when you begin looking for outside investors, the more clearly you can demonstrate "proof of concept" and the easier it will be to sell investors on the business vision. This means that the up-front investment is a critical factor, not only in early-stage success, but also in subsequent financing rounds. It is very instrumental in building a business that has traction.

Yes, it's a fact! Women generally have less cash to "seed" fund their own ventures. They must rely on founding partners, family, and friends to help launch their businesses. With lower founding investments, they must turn to outside investors much earlier in the new venture's life, which might disadvantage them in attracting capital to the enterprise and in negotiating favorable terms. However, the level of their investment does not tell the whole story. It does not support a conclusion that women lack commitment to the enterprise and its success. In fact, those who do start businesses do very well. Business ownership is one of the most effective means of improving women's economic well-being. In 1998, women householders who had founded a business had an average income level 2.5 times that of those women who were wage earners, and their net worth was more than 6 times greater than that of those without a business.[15]

Do Women Have the Requisite Financial Knowledge, Skills, and Experience?

Are the assumptions that women lack the appropriate knowledge, skills, and experience to be good financial managers accurate? Is it reasonable to believe that women aren't good business managers because they suffer from "math anxiety?" There is strong evidence that, for decades, girls and young women did experience strongly gendered influences in the educational process. The result was that they were less likely to study mathematics, accounting, and finance in school. Historically, women concentrated their studies in language arts and social sciences rather than in physical sciences, engineering, finance, or accounting. That path led them to choose careers in human resources and personal services, often favoring administrative roles over strategic or operational positions. These careers provided few opportunities to develop skills in negotiating loans, managing financial controls of the business, or engaging in effective investor relationships—skills prized by investors.

However, things have changed. National Science Foundation (NSF) statistics indicate that in the high school graduating classes of 1998, the female students were more likely than their male classmates to have taken geometry (77.3% vs. 73.7%), algebra II (63.7% vs. 59.8%), and trigonometry (9.7% vs. 8.2%). They were only slightly less likely to have taken precalculus (22.9% of the females vs. 23.0% of the males) and calculus (10.6% vs. 11.2%). Furthermore, NSF reports from 1990 through 1998 show that women consistently earned the lioness's share of bachelor's degrees (53.3% in 1990 and 56.2% in 1998) and, in 1998, women collected almost half (46.8%) of the bachelors degrees in mathematics.[16] However, women do lag men in two critical areas. They represent only one third of the current graduates of leading masters in business administration (MBA) programs and fall behind at the highest levels of education. Women earned 43% of the Ph.D.s granted in biological sciences in 1999, but only 35% of the science and engineering Ph.D.s.[17]

Although American women are still viewed as below average in basic math and finance, that belief is not borne out by these statistics. The math skills hurdle is one of perception rather than reality, yet its persistence continues to plague women seeking capital. If doubts about women's business and financial skills are based on "yesterday's news," the media has done little to dispel them.

There are very few high-visibility women in leadership roles at large corporations and powerful financial institutions. Drawing from the current managerial ranks, print and broadcast media reinforce prevailing images of what business leaders and entrepreneurs look like and how they act. True, *Fortune* devotes one issue each year to the 50 most powerful women in business in the United States (and to the 50 most powerful women in global businesses), but there are remarkably few women featured throughout the remainder of the year. Abby Joseph Cohen, Maria Bartiromo, and Laura D'Andrea Tyson are recognized experts on business and financial matters, but the vast majority of the commentators on the stock market, financing, and economic forecasting are men.

When the popular business media are just as likely to feature a female CEO or CFO (and gender is not the primary focus of the article), the perception that women are not qualified to take leadership responsibilities will begin to dissipate. Of course, that will only happen when more women succeed in taking top spots in highly visible companies. In the meantime, what people see is important, but what they don't see in the media is just as important in determining attitudes and expectations. The absence of women as leaders in the business headlines reinforces the belief that women and business simply don't mix.

Attitudes and expectations are also shaped by the leadership research and theory development that is based almost entirely on studies of men. The models of appropriate leadership styles and the definition of recognized paths to success are derived from these studies of men, so it is no wonder that they have a distinctly male style. A leadership approach that differs from the established model is considered an anomaly and might be dismissed as a weakness rather than a strength. For instance, cooperation rather than competitiveness might be perceived as less desirable in a fast-growth venture even though it can be just as effective in achieving the company's goals. The ability to make hard and fast decisions is not one of the classically defined feminine attributes. In fact, when women exhibit these capabilities, they are often characterized as "bitchy."

Lending officers use education as a proxy for human capital and are more likely to grant loans to those who can demonstrate educationally based expertise.[18] Women who operate businesses in sectors commonly seen as "male" (e.g., manufacturing, or based on high technology) might find it especially difficult to overcome industry-based stereotypes, unless they have deep experience in the field. Many women have been unsuccessful in translating their background experiences in a way that overcomes stereotypes about what it takes to run a growth business in these sectors and inspire investor confidence.[19]

Women frequently run into serious barriers when they seek their first round of external funding, whether it is debt financing from a bank or a private equity investment from angels or venture capitalists. Take, for example, Saman Dias, who reported, "When you are starting a business, nobody wants to give you money."[20]

Saman Dias, CEO of Walnut Creek-based AIM Computer Training recalled the painful process she experienced when she first sought bank financing. She had operated her ser-

vice business successfully for several years, but when she needed additional cash for growth and expansion, she found the lending process intimidating. She filled out applications and met with teams of bankers from 10 different institutions, only to be repeatedly rejected.

Although there are large numbers of women entrepreneurs who actually have appropriate skills, the perception that they are less competent as business leaders and financial managers remains a challenge. In cases where they make lenders and investors hesitate to commit, misconceptions can provide an unusually high hurdle for women entrepreneurs. If funding is denied or delayed simply because a woman entrepreneur is assumed to be less "financially capable," the enterprise will be handicapped and the woman will have to work harder, not only to prove her own abilities, but also to make the business succeed. Fortunately, there is evidence that things are changing.

Since the 1960s, each new generation of American women has been better trained in basic business skills and has gained deeper managerial experience. The number of women gaining managerial experience in the corporate ranks and experience on start-up teams is growing. In 1999, women made up 46% of business decision makers. Approximately 9.4 million women reported that they held executive, administrative, or managerial positions. The fact that women represented 57% of the executives under 25 and 52% of those under 35 provides evidence that there is significant change afoot.[21] Throughout the 1990s, women started new ventures at nearly twice the rate of men and their businesses are not only surviving, but also thriving.[22] Debt capital has become widely available to women-led businesses that can demonstrate a track record, and women are recognizing the importance of drawing on multiple sources of capital. As a result, there is a growing cadre of women entrepreneurs who have the requisite financial experience and business savvy to run large entrepreneurial organizations.

Despite these gains in the debt markets, few women business owners have been successful in securing private equity investments.[23]

Women have a very difficult time convincing equity investors that their businesses represent more opportunity than risk and that an investment will be well rewarded. Many investors are still concerned that there are substantial risks associated with women-led businesses, but there is not a sufficient countervailing "upside" to be had. Female entrepreneurs are considered a good bet in that they are no more likely than men to default on their loans. They are, however, seen as less likely to soar to great heights (and provide big payoffs), primarily because they are considered unwilling to take the big risks necessary to win.

Equity investors see that women are more likely to avoid debt and less likely to put personal collateral at risk[24] and, from that evidence, they infer that women are risk averse. These observations are deeply ingrained, coming from impressions formed on the playgrounds of America and reinforced by the educational system and early career paths. Girls are viewed as more cautious than boys in play settings; men are known to love fast driving and, by extension, seem to be more at home with riskier financial situations than women. Because risk is considered to play a central role in entrepreneurial decision making,[25] assumptions about women's personal risk preferences have a "spillover" effect on assumptions about their tolerance for risk as business owners.

Research on risk reveals that women are generally less tolerant than men on a variety of dimensions. For example, they are much more concerned about being caught and convicted of speeding than are men.[26] They also exhibit a greater preference for making "safe" choices in personal behavior including decisions about smoking, seat belt use, and preventative dental care.[27] They have also been shown to choose a more cautious approach to personal financial management. Men allocate a higher proportion of assets to stocks (riskier strategy)[28] and select less conservative positions relative to their portfolio's volatility, individual stock volatility, and size of investments[29] than do women.

However, women can offset risk aversion through education and experience. Research shows that having a college education increases the likelihood that women will seek debt financing.[30] Women have now achieved higher levels of education than men business owners.[31] Furthermore, it appears that although some women adopt lower risk strategies (which could lead to lower returns), the overall performance of their businesses is on a par with their male counterparts. In other words, women are more likely to "hit their target."[32]

There is also evidence that many highly skilled corporate women who choose entrepreneurship do not shy away from risk. In a recent study conducted by Korn Ferry and Columbia University, *Fortune Small Business* found that executive women leaving the corporate ranks to start new ventures were not any more risk averse than their male colleagues. "Their primary reason for starting new ventures was the adrenaline factor. An 'opportunity to take risks' was cited by a stunning 77.8% of respondents. Next up (66.6%) was another hard-headed goal: the chance to make more money. And rounding out the top three was clout, the ability to make strategy."[33]

Even if they are risk tolerant, women who succeed in attracting investment capital might find that their management and financial skills are in question. If they are perceived as higher risk investments, they might have to pay a higher premium for an equity investment. Those fortunate enough to secure funding might find that their angels and venture capitalists provide closer oversight because women CEOs are less "trusted" in their financial expertise.[34]

Separating the High Potential, High Performers from the Rest

Almost all of the concerns about women business owners as high-potential, high-growth entrepreneurs are based on generalizations about all women as business owners. Where there is truth to the assumptions, they tend to explain why the vast majority of women entrepreneurs have chosen small, closely controlled, income replacement businesses rather than high-growth enterprises. In 1997, almost 85% of all women-owned businesses were sole proprietorships with average annual receipts of $31,000 (as compared to the 74% of all U.S. businesses that were sole proprietorships with average annual receipts of $58,000).[35] Only 5.8% of women operated their businesses as C corporations and 6.2% were organized as Subchapter S corporations in 1997.[36] The vast majority of men, as well as women, who start businesses, tend to create small, local enterprises that provide good income and a personal stake in the business, but the men are much more likely to hit higher revenue targets. In fact, in 1997, only 13% of the women sole proprietors had receipts in excess of $50,000 and 2.7% reported receipts over $200,000.[37]

However, generalizations fail to take into account the exceptions. Just as there is a small cadre of highly motivated, highly qualified male entrepreneurs, there is a subset of highly focused, highly performing women entrepreneurs who want to grow large, vibrant businesses. The main difference seems to be that where men are concerned, these differences are clearly recognized and actively searched out, whereas, with women entrepreneurs, the assumption seems to be that one size fits all cases.

Katherine Gray, another seasoned entrepreneur, experienced what appeared to be gender-based biases when she undertook a search for private equity. She wrote to the Diana Project team for help:

Dear Diana,

I was reading *Fortune Small Business* and came upon the Ol' Gal Money Hunt[38] article, about your research. I hope you can help me. I am a 54-year-old health care professional. I have a Ph.D. in educational psychology and developmental psychology with an undergraduate degree in

Business Administration–Marketing. I completed a post-doctoral year in gerontology (study of the elderly) at the University of Minnesota and have since served in senior executive positions at several heath care companies. At one, I managed a start-up subsidary that developed and produced software. I have had as many as 275 staff reporting to me.

Five years ago I started Sage Health Management Solutions, a company that improves the quality of health care by using the Internet to manage diagnostic test orders. I have patented the software and business method. I am convinced that the market potential for our products will increase dramatically in the next five years due to the growing elderly population needing health care services, new regulations for security in transmitting patient data, increased pressure from all sides to lower health care costs and, most importantly, the recognition of the need to improve the quality of the care provided. Our software addresses each one of these issues.

I have bootstrapped the company to this point, relying on money from family, mortgaging our home (twice), and even have angel investors who have provided me with financing. But now I need a venture capitalist who will make a substantial investment in the company so we can expand into the marketplace. I've been to several networking events where I have met with venture capitalists, but they seem reluctant to invest. They don't seem to realize that I've been able to put together the seed capital to get the business to this point, and am capable of taking it to the next level. Do you have any advice for me?

V. Katherine Gray
C.E.O. & President, Sage Health Management Solutions

Katherine Gray typifies the challenges that women entrepreneurs face in equity fund-raising for expansion.

All too often, the assumptions about women entrepreneurs are generalized to all, without recognition of the capabilities and ambitions of a subset of highly qualified women who are ready to lead high-growth organizations. The last big nut to crack is how capable women who want to lead high-growth enterprises break the stereotypes and find creative ways to tap into angel and venture capital.

The Springboard Survey:
A Study of Women Entrepreneurs
Leading High-Potential Enterprises

A recent survey of more than 100 women-led businesses that were seeking equity investments in 2000–2001 provides insights into how women with high-growth intentions can address the challenges of funding their young enterprises. The survey examines how these women bootstrapped (self-funded) their product development and the development of the business itself. The findings demonstrate how they countered the negative stereotypes, demonstrated their capabilities, and created enough confidence in themselves and their enterprises to engage financial partners. The survey was one of many instruments used to develop an understanding of how these ambitious women (selected because they were actively seeking equity funding through the Springboard Venture Forums) organized their businesses and developed credible bases of operations before seeking external funding. The survey included questions about two broad categories of bootstrapping: those directed at product development and those that were more far reaching and focused on development of the business as a whole.

Product development options are directed at providing the resources needed to move from the "good idea" stage, to working product concept, to a functioning prototype, then beta testing and establishing channels of distribution, and creating the marketing strategies appropriate to building a customer base. Entrepreneurs often rely on advances from customers or negotiate special deals for manufacturing equipment to fund this stage. They are also likely to seek research grants such as those available through SBIR or work with university-based research programs where they can share labs or equipment. They might require prepayment on licenses or royalties to fund this development stage. The ultimate goal is to get the product or service to market with the minimum cash outlay.

Business development includes all the activities associated with building the enterprise. Although entrepreneurs use a wide variety of bootstrapping techniques to fund the early growth of the business organization, there are two major categories of bootstrapping that capture the essence of how the funding can be managed. The first is bootstrapping by minimizing the demand for capital and the second category is bootstrapping by finding alternative ways to meet capital needs.

Minimizing the need for capital really means that the entrepreneur focuses on controlling rather than owning resources. For example, she chooses to lease rather than purchase expensive equipment that would require large cash outlays and commit the business to a specific direction for the long term. Instead of hiring full-time employees, the entrepreneur will use temporary personnel or short-term contract labor to reduce overhead expenditures. They employ relatives at below market wages or pay with equity compensation while they work with little or no salary for themselves. Many entrepreneurs negotiate deals with service providers (lawyers, accountants, public relations firms) at below-market rates with the promise of long-term relationships at full price in return.

Most entrepreneurs monitor both accounts payable and accounts receivable closely and ease cash flow crunches by collecting early and paying late. Establishing routines for speeding up invoicing, offering the same conditions to all customers, or even ceasing business relations with late payers can minimize accounts receivables, and get cash into the business more quickly and effectively. Other "minimizing" boot-strapping techniques include the creation of systems to reduce stock (building "just-in-time" delivery systems) and negotiating the best possible terms with suppliers to minimize capital invested in inventory. Using internally generated cash is another alternative that can minimize the need for raising capital as the business grows.

In contrast, bootstrapping options that rely on alternative ways to meet capital needs usually involve owner financing. The focus of these alternatives is on raising capital quickly without having to pledge substantial collateral that the growing business might not yet have. Personal and business credit cards are a common source, as are personal bank loans, home equity loans, or personal savings. Selling accounts receivables (factoring) and borrowing from previous employers, are alternatives that can help the business get to a position where it is attractive to outside equity investors.

The results of the Springboard survey (see Table 6.1) show that the women who succeeded in attracting outside equity investments were far more likely to have used bootstrap financing options to build their businesses than were those still seeking equity. The most pronounced differences between the successful venture capital seekers and those still on the hunt were their use of product development bootstrap techniques and their ability to minimize business development capital requirements. The groups were more similar in the ways they met the capital needs of their growth businesses. Nearly 90% had used personal savings to bootstrap the business and more than half had used personal and business credit cards. Less than 40% reported getting loans from family and friends, and less than 20% reported taking out personal bank loans to support business development and growth. Less than 5% had factored (sold or pledged) accounts receivables to raise capital.

TABLE 6.1   Use of Bootstrapping Options by Springboard Applicants

	No Equity	Got Equity	Total
Bootstrapping product development			
Prepaid licenses, royalties, or advances from customers	16%	35%	24%
Customer-funded research and development	14%	33%	22%
Bootstrapping business development			
Minimizing capital need			
Leasing equipment	16%	60%	35%
Temporary personnel	57%	60%	58%
Credit from vendors	12%	53%	30%
Interest on overdue payments from customers	4%	8%	6%
Delayed compensation for founding team	61%	88%	73%
Deals with service providers (e.g., lawyers) at below competitive rates	52%	58%	54%
Using retained earnings	26%	18%	23%
Meeting capital need			
Personal credit cards	57%	60%	58%
Business credit cards	47%	55%	51%
Personal bank loans	16%	20%	18%
Personal savings	94%	80%	88%
Selling or pledging accounts receivables (factoring)	4%	5%	4%
Paying employees with company stock	33%	75%	52%
Loans from family and friends	39%	38%	39%
Loans from partners' families and friends	20%	18%	19%
Loans from previous employers	2%	5%	3%

One of the greatest differences between the two groups was their ability to use other people's resources. Requiring prepaid licenses, royalties, or advances from customers; having customers fund research and development; and getting credit from vendors distinguished those who got outside investments. Similarly, almost 60% of those getting equity reported leasing rather than purchasing equipment in comparison to just 16% of those still searching for an outside equity investment.

Of those who were successful in getting equity investments for their companies, more than 35% had founding teams with accounting experience and almost 40% had teams with financial planning experience. Thirty-five percent of the businesses still seeking external investments had financial planning experience on the top management team, in comparison to 46% of businesses that had already gotten investments (not statistically different). Women who demonstrate a competence in cash flow management and financial recordkeeping, as well as an in-depth understanding of financial or accounting exigencies, whether learned in school or in prior employment, convey the financial sophistication that inspires trust in financiers and investors.

Over 90% of those who were successful in getting outside equity reported some or all of the investment came from private investors (individuals or groups), although half reported having gotten funds from a venture capital firm. The heavy reliance on angel funding corresponds to findings in other studies. The Global Entrepreneurship Monitor (GEM) study reports that in some nations more than 90% of investment capital in entrepreneurial companies (male- or female-led) comes from informal angel investors.[39] What is unusual is that 50% of the entrepreneurs in the Springboard study reported funding from venture capital firms—evidence that sponsoring forums like Springboard 2000 (now Springboard Enterprises; *www.springboardenterprises.org*) can greatly increase the odds of success in finding funding.

Since the initial Springboard forum in Silicon Valley in 1999, more than 230 women-owned businesses have presented at nine venture forums in seven U.S. markets and have secured, to date, close to $2 billion in investments.

The Springboard findings are consistent with other studies that have identified bootstrapping as an effective strategy for financing a new enterprise's early stage growth and positioning the firm to be attractive to outside investors in subsequent rounds of financing. Bootstrap financing was used by 94% of new technology-based firms (see Table 6.2) and was the preferred source of more than 80% of the Inc. 500 fastest growing privately held firms in the United States.[40]

TABLE 6.2   Sources of Equity Investments

Sources of Equity	
Private investors—individuals or groups	93%
Bank where you had debt	8%
Venture capital firms	50%
From pension funds/insurance companies	5%
Publicly issued stock	5%
Investment from a small business investment corporation	8%

What Can Women Do to Clear the Financing Hurdles?

To Overcome Any Shortfalls in Initial Funding

Build Personal Reserves

The earliest investments will be your own and those of your cofounders. The more cash that you can set aside for the early-stage development of the business, the stronger the position you will have when you seek outside investors. Use the time before you start up the business to cultivate your network of business and professional contacts who can assist in the start-up and development of the business— either directly as partners, investors, clients, or customers, or indirectly as references and conduits to other interested partners.

Consider Founding with a Partner or a Small Team

Most complex businesses are created by small teams of entrepreneurs rather than by individuals. Consider your goals and your capabilities, then organize a founding team with multiple talents and resources and draw on the shared pool of financial resources to get the business off to a flying start.

Creatively Finance the Business to Show Proof of Concept and Capability for Growth

Women must raise their initial capital creatively, including using bootstrapping techniques. Bootstrapping by minimizing capital requirements can enable the team to demonstrate product viability, build market interest, and prove management capability. That level of success already achieved is the proof that enables women to take the next step and engage debt and equity investors. The Springboard survey results provide a good comparison of women who were successful in securing outside equity investments and those who were not. What the winners had in common was their ability to bootstrap the early stages of growth. The personal savings of the start-up team funded 90% of their ventures in the early stages. The next most popular strategy was delaying compensation for the founding team to help build the business (73%).

However, there were distinct strategies that differentiated those ventures that succeeded in getting equity investments from those that are still trying. Among these are bootstrapping options that use "other people's money" (i.e., customers, vendors, and employees) and control resources the business doesn't own (e.g., leasing equipment). Bootstrapping was critical for positioning the businesses for subsequent investment by external investors; a well-disciplined financing strategy increases the chances of the firm's later success and increases the venture's access to outside investors. Women-led businesses that use bootstrapping as part of their financing strategy are more likely to be successful in securing equity financing. These women have been able to demonstrate the success potential of their businesses while developing greater skills as leaders.

If women have not had the opportunity to learn how to plan and execute bootstrap financing through firsthand industry and start-up experience, attending programs to learn about these options is advisable. Leading a fast-growth business is challenging. Bootstrap financing is essential to getting off to a good start.

To Demonstrate Financial Knowledge and Management Savvy

Understand Capital Types

The amount of information women have about various sources of financing will directly affect their financing strategy. When entrepreneurs are unaware of capital alternatives, their choices are limited and they are likely to rely on expensive and inefficient capital sources (e.g., credit cards because they're short term with high interest). As a result, they will pay more for the money, incur higher risks, and ultimately lower the value of the firm.[41] By familiarizing themselves with the advantages and disadvantages of the full range of capital options, women will be in a better position to price and negotiate the investment.[42]

Investors are quick to see an entrepreneur's knowledge or information gap and are likely to judge the firm less worthy of investment if the entrepreneur has not already demonstrated her ability to create value through bootstrapping. Although information on capital types can be gleaned incrementally as the firm moves through the various growth stages of the business, having the information early in the company's development will allow the management team to drive the growth of the company rather than having to constantly be in a reactive mode.

If the relationship between the entrepreneur and the financier hinges on the degree of confidence inspired, then women who understand capital types and know how to leverage debt and equity will have a far greater chance of gaining the investments they need for their fast-growing or "gazelle" business.[43] Having information on financial products will increase women's confidence and help them more effectively negotiate the terms of financial contracts and facilitate compliance and renegotiation.[44]

Understand Requirements of the Industry

Different industries have different capital requirements, which increases the need for a coherent financing strategy. In manufacturing, more capital is needed to finance production facilities, equipment, inventories, and working capital and to cover the initial operating losses the business is likely to incur. Similarly, technology-based companies will require more up-front capital because they often face long lead times developing and transferring new technology into the marketplace. Businesses started in retail or personal and business services have lower capital requirements because they need less equipment or inventories but might need more money for marketing so they can generate sales and profits rapidly.

Understanding the underlying factors in the industry and how those factors impact capital requirements will improve the effectiveness of financial planning and success in securing investments. To some extent differences between industries might be offset by the skills and experiences of the top management team. This means that entrepreneurs need to carefully evaluate the skills and abilities of the management team and determine whether skills can be substituted for financial capital within the particular industry constraints.[45]

Understand the Motives of Lenders

Investors have differing motivations for investing in growth companies and the outcomes they expect will vary. Equity investors are interested in return on investment and can expect as much as a 50% annual return. Debt investors, on the other hand, will be more interested in how risky the loan is and the extent to which it can be covered with collateral. Understanding the differences in motivations and expectations will help you evaluate the pros and cons of financing alternatives and choose the sources most appropriate to your business.

To Overcome Concerns about Ability to Manage Risk

Develop a Process for Risk Management

Information, skills, and abilities increase risk tolerance. People with higher levels of formal education as well as industry, managerial, and previous start-up experience are more likely to invest personal resources in their business and seem to take greater risks with their financing strategy overall.[46] Essentially, these nonfinancial resources mediate the risk relationship. Investments entrepreneurs make in information gathering, knowledge, and skills, will likely translate into their willingness to take more risk. The enhanced information gives the entrepreneur a greater ability to make good choices. Understand that every round of financing takes twice as long as you anticipate it will, so start early and manage cash carefully.

Work with Reputable Professionals to Expand Your Knowledge and Your Network

Lawyers, accountants, and consultants can help you fill in the gaps in your knowledge of specific financing alternatives, can make referrals and introductions, and can point out potential pitfalls. It is particularly important that you have a full understanding of the deal terms and that you protect your own interests as you take in new partners.

Notes

1. U.S. Small Business Administration Office of Advocacy. 2001. *Women Owned Businesses, 2001.*
2. Federal Reserve Board. 1999, March 9. *Remarks by Alan Greenspan: Changes in Small Business Finance.* Federal Reserve System Research Conference on Business Access to Capital and Credit, Arlington, VA.
3. Harris, S. 2000, January 31. Taking aim at the male/female wage gap. *Christian Science Monitor.* csmonitor.com.
4. National Committee on Pay Equity. *The Wage Gap Over Time: In Real Dollars, Women See a Continuing Gap.* www.feminist.com/fairpay.

5. Ibid.

6. U.S. Small Business Administration Office of Advocacy. 2001. *Women Owned Businesses, 2001.*

7. The Glass Ceiling Commission. 1995, March. *Good for Business: Making Full Use of the Nation's Human Capital.*

8. Small Business Administration press release. 2003, October 10. SBA Sets 50-Year Record in Loans to Small Businesses, Registers 29% Increase in FY 2003; Loans to Minorities Up 38%. *www.sba.gov.*

9. Center for Women's Business Research. 2001. *A Compendium of National Statistics on Women-Owned Businesses in the U. S.*

10. Center for Women's Business Research. 2001. *Entrepreneurial Vision in Action: Exploring Growth Among Women and Men-Owned Firms.* Washington, DC: Center for Women's Business Research.

11. *www.sba.gov.*

12. Center for Women's Business Research. 1998. *Capital, Credit and Financing: An Update Comparing Women and Men Business Owners' Sources and Uses of Capital.* Washington, DC: Center for Women's Business Research.

13. Ibid.

14. Coleman, S. 2002. Constraints faced by women small business owners: Evidence from the data. *Journal of Developmental Entrepreneurship.* 7(2): 151–173.

15. U.S. Small Business Administration. 2001. *Report on Women in Business, 2001*, p.4. *www.sba.gov.*

16. National Science Foundation Web site, Division of Science Resources Statistics. 2002. *Women, Minorities, and Persons with Disabilities in Science and Engineering Report.*

17. Ibid.

18. Coleman, S. 2002. op. cit.

19. Hisrich, R. D., & O'Brien, M. 1982. The woman entrepreneur as a reflection of the type of business.

20. Levine, D. S. 2002. Show them the money. *San Francisco Business Times*, May 31–June 6, p. 44.

21. U.S. Small Business Administration Office of Advocacy. 2001. *Women Owned Businesses, 2001.*

22. Ibid.

23. Brush, C. G., Carter, N. M., Gatewood, E. J., Greene, P. G., & Hart, M. 2001. Women business owners and equity capital: The myths dispelled. *Insight Report.* Kansas City, MO: Kauffman Center for Entrepreneurial Leadership.

24. Carter, S., & Cannon, T. 1992. *Women as Entrepreneurs.* San Diego, CA: Academic Press.

25. Forlani, D., & Mullins, J. W. 2000. Perceived risks and choices in entrepreneurs new venture decisions. *Journal of Business Venturing.* 15(4): 305–322.

26. Brinig, M. 1994. Why can't a woman be more like a man? Or do gender differences affect choice? in R. J. Simon (Ed.). *Neither Victim nor Enemy.* Iowa City, IA: University Press. *www.uiowa.edu/~mfblaw/.*

27. Hersch, J. 1996. Smoking, seat belts and other risky consumer decisions: Differences by gender and race. *Managerial and Decision Economics.* September: 471–481.

28. Jianakoplos, N. A., & Bernasek, A. 1998. Are women more risk averse? *Economic Inquiry.* 36(4): 620–630.

29. Watson, J., & Robinson, S. 2002. *Risk adjusted performance measures: Comparing male and female controlled SMEs.* Presented at the International Council for Small Business, Puerto Rico.

30. Coleman, S. 2002. Constraints faced by women small business owners: Evidence from the data. *Journal of Developmental Entrepreneurship, 7*(2), 151–173.

31. National Science Foundation Web site, Division of Science Resources Statistics. 2002. *Women, Minorities, and Persons with Disabilities in Science and Engineering Report.*

32. Watson, J., & Robinson, S. 2002. op. cit.

33. Smith, S. 2001, February 2. The great escape: What do women think when they leave the mother ship to launch their own business? *Fortune Small Business.*

34. Brophy, D. 1992. Financing the new venture: A report on recent research in D. L. Sexton, & J. Kasarda (Eds.). *The State of the Art of Entrepreneurship* (pp. 387–401). Boston: PWS Kent.

35. U.S. Small Business Administration Office of Advocacy. 2003, March. *Dynamics of Women Operated Sole Proprietorships* 1990–1998.

36. Ibid.

37. Ibid.

38. Montandon, M. 2002, March 28. The Ol' Gal Money Hunt. *Fortune Small Business.*

39. Zacharias, A., Neck, H., Bygrave, W, & Cox, L. 2001. *Global Entrepreneurship Monitor: National Entrepreneurship Assessment, United States of America.* Kansas City, MO: Kauffman Center for Entrepreneurial Leadership at the Ewing Marion Kauffman Foundation.

40. Freear, J., Sohl, J. E., & Wetzel, W. E. 1991. Raising venture capital to finance growth, in *Frontiers of Entrepreneurship Research.* Babson Park, MA: Babson College; Bhide, A. 1992. Bootstrap finance: The art of start-ups. *Harvard Business Review.* Nov.–Dec.: 109–117; Van Osnabrugge, M., & Robinson, R. J. 2000. *Angel Investing: Matching Startup Funds with Startup Companies.* San Francisco. Jossey-Bass.

41. Van Auken, H. 2001. Financing small technology-based companies: The relationship between familiarity with capital and ability to price and negotiate investment. *Journal of Small Business Management.* 39(3): 240–258.

42. Ang, J. 1992. On the theory of finance for privately held firms. *The Journal of Small Business Finance.* 1: 185–203.

43. Center for Women's Business Research. 2001. *Entrepreneurial Vision in Action: Exploring Growth Among Women and Men-Owned Firms*. Washington, DC: Center for Women's Business Research.

44. Scholtens, B. 1999. Analytical issues in external financing alternatives for SBEs. *Small Business Economics*. 12: 137–148.

45. Chandler, G. N., & Hanks, S. H. An examination of the substitutability of founders human and financial capital in emerging business ventures. *Journal of Business Venturing*, *13*(5): 353–369.

46. Johnson, J. E. V., & Powell, P. L. 1994. Decision-making, risk and gender: Are managers different? *British Journal of Management*. 5: 123–138; Sykes, H. B., & Dunham, D. 1995. Critical assumption planning: A practical tool for managing business development risk. *Journal of Business Venturing*. 10: 413–424; Gifford, S. 2003. Risk and uncertainty, in Z. J. Acs & D. B. Audretsch (Eds.). *Handbook of Entrepreneurship Research*. Boston: Kluwer.

7

GROWTH ORIENTATION AND STRATEGIES

You've taken the plunge and started your business. Armed with a great idea that you are passionate about, you're on the road to success. But are you on the right track? This chapter explores the factors influencing growth and the challenges you might face as you try to take your business to the next level.

Growth is a choice. You might be committed to creating a large-scale, high-growth enterprise—envisioning your start-up as just the early stage of a global-scale enterprise or a public company traded on the NASDAQ or NYSE. Alternatively, you might prefer a manageable lifestyle business. Perhaps your dream falls somewhere in between the two. Whatever your plans, the opportunities for growth depend on strategic choices that you make at the outset. These choices include the venture concept, industry, market niche, and potential scalability of the business. If the industry is mature and slow growing, the market niche is small or crowded, or if the concept is hard to scale and expand, then your business is unlikely to be a blockbuster in terms of growth and size. At the same time, business concepts that replicate existing ideas or are highly dependent on the entrepreneur's personal involvement (e.g., a catering service or graphic design business) also have low growth potential. Then, from an investor standpoint, the sector you compete in directly affects your ability to raise growth capital. Angels, venture capitalists, and corporate investors are quick to identify those sectors with the greatest promise for innovation and financial returns, then direct their investment dollars to those industries.

Biotechnology, software, telecommunications, medical devices and equipment, media and entertainment, semiconductors, computers and peripherals, IT services, and industrial energy captured more than 90% of the venture capital investment dollars in the third quarter of 2003.[1] Less than 10% found its way to consumer products and services, business products and services, electronic instrumentation, health care services, retailing and distribution, and financial services. Investors devote significant time and effort to specializing in particular industries as part of their personal or firm strategies. Because technology-based businesses are those that solve big problems (e.g., medical diagnostics, faster information delivery, cures for diseases), they usually have the highest probability for returns. It quickly becomes apparent that the vast majority of very high-potential businesses have a technology base. By contrast, the majority of women owning firms in these segments is comparatively small. As we noted in Chapter 1, more than 55% of all women-owned businesses are in services and an additional 17% are in retail. Although it is estimated that more than 250,000 women lead companies in manufacturing, telecom, medical, and other areas,[2] the pool of women-led businesses in industry sectors with high growth potential is still comparatively small.

Now, this is not to say that all businesses in retail lack growth potential, because, of course, there are exceptions. Mrs. Field's Cookies, Liz Claiborne, DKNY, and Mary Kay Cosmetics are well-recognized examples of multimillion-dollar companies that grew in highly competitive retail sectors. However, the present and future reality is that innovative concepts in biomedical, nanotechnology, or photonics that have multiple applications stand a much better chance of growing large and fast.

As you think about growth, no matter what your aspirations might be, the initial choices of industry, concept, and market position will either facilitate or limit your business's potential from the outset. So, when setting your goals and seeking potential investors, it's important to have a realistic perspective and assessment of both your industry and your concept.

If you have considered the opportunities and limitations of these initial strategic choices carefully, how do you take your new venture to the next step?

The answer depends on your aspirations, personal capabilities, resources you will need, and your ability to capture those resources.[3] Every venture choosing growth will require a wide variety of resources, including money, facilities, equipment, information, people, and contacts. High-growth ventures require more resources faster. For either choice, the way these are acquired and used in the business directly affects the growth pathway you follow.

There are so many factors involved in gaining resources and influencing growth you would not expect gender to be one of them. Whether the founder is male or female shouldn't make a difference because there are just so many variables involved. Surprisingly, however, this is not the case.

Hagit Glickman has a Ph.D. in clinical psychology and more than 10 years of experience in managed care. Her business, MyPsych.com combines e-commerce and health care, providing an online service linking mental-health-care providers with their patients. However, when she sought funding from investors, they were not just dismissive, but insulting.

> "The message I got was, 'There, there honey,'" says Glick-
> man. "Here I am, a professional woman and a recognized
> expert in my field. I go into meetings with potential busi-
> ness partners, venture capitalists and angel investors, and
> all I hear is 'This is a really sweet, cute little idea. But, it
> will never go anywhere.' It was shocking to me."[4]

Glickman's concept combined proprietary knowledge and technology, and the potential market of psychiatrists and psychologists who
could use it was large, but she was still not taken seriously. Like Hagit
Glickman, it's not uncommon to hear, "She's not serious about her
business, it's just a little hobby," or "Women are good at running lifestyle businesses," or "She's not a strong enough leader to run a big
company." No matter what growth plans women have, it's frequently
assumed they can't or won't grow them beyond a certain size and are
destined to stay small.

In other words, no matter what type of business or industry women
compete in, many people believe that they pursue slow-growth strategies because they have limited ambitions, capabilities, and resources.
Where do these perceptions come from? To what degree are they true?

Are Women-Owned Firms Smaller?

Yes, there is some truth to the perception that women own smaller firms.
As we noted earlier, women are majority owners in about 28% of all privately held firms, or 6.2 million businesses.[5] At the same time, between
1997 and 2002, the number of women-owned firms grew at more than
1.5 times the average of all firms. Keeping in mind that the vast majority
of all U.S. firms are small in terms of revenues and employees, when we
consider women separately, we see that a large proportion of their firms
remain small. The number of women who are self-employed (rather than
employers) is 84.8% of all women-owned businesses as compared to

72.6% for all U.S. businesses in 2003. According to the Center for Women's Business Research, in 2000, nearly 60% of women-owned firms had less than $500,000 in revenues, compared to 44% of all firms with revenues of that level. At the midrange sales level, the percentage of women-owned businesses was fairly similar to that of all other firms. Approximately 16% of women-owned firms had revenues between $500,000 and $1,000,000, whereas 17% of all firms were found in this revenue category. However, these revenue sizes are generally small, enough to support only the owner and a few employees at best.

We also see that, on average, women-owned businesses also employed fewer workers, although the gap with other firms is narrowing. In 2000, 77% of women-owned firms employed fewer than 5 employees, compared to 74% of all firms; 19% of women-owned firms employed 5 to 19 employees compared to 20% of all firms; and 4% of women-owned firms employed 20 or more employees compared to 6% of all firms.[6] Women employed almost six employees per firm compared to a little over nine employees for all firms. From these statistics, it's pretty clear that many women-owned firms are smaller in both employees and revenues. This raises an important question.

Why Are Women-Owned Firms Smaller?

As we discussed in Chapter 4, one reason that women's firms are smaller is that women have lower growth aspirations for their firms and value growth less than men. The motivations and goals of both men and women influence the performance of their firms.[7] Owners can strive to grow their business or can rein in growth by investing fewer resources, limiting customers, devoting fewer hours to the business, or making a number of other conscious or unconscious decisions that will limit the growth rate of the firm.

Then, as we pointed out in Chapter 5, company size can be related to the entrepreneur's experience and education. Owners with more industry experience and a higher educational level are more likely to grow their firms successfully. At the same time, entrepreneurs with past experience growing a firm are more likely to have the skills and confidence necessary to take a business to the next level.[8] Women with less business or entrepreneurial experience or business education might have lower aspirations or capabilities for growth.

Finally, women's companies might be smaller because they tend to start or acquire firms in less promising industries, restricting their chances of growth.[9] As we pointed out at the beginning of this chapter, industry choice constrains growth when, like retail clothing or a restaurant, the chosen industry is highly competitive with higher failure rates and less growth potential. Why do women start firms in slow-growing, mature industries? It's possible these industries were easier for women to enter, requiring less capital, technical skills, equipment, staff, or management experience.

Alternatively, women might start a restaurant, retail boutique, or consulting service because they are seen as more "suitable" industries for women, or require less financial investment.[10] Finally, many women have greater domestic responsibilities, which results in limited time and commitment to their firms. Some women operate their businesses on a part-time basis as a means of supplementing family income, but this part-time approach directly affects the size and performance of a business.[11]

So, yes, it's true that the majority of women-led ventures in the United States are small, but, so are the vast majority of men-owned business. As we noted earlier, the vast majority of businesses in the United States are started as a lifestyle choice (income alternative) and these ventures are not wildly innovative or fast growing. This means the vast majority of men-led businesses are also small, slow-growing, and in competitive industry sectors.

There is wide variation in size, industry sector, and performance of all entrepreneurial businesses, and we can't simply paint all women-led ventures with a single broad brush suggesting that they are hobby type, small, and have no intention to grow. Clearly there are a variety of approaches to growth, and it is not surprising that it is almost impossible to identify a single, "successful" strategic approach. There is also a rising population of women who seek growth and expansion for their companies. However, the variety of strategic approaches in terms of type of business, size, and future growth intentions is often not recognized for women. Instead, women are often lumped into one generic category, where their business goals and business potential are generalized as being the same.

However, society, investors, and others in the business world do not infer from these data that all men don't want to grow their ventures, are in the wrong sector, or have inappropriate management styles. Instead, these attributions are reserved for women and these create higher hurdles for those women desiring growth.

Why Are Women-Led Ventures Perceived Differently?

There are two possible explanations: the way data are presented and that women are later entrants into the game.

The way data are presented creates perceptions about women's businesses different from those about men's businesses. Women-owned firms are those in which a woman, or women, own 51% of the equity. The comparative (men-owned firms) actually includes other types of businesses—whether majority-owned by men, or larger, more widely diffused ownership, either in private or public companies. This unfairly presents or contrasts the more closely held women-led businesses with all others, rather than those of similar ownership structure. In other words, women-owned firms are presented as the exception or difference from all businesses rather than as a separate category.

On the other hand, women are later entrants into the game. Women's entrepreneurship is a comparatively new phenomenon. Their firms are younger and generally at an earlier stage of development. The fact is that younger firms, whether owned by a man or woman, are faster growing than their older counterparts, have higher revenues, and employ more workers. Of these, about 44% of women owners of high-growth firms are under 45 years of age, compared to only 26% of non-high-growth women owners. Women-owned firms started or acquired in the last 10 years have reached the same revenue and employment distributions as those owned by women for more than 10 years; in fact, more than 20 years. The younger women owners have taken less than 10 years to accomplish the size distribution that their older counterparts needed many more years to reach.[12]

So, even if we consider that there are two tangible explanations for the differences in how women-led firms are perceived, this still doesn't fully explain the perceptions that Hagit Glickman encountered in her attempt to seek capital. What other explanations might we suggest for expecting that women can't or won't grow their firms? Some might say women just aren't as serious about growing a business, and others might offer that women are better at leading people-type service businesses and not as good at technology ventures. Where do these two perceptions come from?

Women Aren't Serious about Growth

Without a doubt, men and women are socialized differently when it comes to career plans, jobs, and business choices. Because children are influenced by the family and work roles of their parents from the time they are young, it is no surprise that by the time they are adults, their attitudes about work are firmly established.[13] Teenage boys are often provided more information about which jobs are appropriate for them, which guides their choices of jobs and careers. As a result, men's pathways are better defined, have a more linear progression, and are more orderly, whereas women are often guided into less secure and lower paying jobs.[14]

How does this happen? When girls plan their careers, they face dilemmas about family life that men do not. Whether or not they choose to have a family, however, they are often guided into less rewarding, slow career progression jobs that drive them to choose family over career.[15] Men might more often be fast-tracked, where they are introduced into business networks to gain advice, referrals, and recommendations. The net result is that women are often tracked into positions and occupations having less responsibility, and then perceived as having lower expectations for career success and accomplishment.

Besides, men's jobs are taken more seriously than women's jobs. Sometimes even when men and women have the same jobs (e.g., both teachers, both doctors, both managers) the man's job will be treated more credibly because he is viewed as the head of household and major provider for his family. At the same time, women often encounter greater emphasis and interest in a man's job rather than a woman's. How many times have you been asked, "What does your husband do?" when you are the successful entrepreneur?

Educational texts and the media perpetuate gender role stereotypes. Take, for example, any of the hundreds of books on Amazon.com about entrepreneurship. The vast majority of the stories, examples, and vignettes about successful entrepreneurs are about men. Few stories present women as role models in high-profile companies, and the few that do are likely to feature women in service or retail-type enterprises. By contrast, stories of male entrepreneurs who have grown large software, manufacturing, or high-tech companies are ubiquitous. Open any newspaper and you will likely see women featured in the gardening and art sections, whereas men are prominent in the business section.

If you seek growth, the bar is just a little higher if you lead a high-tech venture, but if it's low tech, you might be perceived as having an advantage.

Women Are Better at Low-Tech Service Ventures

An outcome of the socialization of career paths is occupational segregation. How does this work? This means that women face limited opportunities in certain careers and management positions. If we recall recent regulatory history, legal and policy changes such as Affirmative Action (1965) made it easier for women to enter different work in industries, but occupational segregation still exists in many sectors of the United States. In 1995 in the United States, more than 95% of secretaries were female. This trend is also apparent worldwide. In 1992, women in Europe held more than two thirds of the jobs in health, teaching, and domestic service, and women clerical workers comprised 66% of this workforce.[16] Similar trends are evident in Sweden, where 90% of jobs as typists, nurses, and housekeepers are filled with women, as are 60% of all public-sector jobs. Australia, Finland, and Denmark report similar levels of occupational segregation.

Then, the effects of occupational segregation are compounded by women's participation in managerial positions. Even though significant progress has occurred since 1990, in that 38% of all Fortune 500 companies (188) have at least a single woman director, this is still a small number.[17] They represent only 15% of all directors. The industries with the most board seats held by women are soaps and cosmetics, savings institutions, publishing and printing, and scientific and photographic and control equipment. Notably, companies like Avon and TIAA CREFF[18] have the highest numbers of women board members. The Federal Glass Ceiling Commission examined several industries, and found that utilities, transportation, and communications had fewer than 30% women managers and ranks above, whereas retail trade and insurance neared 50% each.[19]

The result of years of occupational segregation means that women are less visible leading companies in certain sectors. The small numbers of women working in specific sectors such as engineering, construction, freight delivery, and investment banking creates the perception that women are less capable of running businesses than men. When women wish to grow a company, especially in technology or manufacturing, the lack of examples of women as senior executive leaders creates the perception that these women are pioneers and less competent as leaders of ventures. Because women have succeeded in perpetuating small service and retail businesses, even dominating some business types (e.g., real estate, beauty supply, clothing boutiques) its assumed women prefer to and are just better at running small companies.

The tradition of role socialization and occupational segregation results in generalizations about women that just do not fully apply. Not only does this make it harder for women to forge ahead on the pathway to growth, but it also fails to recognize the new generation of women entrepreneurs.

The New Generation of Women Entrepreneurs

Consider the example of Sandra Wear.

> **Sandra Wear, founder of DocSpace Co., Inc., a document management software company, achieved her strategic goal when she sold her company to Critical Path, Inc., for $568 million. Despite her personal success, Wear believes that women are slow to make inroads into the high-tech industry because engineering and computer science are still perceived as "geeky." As a result, these professions remain dominated by men.[20]**

Is there a new generation of women business owners that is different than the older generation of women owners? Arguably this is the case. Younger women owners are more likely to have MBAs, have experience in software or technology-based firms, and be socialized to consider entrepreneurship a viable career from the start, not just careers for their fathers or husbands. They are set apart from the older generation of women who might be reluctant to expand or adopt state-of-the-art technology.[21] As a result of different growth goals, this younger generation of women-owned firms are more likely to own firms in fast growth sectors. Forty-three percent of younger women business owners' firms grew at least 30% in revenue or employment in the last three years, surpassing the 38% of young male owners' businesses that grew at this rate.[22] This differential is noteworthy because both groups had a similar amount of start-up or acquisition capital—a marked change from previous generations of women who consistently used smaller amounts of capital to start or acquire their businesses than male business owners, regardless of their generation.[23]

Our research showed that women applying for money through the Springboard Venture Forums were more similar to male entrepreneurs seeking capital than to women owning small firms (see Table 7.1).

TABLE 7.1   Profile of Springboard Applicants Women-Led Ventures Seeking Capital in 2000

Total capital sought	$1.02 billion
Average sought	$2.5 million
Round funding	2nd round
Percentage with revenues	60%
Percentage desiring rapid growth	80%
Most popular business sectors	Technology, life sciences, software, communications
Average number of employees	25
Average management team size	4
Percentage of team with previous start-up experience	40%
Team average industry experience	39 years

Note. N = 900.

We examined the applicant pool from the Springboard Forums in 2000 to determine the strategic characteristics of the proposed businesses. Most of the 900 applicants were competing in technology sectors, such as telecommunications, Internet, software, biotechnology, and medical technology. More than 80% of the applicants sought rapid growth and indicated that they would consider public or private sale to achieve liquidity. An indicator of the aggressiveness of new ventures is the size of the market they target. More than half of the Springboard applicants estimated the size of their target market to be more than $15 billion and international in scope.

Approximately 53% of all applicants were in the beta stage of development, and 47% had commercially launched their product or service. These applicants were further along in the development of their businesses than the average early-stage recipient of men-led ventures seeking funding. We also compared those applying to the Forum to the 84 selected to present their plans to investors. Presenters were more likely to be larger, to have launched a product, and to be business-to-business Internet providers (at a time when this category was still attractive to the venture capital community). Presenters sought an average of $10 million for second-stage financing and often had patented products.

Although the sample of Springboard applicants is biased because the applicant pool largely included only technology, life sciences, and new media companies, it is nevertheless representative of the types of businesses most often funded by investors. Over the first two years of Springboard Forums more than 1,700 women applied and after several screenings and evaluations, 170 were selected to present.[24] More than 350,000 women have sales of greater than $1 million, suggesting that there is a significant population of women entrepreneurs desiring to grow and expand their businesses.

Therefore, our discussion to this point shows that yes, the vast majority of women-owned firms are small, owing to a variety of reasons including choice, industry sector, and experience. However, many of the same factors influence men-led ventures and their growth as well. What's different is that all women-owned businesses are perceived as being smaller service businesses due to historical occupational segregation and socialization. Our analysis shows that, in fact, these broad generalizations just don't apply to all women. There is a distinct subset of women who seek fast growth, and, there is a large subset who seek some growth.

If you are one of these women seeking growth, the challenge is how to overcome the broad expectations and misperceptions. You begin by having a clearly thought-out strategy.

Strategies for Growth

If you choose to grow, you first need to consider your industry sector. If your business is in a very high-growth sector, you next need to look at the structural forces at work in that field. Who are the other potential players, whether new entrants or incumbents? Are there barriers to entry or exit? How powerful are the suppliers and customers? Does government policy support (e.g., tax incentives) or encourage growth? Can you protect your business from competition through patents, exclusive relationships, or preemptory market positioning? On the other hand, if your business is in a highly competitive sector where concepts are easily copied and products are not well differentiated, the challenge is to meet or beat competition by developing unique capabilities or perceived differences in the mind of the consumer. In other words, your starting point for a growth strategy begins with a clear understanding of the industry growth, bases of competition, and role of customers and suppliers.

Then, given your choice of venture concept and the industry you compete in, there are several approaches to growth, depending on your personal capabilities, goals, and resources. Rebecca Reynolds Moore and Jennifer Lane chose two dramatically different approaches. Each strategy led to success.

While completing her MBA with a concentration in non-profit and public management from Boston University, Rebecca Reynolds Moore conducted a term project that concluded that the vast majority of museum retail stores were barely profitable. She found most were staffed with volunteers and sold items only to their visitors or a select local mailing list. After spending hours attending retail conferences and visiting museum stores and trade association meetings, Reynolds Moore concluded that 75 of the medium to large museum shops (sales more than $500,000 a year) might benefit from aggregated advertising on the Web, which would give them greater exposure to customers outside their geographic areas. She estimated that over 70 million adults visited a museum an average of three times a year and that shoppers in museum stores would spend more than $1 billion by 2001.[25] Her research also showed that consumers of online retailing would like the chance to purchase museum gift items from a variety of museums in a single transaction. She saw this as an opportunity to connect museum partners with electronic retailing services to a global audience.

For three years Reynolds Moore worked hard developing custom software, negotiating strategic partner arrangements, and marketing the business. By the end of 2000, her persistence paid off. Museumshop.com was operating, offering the largest selection of museum products online (more than 3,500) and publicizing exhibits for more than 40 U.S. and international museum partners. Even with her early success, Reynolds Moore had greater aspirations. She desired to grow and expand her business. However, to achieve her vision, Reynolds Moore needed growth capital. Her challenge was to locate capital providers and to persuade them that her venture was a viable and attractive investment opportunity.

Jennifer Lane took a different strategic approach.

As a young girl, Lane had always wanted to be a professional woman making a difference.[26] As the owner of Compass Planning Associates with offices in Boston, her dream had come true. She was helping people, usually women, attain financial security. However, her pathway to business ownership was nontraditional. Lane graduated from Embry-Riddle Aeronautical University in 1989 and became a commercial pilot. After two years, she decided to make a career change and took a position with the John Hancock Insurance Company. She earned a financial planning certificate and another two years later, set up her own office in Arizona. Using her personal network, she served a variety of clients, and relied on her mother and younger sister for assistance. "I have a lot of patience and the clients who work particularly well with me are having a lot of stressed-out issues around their money," said Lane.[27] After 10 years, she hopes the business will eventually support four full-time financial planners and several subcontractors. "I want to grow enough to have longevity and to provide services to a large number of people, but I don't want to grow so much that we lose our individual touch."[28]

These two stories reflect different strategic approaches to growth. One highlights significant goals in an innovative and growing industry, whereas the other reflects modest growth plans in a more traditional business.[29] Business growth goals include geographic scope, which can be local, national, or global; as well as the sheer size based on employees or gross sales. Reynolds Moore pursued a strategy that created a new business model. By aggregating multiple museum shops into a single online retail and information site she was able to expand her business internationally, increase online services, and eventually vertically integrate. The venture was a candidate for equity funding because of its potential for growth and innovation. For Jennifer Lane, the business goals were different. She self-financed her business and sustained slow incremental growth through cash flow.

These two examples demonstrate just two of the many strategies you can adopt. Some entrepreneurs choose a low-cost strategy, whereas others offer high quality or other ways to achieve unique differentiation. For example, if you want to grow geographically, you might consider adding new products or services, selling to a new market, expanding distribution channels, expanding advertising and promotions, researching new markets, and expanding the scope of operating activities.[30] If your goal is to minimize costs and increase your scale, you might focus on product standardization, improving internal operations by acquiring more efficient equipment, computerizing current operations, or upgrading systems.

Strategic approaches fall along two basic dimensions: individual goals and capabilities, and venture resources. Individual goals are the growth orientation or the aspirations and vision you have for the future of your business. As we discussed in Chapter 4, you might have modest goals for a small manageable business or high hopes for a large, significant venture. These goals combine with your personal skills and capabilities, which include your financial savvy, experience, education, and business skills. At the same time, a growing business requires significant resources (e.g., money, facilities, information, equipment, trained personnel, technology, and company alliances). Figure 7.1 shows how different levels of resources and individual capabilities and goals affect growth strategies.

Each strategy has different business characteristics and requires a different combination of capabilities, goals, and resources, which are described next.

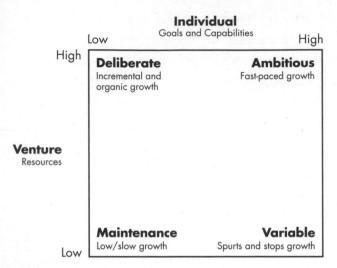

FIGURE 7.1   Approaches to growth.

Ambitious Strategy

To pursue an ambitious strategy you need grand goals, strong personal experience and expertise, and significant resources. Entrepreneurs and ventures suitable for this strategy are in a very small minority, with less than 1% of all businesses receiving institutional venture capital, which translates into fewer than a couple thousand businesses per year. Even including those receiving substantial private equity investment, or angel financing, the number of businesses suitable for ambitious growth is probably less than 10,000 at any given time. Why are so few businesses right for ambitious growth?

First, you need an extensive network of funders, business associates, and advisors; a solid management team; and a proven business concept. Through this network, you can make contacts with those who would fund your business. Second, most investors are only interested in businesses that operate in large and rapidly growing industries, where it is harder, rather than easier, to enter in terms of start-up costs, regulatory approval, competitive dynamics, or distribution channels. Third, an ambitious strategy generally means developing a unique advantage that is not easily copied. Unique advantages are those protected by copyrights, patents, or hard-to-replicate learning and practices. As the business grows, it will seek innovation and change, move into markets quickly, and expand into business sectors that are growing and innovative. Fourth, your experience, expertise, and personal leadership capabilities must be outstanding.

For instance, telecommunications and bioengineering are examples of industry sectors that reflect these characteristics. The entrepreneur's strategy would reflect a strong personal desire to grow the venture, a motivation to devote significant time and energy to make the business succeed, and the willingness to give up ownership control to exit the venture and move on at the appropriate time.

Kim Polese cofounded Marimba Software, a venture that develops, supports, and configures software. She followed an ambitious strategy. Marimba, which popularized Sun's Java computer programming language, allowing software developers to write their programs, created packages to serve Fortune 100 customers as well as many multinationals around the globe. Polese had personal expertise and experience in software, as well as high hopes for its success. "I'm the kind of person who needs to be in a wild, seat-of-the-pants-type organization," Polese says.[31]

Deliberate Strategy

A deliberate strategy is for women who have adequate or significant resources, but often have lower capabilities or goals. For instance, you might have top-quality employees, up-to-date facilities, and adequate cash, but maybe you just want to keep the business manageable, rather than beyond your control. On the other hand, you might have high aspirations and adequate resources, but perhaps you need to develop your management and leadership skills. Either way, you would follow a deliberate, well-thought-out, and incremental approach to growth.

Small, focused ventures are those that have a special niche in an industry, or focus on a particular customer group. Kate Spade began by making only high-end designer fashion purses, a narrow niche in the fashion accessories industry. She emphasized quality and high value, growing incrementally in a highly competitive and somewhat slower growing industry. Similarly, E. G. Carol Howe started CBR with one "concept" store in the Minneapolis airport in 1995. She now operates 10 concepts (36 total stores) at 12 major-hub airports across the country. The success of CBR Incorporated has depended on Carole's ability to identify trends and translate them into award-winning stores like Spirit of the Red Horse (a Native American jewelry store), toto (a trend gift store), and Radio Road (a fresh and classic clothing store) while keeping the company's focus on a narrow segment of the retail industry. By expanding in spurts when resources from the success of one concept were available to fund introduction of the next, Carole has delivered 29 years of revenue growth without ever receiving an outside equity investment.

Variable Strategy

You might have high aspirations but your resource base might not be adequate to make it work. For instance, maybe you hope to have a large, fast-growing venture, but developing the technology or raising money is going slower than planned. Chances are you might have good experience, lots of confidence, and strong leadership skills, but the resources just aren't available when you need them. In this case, you follow a scrappy approach, bootstrapping heavily and expanding in spurts as resources are raised and acquired. It's possible you are also in a very competitive industry, like retail or business services, and sometimes the concept can be copied. Even if the business is low technology, or can be copied, it is possible to grow by a standardized approach to volume expansion through multiple locations or franchising. Strong marketing and human resources skills are usually needed for this entrepreneurial approach.

Marlene Carlson had little industry experience when she invented Puzzle Toes, shoes that feature a picture of a dinosaur—the right shoe having the front half of the dinosaur and the left shoe having the back half. Between 1994 and 2000 she invested significant time and money with dreams of getting her product into Wal-Mart. When the large retail chains resisted, Carlson first filed a patent on the design and image of the shoes, then hired an industry professional to help her gain access to the appropriate trade shows and distribution channels. Progress was slow, but by keeping her options open she negotiated a licensing agreement with Quest Products. Puzzle Toes are now sold at Wal-Mart stores nationwide.[32]

Maintenance Strategy

The vast majority of businesses in the United States follow maintenance strategies. Many of these are income-replacement ventures with a single location. These are frequently personal or business services that have little potential for growth. The entrepreneur prioritizes business time relative to nonwork time, and is less willing to commit to 80-hour weeks and no vacations. These businesses can be home based or part time. The entrepreneur might wish to control the business by maintaining strong personal involvement in all aspects of decision making, customer, supplier, and employee relationships. There are many reasons why this might be appropriate: It could be competition, or it might be that you just don't want to take the risk. Others just make a substantial income from a known effort and pursuit. If you have low aspirations and don't plan to grow beyond a small size, chances are you are following a maintenance strategy. Jennifer Lane's business described earlier is a good example of an income-replacement venture. Others include a local flower shop, an attorney's office, or a gift shop.

Of course businesses can change strategies. For instance, a biotech company might start out with a variable strategy, but once clinical testing is completed and funding acquired, it might move toward an ambitious strategy. On the other hand, starting a cookie business like Mrs. Field's could be considered competitive and easily copied, but that company followed an ambitious growth strategy by franchising the concept. Once you have identified your strategy, how do you clear the challenge of differing expectations?

Overcoming High Hurdles

> *Don't become an entrepreneur because you want power and control. Do it because you believe in what you want. And, look at the broader picture; don't get hung up on the details—let certain things go.*

So you have determined your strategy and want to grow your business, but you have come up against expectations that you can't or shouldn't grow your venture. What should you do? The following are some suggestions.

1. Determine what your personal definition of success is: Fast growth? Personal wealth? Large sales? Great profits? What exactly is your plan for the future of the business? Reflect on your personal goals as well as the business needs. The strategic approach for the business will be directly related to the goals — some strategies will not permit fast growth, whereas other strategies demand it. Recognize the trade-offs. For instance, if you have a high need for control—want to manage, be involved, be personally connected to staff and employees, and personally make decisions rather than delegate—chances are your business goals will not be consistent with fast-growth, large, equity-funded ventures.

2. Understand that not all industries are appropriate for equity financing. What are the patterns of financing for your industry sector? Chances are this depends on the asset base (capital intensiveness), growth rates, and innovativeness of the businesses in

this area. If companies have received investment capital, what is their profile? If companies are more often financed by debt or earnings, be knowledgeable about why this is the case.

3. Develop a strong market focus, know your industry, and establish contacts with the players. There is no substitute for market understanding, industry knowledge, and contacts. Investors, and bankers for that matter, want to know how you plan to grow your venture. You need to know the facts of your industry from growth rates, to market share of competitors, to their strategies, as well as have personal relationships. You can't grow the business without being able to "name your customers" and explain why they will buy your product or service. This generally comes from work experience in the industry (or related industries, such as those of suppliers or customers), but in some cases, key information can be gained from studying trends or having advisors or management team members to assist.

4. Be able to articulate why your venture is appropriate for growth capital. Does it have sizable potential? Can it provide expected returns to investors? You must think "big" enough— ask for enough money, and be able to explain how these funds will be used, and why they are appropriate for a venture with this potential size and scope.

5. Be aware of the expectations and tendency for people to generalize about women-led ventures. You might be the first woman to lead a venture in your sector. If this is the case, understand that you might need to overcome perceptions about size and growth. How can you do this? Remember that the presence of the stereotype is a subconscious reaction to prejudge someone or something. To counter this, present your proposal with facts and help the potential funder see you as a competent businessperson.

Summary

We explored strategies and growth orientation of women-owned businesses in this chapter. Existing perceptions suggest that women prefer to run small, hobby-type service ventures that don't grow. In the past, most women-led ventures fit this description, but today women start and grow ventures in all industry sectors and there is a significant population who wish to grow their businesses. Yet, there is some truth to these perceptions because on average, the majority of women-led ventures are smaller in revenues and employees. However, believing that all women run small, slow-growth service ventures is overgeneralizing across a diverse and very large population of entrepreneurs. Like their male counterparts, women entrepreneurs cannot be lumped into single categories. Their business purposes, strategies, and growth goals vary widely. Aspirations and personal capabilities influence size and growth of women- and men-led ventures. Painting all women with a single brush stroke is a mistake. Unfortunately, because swift-growing women-led ventures are a comparatively new phenomenon, and data categorizations are limiting, misperceptions do persist. Aspiring women entrepreneurs need to be knowledgeable about these beliefs and be prepared to counter these with solid industry information when they meet with potential investors. In addition, matching your business strategy and growth goals to those of investors is the next step. What is the nature of the venture capital industry? Who makes decisions about providing money to new ventures? These questions are explored in the next chapter.

Notes

1. National Venture Capital Association Web site: *www.nvca.org*.
2. *Women in Business, 2001*. Washington, DC: U.S. Government Printing Office, Office of Advocacy.
3. See Figure 2.1.
4. Osborne, D. M. 2000, September 1. *A Network of Her Own. www.inc.com/articles/ start_biz/20125-print.html*.

5. Center for Women's Business Research. 2001. *Removing the Boundaries.*

6. Ibid.

7. Bird, B. J. 1989. *Entrepreneurial Behavior.* Glenview, IL: Scott Foresman.

8. Kolveried, L., Shane, S., & Westhead, P. 1993. Is it equally difficult for female entrepreneurs to start businesses in all countries? *Journal of Small Business Management* 31:4, 42–51; Cliff, J. E. 1998. Does one size fit all? Exploring the relationship between attitudes towards growth, gender, and business size. *Journal of Business Venturing, 13*(6) 523–542; Davidsson, P. 1989. *Continued Entrepreneurship and Small Firm Growth.* Stockholm: Stockholm School of Economics; NFWBO. 1994. *A Compendium of National Statistics on Women-Owned Businesses in the U.S.* Silver Spring, MD: NFWBO.

9. Loscosco, K. A., Robinson, J., Hall, R. H., & Allen, J. K. 1991. Gender and small business success: An inquiry into women's relative disadvantage. *Social Forces,* 70:1, 65–85; Chaganti, R., & Parasuraman, S. 1996. A study of the impact of gender on business performance and management patterns in small businesses. *Entrepreneurship Theory and Practice.* 21:2, 73–75.

10. Ehlers, T. B., & Main, K. 1998. Women and false promise of micro-enterprise. *Gender and Society.* 12:4, 424–440.

11. Goffee, R., & Scase, R. 1985. *Women in Charge.* London: Allen & Unwin; Kaplan, E. 1988. Women entrepreneurs: Constructing a framework to examine venture success and business failures. In B. A. Kirchoff, W. A. Long, W. E. McMullen, K. H. Vesper, & W. E. Wetzel, Jr. (Eds.). *Frontiers of Entrepreneurship Research.* Wellesley, MA: Babson College. 625–637; Lee-Gosselin, H., & Grise, J. 1990. Are women owner-managers challenging our definitions of entrepreneurship? An in-depth survey. *Journal of Business Ethics, 9*(4/5), 432–433; Belcourt, M. 1990. A family portrait of Canada's most successful female entrepreneurs. *Journal of Business Ethics, 9*(4/5), 435–438; Chaganti, R. 1986. Management in women-owned enterprises. *Journal of Small Business Management,* 24:4, 18–29.

12. Center for Women's Business Research. 2001. *The New Generation of Women Business Owners: An Executive Report.*

13. Gilligan, C. 1982. *In a Different Voice.* Cambridge, MA: Harvard University Press.

14. Smith, D. 2000. *Women at Work: Leadership for the Next Century,* Upper Saddle River, NJ: Prentice Hall.

15. Morrison, A. M., White, R. P., & Van Velsor, E., and the Center for Creative Leadership. 1992. *Breaking the Glass Ceiling.* Reading, MA: Addison-Wesley.

16. Ducheneaut, B. 1997. Women entrepreneurs in SME's. *OECD Conference on Women Entrepreneurs in Small and Medium Enterprises: A Major Force for Innovation and Job Creation.* Paris.

17. Fact Sheet. 1998. Catalyst Census of Women Board of Directors of the Fortune 500.

18. The world's largest financial service provider for U.S. educators.

19. *Good for Business: Making Full Use of the Nation's Human Capital: The Environmental Scan.* 1995. Report commissioned by Secretary of Labor Robert B. Reich.

20. Evans, M. 2001. Springboard Female Entrepreneurs to Riches, *Financial Post.*

21. Rosa, P., Carter, S., & Hamilton, D. 1996. Gender as a determinant of small business performance: Insights from a British study. *Small Business Economics.* 8:4, 463–478.

22. The National Foundation for Women Business Owners. 2001. *Entrepreneurial Vision in Action: Exploring Growth Among Women and Men-Owned Firms.*

23. Center for Women's Business Research. 2001. *The New Generation of Women Business Owners: An Executive Report.*

24. *www.springboard2000.org/p/l1.asp?PID=2&SID=2,* Springboard Enterprises Home Page, About Us.

25. Rebecca Reynolds Moore, class visit to Boston University, Spring 2002.

26. Adapted from published story and interview by Graves, H. 2003, June. Certifying financial security is Jennifer Lane's mission. *Women's Business Boston,* pp. 7, 13.

27. Ibid.

28. Ibid.

29. The National Foundation for Women Business Owners uses two dimensions to characterize high-growth firms: past growth performance and future growth strategy. High-growth performance was defined as 30% or more growth in revenues or employment over the last three years. Future growth strategy was defined as planning to expand at a solid rate or to growing into a large enterprise that might go public or be sold.

30. Churchill, N. C., & Lewis, V. 1983. Five stages of business growth. *Harvard Business Review.* May–June, 30–50; Gundry, L. K., & Welsch, H. 2001. The ambitious entrepreneur: High growth strategies of women-owned enterprises. *Journal of Business Venturing,* 16:5, 453–470.

31. Hamm, S. 1997, August 14. Kim Polese–CEO, The next generation. *Business Week. www.businessweek.com/1997/34/b354164.htm.*

32. Deblak, D. 2003, November. The big picture. *Entrepreneur Magazine.* 144–145.

8

BUILDING USEFUL NETWORKS AND CASHING IN ON SOCIAL CAPITAL

Your social networks are affiliations—either formal or infor-mal—with people who share a common set of interests and who interact with you and each other on a repeated basis. Your managerial network is that set of relationships critical to your ability to get things done professionally.[1]

Your social capital is the collective value of all your "social networks" (who you know) and the inclinations that arise from these networks to do things for one another ("norms of reciprocity").[2]

Many people argue that women are simply not plugged into the most effective business networks. If this is true, and they don't have any meaningful connections with the people who count in the financial world, women will have difficulty getting their business plans reviewed or their financing cases heard. If they are able to get access through an intermediary, but haven't accumulated any relevant social capital, female entrepreneurs will find striking a good deal almost impossible. Of course, many women are well-connected and are able to capitalize on their social capital. For example:

> **When Robin Chase wanted to find investors for the new Zipcar venture, she first contacted her friend and mentor at MIT's Sloan School of Management. She knew that he valued her skills and recognized her achievements. Because of their long-standing relationship, he was willing to read the plan, make comments and suggestions, and introduce Robin to several business people who might provide additional help, serve as board members, or consider investing.**

Chase was well connected to the MIT network and had accumulated substantial social capital during her years as a student and, later, through her professional career. She kept in close touch with some of her faculty advisors and was able to use both her network and her social capital within that network to gain access to important partners and advisors. Linda Mason and Roger Brown, founders of Bright Horizons, also cashed in on their social capital and business networks when they launched their new venture in 1986.

> **Linda Mason and Roger Brown had a revolutionary idea for a chain of high-quality day care centers located in the workplace. They asked employers and real estate developers to provide space and necessary equipment, so that they could minimize their capital investments. Nonetheless, they estimated that they would need several million dollars to launch their concept and to demonstrate its value.**

They were well-armed with education, experience, and a very strong network of potential investors before they ever sat down to write a plan. The two had met while students at the Yale School of Organization and Management. Both had extensive work experience with children, managing refugee programs in Thailand. When they returned from Thailand, they co-authored, *Rice, Rivalry, and Politics,* a book based on their relief work. Later, they accepted the challenge of running the Save the Children Federation in the Sudan, a $14 million project staffed with 600 professionals.

Both had served as management consultants, Brown with Bain and Mason with Booz, Allen, and Hamilton. Their credibility in their chosen field and their demonstrated business capabilities stood them in good stead. In 1986, the two raised $2 million in venture funding from Bain Capital and Bessemer Ventures. They also secured their first commitment for a day care center from the developer of One Kendall Square in Cambridge, Massachusetts. Their direct links to the investment community and their experience and expertise enabled them to get access to the right decision makers and to clinch the deals.

How well equipped are you to capitalize on your networks and to trade on the social capital you have created? You will need both to find highly skilled managers to fill out your founding team. If you find them, you need connections and credibility to entice them to leave their secure, well-paid positions to join you in your new venture. Can you get access to the people who have the talent and resources you need to make your dream a reality?

Consider this scenario: You have created a spectacular new business concept and developed a detailed plan for making it happen. You have successfully cleared the start-up hurdles and the business performance, to date, has demonstrated that you have the leadership skills, the technical knowledge, and the financial savvy to run a rapidly growing venture. The industry you have chosen has great growth potential and your venture seems well positioned within the industry. With these challenges behind you, you might think that getting additional resources necessary to start and grow the business would come easily. However, there are still more hurdles to overcome.

Getting the human and financial resources you need is really dependent on the networks in which you operate (who you know) and, even more important, who knows and values you as a great businessperson (the social capital you have developed within that network). Successful entrepreneurs—both men and women—not only know a lot about the businesses they are starting, they are also well-known and highly regarded by the business and financial communities that can assist them. They have built up relationships over time that are invaluable in the course of starting and running a new venture.

Are Women Unplugged from the Right Networks?

The effective use of social and professional networks is, without a doubt, one of the most important parts of doing business. Research shows that successful managers spend 70% more time engaging in network activities than do their less successful counterparts.[3] For entrepreneurs, the benefits of having effective networks include more timely and efficient access to information, advice, and resources. Networks also include direct links to other human, financial, and material resource providers.

Of course not all networks are alike. Most people engage in at least three different types that serve very different purposes. For example, there are task networks that are very specific to the exchange of work-related resources—information, expertise, advice, and even material resources. There are also career relationships that you build to provide direction, guidance, and sponsorship in your own career development. Perhaps the most important in your life—although not necessarily in your entrepreneurial efforts—are the social networks that provide closeness and build high levels of trust.[4] Of course, these networks are not mutually exclusive. Many individuals whose primary contact is through your workplace might also be members of your social network, for example.

The business and social connections among lawyers, accountants, technical service providers, investors, and others provide a communications infrastructure that enables members to share information and resources. Connections among the members of a network are often very tight, particularly among those whose repeated interactions support high-potential businesses. Entrepreneurs who try to gain access to this network often find they need to be introduced or "sponsored" by the initiated, either by successful entrepreneurs who have already gained admission or by their investment bankers, attorneys, or venture capitalists.[5] Women generally have fewer entry points, so they find breaking into these networks especially daunting. As a result of being "outsiders," they have more difficulty making contacts that can result in securing financial resources or technical expertise.

Many entrepreneurs decide that networking is an important part of building assets and they deliberately become more active in business and professional groups. However, it is important to note that real networking is not just meeting someone at a cocktail party or a professional trade show and exchanging business cards. It is the management of all the activities associated with developing and maintaining ongoing relationships.[6] It includes repeated interactions and mutual exchange of valuable information and resources.

Why can't qualified women entrepreneurs get access to the critical resources they need? Two closely related explanations shed some light on the problem:

- Women are not "dues-paying" members of key business networks.

  – Their work experience does not provide them frequent interaction with those who control vital resources and with important deal brokers.

  – Social and cultural norms often preclude women from participating in networks that mediate access to money and financing.

- Women lack the appropriate social capital to make meaningful exchanges within business networks.

Let's look more closely at how business and financial networks operate, what benefits they offer, who is included, and how transactions are actually made.

Formal Networks

Networks consist of both formal and informal relationships in which individuals have repeated, noneconomic interchanges. Formal networks (sometimes called *prescribed networks*) involve individuals engaging in organizationally defined tasks.[7] These networks exist in the workplace, in professional organizations, and in voluntary associations. For example, the senior management team and the board of directors constitute a formal network that oversees the business and provides governance. At an entirely different level of the organization, a new product development team might also represent a formal network of people drawn from many different areas of the company on a temporary basis. A professional organization (e.g., the state bar association) can function as a very large network at one level, but can also include several more tightly connected network subsets within its committee structure and special interest groups.

Many voluntary associations have formalized their networks by developing very explicit rules of conduct. For example, the chamber of commerce offers a roundtable program for its members where local entrepreneurs meet on a regular basis to discuss challenges facing their businesses. The roundtables often are self-facilitated and the members determine the agenda. Rules governing attendance and participation, including the membership dues, are set by the chamber. The extent to which these roundtable groups are successful depends, in part, on their cooperation in following and enforcing the chamber's rules and procedures for the roundtables. Members have assigned roles. They might serve as liaison to the chamber officers, be the recorder of the meeting minutes, or take on the role of the monthly leader. Each of the members shares responsibility for accomplishing the common group goal—learning and advising one another about business matters—but within the structure laid out by the chamber program.

Informal Networks

Many networks are informal (sometimes called *emergent*).[8] Like their more formal counterparts, these networks can be work-related, social, or affinity-based. They develop out of people's self-interests. For example, women leading high-growth companies might meet with other women business owners for a monthly breakfast to discuss current challenges facing their businesses. Even though there might be a chamber of commerce roundtable program in the community, these women prefer the friendship and social support they get from their informal gathering. In the chamber of commerce program, participants are assigned to the various roundtable groups based on a set of established criteria (e.g., size of company, industry sector, firm age). In informal networks, individuals have leeway to choose who will participate in the network. Within both formal and informal networks, there is a sense of mutual interest and some commitment to exchange and support, even if limited to trading business cards and making introductions. Because of the expectation of fair exchange (of information, support, referrals, and resources) within the network, membership is generally limited to people at approximately the same level of power and influence, although this operating ground rule is not necessarily explicitly stated.

Benefits of Networks

Networks offer numerous benefits. If they continue to function over a long period of time, they usually engender a strong sense of belonging and become an important forum for exchange of many different kinds of "favors." Individual members use them to facilitate exchange of very tangible resources (materials or physical resources), but they also benefit from the sharing of more expressive resources (friendship) with their network contacts.[9] Networks often provide social support, access to information, referrals for employees and consultants, and introductions to resource providers—including angels and venture capitalists who can be investors. Most women entrepreneurs recognize the benefits of an effective business network, but often they are unable either to identify or to gain membership in those social and business circles that would be most useful to their business development.

For one thing, many of the activities that build and reinforce network ties seem to exclude women either by design or default (e.g., golf, business trips, sporting events). If women do gain access, they often find that they are in a very small minority. Most formal and informal financial associations and business interest groups are predominantly male, so even if a woman is officially a member, she might still be treated as an outsider.

Many people argue that women are not being excluded from business networks, but that they demonstrate an overwhelming preference for a very different kind of network relationship. They assume that women are more likely to become part of expressive networks, those in which emotional intensity, mutual confiding, and intimacy characterize the relationships. These networks are usually small and homogeneous with relationships of long duration built on frequent contact. Although they encourage a high degree of trust and emotional closeness,[10] they are unlikely to include a strong business component. Whether it is by choice or circumstance, many women find it difficult to build effective business network links to the people most likely to offer sound business advice and introductions to venture capital contacts.

Network Boundaries and Barriers

Some of the challenges that women confront in getting access to useful business networks are culturally based norms. There are rules (often unspoken, but generally acknowledged) that govern society and define appropriate roles for individuals. These norms include expectations about how men and women should behave, how they should interact with each other, and who has authority and value. Social attitudes and beliefs help people make sense of these norms.[11] An individual's self-concept (how she sees herself and how she sees others) is an important aspect of the cultural sense making. Self-concept is made up of two components: personal identity and social identity.[12]

Personal identity refers to how women see themselves in terms of their traits or characteristics. For example, if you earned an MBA, worked on Wall Street, or had broad management responsibilities before considering a start-up, you are likely to see yourself as intelligent, capable, and experienced. These perceptions influence your attitudes and behaviors, how you present yourself to others, and your willingness to join networks. If, however, you perceive yourself as somehow less "qualified" than other members of a network, you are likely to shy away from joining the group. As one professional counselor noted, "Successful networking has three main ingredients: know-how, savvy, and guts."[13] How you see yourself will determine how likely you are to have the "guts" to join unfamiliar networks that could benefit your business.

Social identity is the second aspect of an individual's self-concept. Social identity is derived from the attributes of groups to which one belongs. You are born into some groups (sex, race, ethnic group, and age cohort), but you are able to choose many of your associations (college or university, clubs, sports teams, professional organizations). Each group has distinct characteristics that are developed and reinforced by its members. Individuals' distinctions between "I am a member" and "I am not a member" lead them to behave in ways that reinforce the group's norms, even when the group is very large and diverse. For example, individuals in the Generation X age group are expected to behave very differently from those in the Baby Boomer generation who are nearing retirement. They like different clothes and music and apparently hold different work and life values. Their world is totally "connected" through cell phones, instant messaging, and e-mail. Members of a group provide cues about what behavior is appropriate within the network and provide sanctions for deviants. These behaviors are also reinforced by society at large.

All of us participate in many different groups, some by choice and others by circumstance. Each affiliation we have can affect a wide range of life choices. From birth, gender identification prescribes attitudes and behaviors for both men and women. For example, gender lines often influence social and work group decisions. Women are more likely to choose occupations in health care, education, and social work, whereas men are more likely to opt for business, finance, engineering, and science. This means that women belong to different professional networks and develop very different social identities.

Social identity often defines which groups wield power. Dominant groups use their power to impose values and ideologies that legitimate and maintain the status quo.[14] In a capitalist culture in which business is a highly valued activity, professionals in finance, accounting, technology, and manufacturing become very important. Those who are dominant in these professions develop behavioral rewards and sanctions that reinforce their network boundaries and behavioral norms.

Whether consciously or unconsciously, they develop codes and behaviors that can lock others out of these networks. If women are among the "outgroup," they will have a difficult time accessing the information, knowledge, and resources that are shared readily within the "ingroup." This is particularly true of informal networks, where admission standards for membership are not clearly articulated.

Group behaviors are facilitated by symbols and artifacts in the culture and reinforced by the media (magazines, television programs, books, newspapers, videos, etc.). Consider recent television commercials that depict people interacting in a business setting. Is the group predominantly male? What is the breakdown of men versus women in the chamber of commerce, young entrepreneurs organization, or other business association meeting? What behavior is expected of women as a group rather than as individuals? How are messages about these expectations communicated?

The Case for Homogeneous Networks

Cultural and social norms provide sorting tools for determining who belongs to the ingroups and who is relegated to the outgroups. These might include age, sex, and race, but group membership is determined by many other factors, as well. Most affiliations develop simply because people are attracted to others like themselves. They like associating with others who share common feelings and experiences. This attraction can be seen in numerous settings including work groups,[15] interpersonal friendships, and voluntary associations.[16] In other words, birds of a feather deliberately flock together.

By sharing common attributes or interests, groups do the following:

• Invoke feelings of solidarity

• Build trust, empathy, and understanding

• Share business and personal resources

- Exclude those who don't belong to the group—those in the out-group

Individuals attribute common feelings and experiences to other members of their group even before they know them personally, basing their assessments on the stereotype of what membership represents.

To preserve cohesiveness in a group and to define the group standards more clearly, members ostracize minority members. Fearing that others might attribute to them the same negative characteristics that they attribute to this ostracized individual, those in the majority maintain cohesiveness by closing ranks. Is it any wonder that women feel unwelcome in groups dominated by men? By the same token, men are likely to feel uncomfortable in groups dominated by women. However, because the groups that are organized around business, finance, and banking (the groups that exert the most power and influence in our culture) are dominated by men, these patterns of reciprocal exclusion do not have equal ramifications in the business world.

The development of homogeneous networks based on interpersonal attraction is not necessarily bad. Networks made up of people who are alike and who have similar values and interests quickly develop their own shorthand vocabularies, which facilitate quick and clear communication and clarify interpretations. Members of a network can share resources effectively. However, when the network is made up of people with similar backgrounds, little new information and insight will be gained by talking to more than one person in the network because they all share similar experiences and viewpoints. For this reason, there is always a tension between the comfort and solidarity of a well-established network and the need for expansion and greater inclusion.

The Case for Heterogeneity

When a network is made up of individuals with diverse work and social backgrounds, each member is likely to bring a different perspective and provide the entrepreneur with new and nonredundant information. Multiple points of view can offer more than one solution to a problem.[17] Entrepreneurs need information and resources from a variety of sources,[18] so having diverse contacts increases their chances of developing good leads on potential markets, business locations, sources of capital, promising business partners, or key management personnel. Individuals with social networks that include people from a variety of backgrounds enjoy a richness in the information exchanged, attitudes formed, and personal interactions.[19]

Cultural norms explain why networks are homogeneous and why, at the broadest level, men prefer to be with men, and women with women. They provide some understanding of why this segmentation occurs and, by extension, they show why men dominate networks that have the highest financial and human resources capabilities. Of course, there are some women entrepreneurs in these networks. Some women have successfully broken the cultural norms and gained access to individuals in those networks that exercise control and access to the critical human, technical, and financial resources that entrepreneurs need.

Social Capital—The Currency of Network Exchange

Once you have gained access to the right networks, you will need to build your own social capital account. Just what is social capital?[20] Unlike human capital (endowed qualities of appearance and intelligence; acquired skills of knowledge and experience), which resides in the individual, social capital is the medium of exchange that has value in use. It represents a "bank account" of goodwill on which you can make deposits and withdrawals. Over time, you accumulate your own social capital through repeated exchanges with other members of the network in the context of ongoing formal or informal relationships. Mutual obligations are created through these exchanges: "I'll do this for you now, with the understanding that if I need something from you in the future, you'll do that for me" is implied, although rarely stated explicitly. The expectation of even exchange is not specific to a particular point in time. The favor doesn't have to be reciprocated immediately, but can be "banked" with the expectation that it will be returned at a future time. Furthermore, when working within a network, the return of the favor isn't always specific to the person who has granted the favor, but can be generalized. Rather than repaying the favor directly, the kindness can be granted to someone else at a future date. Thus, social capital has both a specific and a generalized aspect.

Entrepreneurs need large reserves of social capital because, at the time of start-up, they are frequently withdrawing more than they are depositing. The moral and social support that family, friends, mentors, and acquaintances offer to an entrepreneur are social capital investments they are making in the entrepreneur. So, too, is the free business advice from work associates or free labor provided by family and friends before the business is able to make payroll. Community support groups, church affiliations, or volunteer organizations can be sources of a wide variety of social capital investments in an entrepreneur's fledgling business—including important business introductions, sale or lease of physical resources at below-market prices, development of potential client bases, and even early customer relationships.

Although each of these examples seems to be one-way—a granting of favors to the entrepreneur—they are more likely to be examples of exchange in which social capital is being repaid. The entrepreneur is calling on her reserves of goodwill built up by services and favors she has already performed or for support and encouragement she has previously provided. Like everyone else, entrepreneurs accumulate social capital over time as they build one-on-one relationships with others. They do so by providing favors and social benefits. Although there is no explicit contract or bargain about what will be given in exchange, there is an expectation that the relationship is mutual and that either party will be able to withdraw some of the accumulated social capital in the future. Friendships facilitate the creation and exchange of social capital that can be used again and again as favors are exchanged and a sense of indebtedness is established.

Reputation and Trust

Your reputation comprises the world's view of your business activities, your record of achievements, and your personal conduct over time. Your reputation is really the estimation that other people make of you and your potential, based on what they know of you from the past. Trust embodies their beliefs about your integrity and also represents the leap of faith that your past behavior is an accurate indicator of your future. Both reputation and trust are important components of social capital that are developed within a given context.

Many aspects of social capital are specific to a particular network and they constantly reinforce the network's cohesiveness. Frequently repeated one-to-one transactions between individuals in a network build up trust, empathy, and familiarity as they accumulate reserves of social capital. But what if you have banked your social capital in one network, only to find that the critical resources are in another? How can you bridge the gap?

Like financial capital, social capital can be borrowed from others who have a surplus. You can rely on other people's reputations to open doors and to vouch for your credibility. When entrepreneurs cultivate contacts and build relationships with influential people, they often tap into their extended network of information, knowledge, or referrals to other key influencers. Building a varied management team provides another way to leverage social capital and reach into multiple networks. You can accumulate personal social capital to be used within your own networks, but you can also position your firm to gain access to resources in other networks through association with others who are insiders. Sometimes, you can gain access through institutions as well as through individuals. For example, if you attended a well-known university or were employed by a prestigious firm, you might gain credibility and access to networks that would otherwise not be open to you.

Spending Social Capital within a Network

Entrepreneurs with growth companies can cash in social capital to get an appointment with potential investors. These decision makers can provide much more than financial resources. They also have information about suppliers, customers, and distributors, and leads on where to recruit key management personnel or potential partners. Rarely do investors give an unsolicited business plan the same attention and consideration as one that comes to them through a trusted referral. The endorsement that such a gatekeeper gives an entrepreneur makes a big difference in whether or not a plan is read or seriously considered. When trying to get that first appointment, the entrepreneur often has to rely on the reputation of her "sponsor," which might carry far more weight than the technical merits of the plan. Because getting the attention of the right people is so important, entrepreneurs do well to find influential people who can assist in getting their plan into the investors' hands. In this case, the old adage, "You are known by the company you keep" can have a very big payoff.

It's not that women don't have social capital. The reality is that women are very good at building deep, trustful relationships within their tight networks of family and friends. However, this social capital might not have much value in the networks that include key business resource providers. Although a woman might have a rich social capital account, it's often coined in the wrong realm for business.

Some Networks Are Like Foreign Countries

It should be pretty clear by now that social capital is a type of currency that can be earned and spent within a specified universe. Just as you can develop your human capital through education and professional experience, you can also consciously create and trade social capital. Consider the entrepreneur who sees tremendous growth opportunities for her company in global markets. She has spent the past two years developing network contacts she thought would be useful. She's been active in her local school's parent–teacher association (PTA), joined a Toastmasters group, and regularly attended a speaker program for local business owners at the community college. Through these associations, she joined a consolidated buying group for her company, hired several new employees, and lent some of her production capacity to an entrepreneur who had an order he couldn't fill with his current plant capacity. In other words, she banked substantial social capital through her interactions.

None of this capital, however, seemed to be of particular value in expanding her company into international markets. The social capital she had accumulated didn't provide a medium of exchange with those who controlled the foreign sources of supply she needed or the international channels of distribution. She had plenty of capital, but it was in the wrong currency. Key contacts in the international market didn't care that she could introduce them to others in her local PTA or that she had excess capacity they could use. Imagine having only Euros in your wallet when you enter the United States with no currency exchanges open.

The human capital she needed could be earned by attending seminars at the local international trade office, by enrolling in the community college's international management lecture series, or by joining a trade mission sponsored by the U.S. Small Business Association. The social capital could be developed through the relationships she built in each of these environments.

In a similar vein, venture capitalists and other resource partners for high-growth ventures operate in a networked world of fast-paced, technically based, heavily resourced transactions. Women business owners often work, socialize, and develop relationships within entirely different networks. Members of each network function well in their own domains where they can freely exchange their social currency and there is no question about its value. However, when women try to enter "a foreign country," they find that the currency they built up is not recognized or valued. Consequently, they need to find willing intermediaries who will lend their credibility and legitimacy through association and referral. To date, women have not been very good at identifying or engaging these currency exchange brokers.

The social networks of men and women are surprisingly similar on many dimensions. Early research indicated that men have larger networks than women,[21] but more recent findings show them as having networks similar in size.[22] Both groups spend a similar amount of time building and maintaining social contacts.[23]

Women Have Diverse Networks

Women entrepreneurs' networks are not nearly as homogeneous as are men's, nor are they made up exclusively of other female entrepreneurs. However, social norms influence women to have other women in their network and because of gender-based work segregation, these contacts would be less useful contacts for advancing an entrepreneurial endeavor.

Research indicates that men's networks are comprised primarily of men. However, women report that their networks include men as well as women.[24] On the surface, this would seem to be good news because, when networks contain people from a variety of ages, sexes, races, and work backgrounds, especially those beyond the immediate work group, they tend to be both powerful and useful.[25] However, if women believe that men are part of their network, but men do not recognize women as members of theirs, there is a basic disconnect and the network connections that women believe exist are weak at best. At least in theory, the diversity found in women's networks should increase access to nonredundant information and a variety of perspectives. However, women report more relatives or kin in their networks,[26] whereas men are more likely to name coworkers.[27]

Men view their networks in terms of what can be gained from membership. They emphasize the exchange of favors and obligations. Women emphasize responsibilities and obligations more than men.[28] Women are more likely to name their spouse as their key network contact[29] and are more concerned with relationships and friendships based on trust.[30] This might explain why they are more apt to turn to family and friends or close business associates than to work associates for advice and support. Women's reliance on relatives reduces the advantage that having a more diverse network might otherwise offer. Relying principally on those with whom you already have close relationships effectively limits access to new perspectives and leads to a very circumscribed resource base. As a result, even though women's networks are nominally more diverse, the choice of members makes it unlikely that information and resource flow will be widely varied. Their networks are actually homogeneous on the family dimension so the related disadvantages persist.

Women Benefit from Strategic Sponsors

Social capital can be borrowed. Women who don't have large reserves of the right social capital can benefit from borrowing social capital from others.[31] In a study of managerial promotion in the high-technology industry, women with the most rapid promotion rate were those who established close relationships with others in their work group and relied on a strategic sponsor other than their immediate supervisor to introduce them to influential contacts. Men, on the other hand, were more successful if they relied on their boss for contacts, as well as establishing relationships with others outside their work group, individuals who were unconnected to each other. Successful men established a broad, flat network of many unrelated contacts ensuring a wide variety of nonredundant information and perspectives. Why wasn't this strategy equally successful for women?

The need for women to establish a strategic sponsor to achieve promotion reflects the lack of legitimacy women have in organizations. Women often don't fit the network profile, so they don't have the opportunity to build relevant social capital. Because women are often viewed as tokens in managerial ranks, top decision makers look to others in the organization to vouch for their credibility before promoting women to broader leadership responsibilities. Whom can they ask? Women's immediate supervisors are expected to speak highly of them because subordinates' actions reflect on their managerial competence. Consequently, their opinions will carry less weight. A strategic sponsor is needed, someone who is positioned at the top of the organization and is well placed to reinforce the immediate supervisor's opinion and vouch for the female protégé, lending her their reputation and giving her the credibility she needs.

For entrepreneurs, mentors can be strategic sponsors. Mentors provide instrumental value (career advice) as well as friendship and moral support. They can extend the entrepreneur's reach into other influential networks by providing introductions and access, effectively lending legitimacy. In other words, women entrepreneurs can use mentors as strategic sponsors who will provide social capital and advance their interests. Our research shows that women entrepreneurs who succeeded in getting the equity investments they were seeking named their mentors as influential in their social networks. More than 60% reported relying on a mentor who was a fellow business owner and 45% said they relied on other mentors.

Creating Effective Networks

Social capital is developed and valued in the context of a specific network. The network provides a conduit for the exchange of information and resources that enhances the success and survival of the business. Networks allow entrepreneurs to gain access to opportunities and resources, save time, and tap into advice and support that might otherwise be unavailable. They influence the social, emotional, and material well-being of their members. As entrepreneurs use their existing social networks, they acquire new information and resources and they begin to create new networks.

One strategy we recommend to women entrepreneurs is to cultivate a wide range of contacts in multiple social networks. This strategy has proven successful for men. Entrepreneurs with wide-ranging and diverse networks are more likely to have contacts that connect them to equity capital markets. Women business owners need to extend their reach beyond their personal networks—parents, siblings, spouse or partner, in-laws, friends, and neighbors—to gain the social capital they need to access resources. Establish relationships with those outside your immediate circle, those that require less emotional investment. Such individuals can act as bridges connecting you to nonoverlapping sources of information or resources. Executing this strategy requires breaking into the "old boy" networks so it can be awkward and uncomfortable. The subtle messages that pervade the business culture sometimes lead to the conclusion that women need not apply, that you are not expected to take part in the influential social and business discussions. Yet, these contacts can link you to information, knowledge, referrals, training, and money, so they are worth the discomfort and effort.

However, just meeting with individuals outside your close circle of supporters isn't sufficient. To make the critical connections in the investment community, you need to rely on alternative networking strategies. Some network relationships involve the exchange of multiple resources, providing instrumental value, like career advice, as well as friendship. Think about your mentors. The strong relationship that develops between a mentor and a protégé increases the likelihood that the protégé will be connected to and benefit from the mentor's own network.[32] For women entrepreneurs, having such strong mentoring relationships and the links that follow can substantially increase the reach of their networks.[33]

Attorneys, accountants, bankers, and technical consultants can also provide bridges into the investment community. Unlike mentors, however, these advisors might be less willing or able to signal that the woman entrepreneur is a legitimate player, and her business a worthy investment. They might have little motivation to lend their reputation to advance the interests of a client or acquaintance they don't know well. Mentors impart legitimacy, provide moral support and friendship, and chauffeur women to capital markets. Mentors who have entrepreneurial experience are particularly beneficial to entrepreneurs. Research shows that advice from other entrepreneurs paid the highest dividends for business owners.[34]

Language and symbols can also create social capital. A polished business plan, or a leadership position in associations, or a reputation for trustworthy behavior can enhance the legitimacy investors are looking for. Commitment and conduct can enhance one's reputation. Creating an advisory board can extend your social capital and enable you to "borrow" from the accounts of the well-connected board members. Finally, cultivate business groups within your community. Numerous business owner support groups meet regularly and offer entrepreneurs an opportunity to air their problems, discuss solutions, and share similar challenges. Many entrepreneurs find such groups not only a source for solace and validation, but also indispensable for referrals and advice.

Notes

1. Ibarra, H. 1995. *Managerial Networks*. Boston: Harvard Business School Note 9-495-039, Harvard Business School Publishing.

2. Putnam, R. D. 2000. *Bowling Alone*. New York: Simon & Shuster.

3. Luthans, F., Hodgetts, R. M., & Rosenkrantz, S. A. 1988. *Real Managers*. Cambridge, MA: Ballinger.

4. Ibarra, H. 1995. op. cit.

5. Alimansky, B. 2000. Eight ways to ruin your chances of raising equity capital. *Journal of Private Equity*. Summer: 78–83.

6. Ibarra, H. 1995. op. cit.

7. Ibarra, H. 1993. Personal networks of women and minorities in management: A conceptual framework. *Academy of Management Review*. 18(1): 50–87.

8. Ibid.

9. Ibarra, H. 1993. Network centrality, power, and innovation involvement: Determinants of technical and administrative roles. *Academy of Management Journal*. 36(3): 471–504.

10. Granovetter, M. 1973. The strength of weak ties. *American Journal of Sociology*. 78: 1360–1380.

11. Mills, A. J. 1988. Organization, gender, and culture. *Organization Studies*. 9: 351–369.

12. Underwood, R., Bond, E., & Baer, R. 2001. Building service brands via social identity: Lessons from the sports marketplace. *Journal of Marketing Theory and Practice*. 9(1): 1–13.

13. Lloyd, J. 1996. Some tips on the fine art of learning to network. *Joan Lloyd at Work*. Internet newsletter at *www.joanlloyd.com/articles/open.asp?art=642.htm*.

14. Calas, M. B., & Smircich, L. 2000. Ignored for "good reason": Beauvoir's philosophy as a revision of social identity approaches. *Journal of Management Inquiry*. 9(2): 193–199.

15. Ibarra, H. 1997. Paving an alternative route: Gender differences in managerial networks. *Social Psychology Quarterly*. 60: 91–102; Kalleberg, A., Knoke, D., Marsden, P., & Spaeth, J. 1996. *Organizations in America: Analyzing Their Structures and Human Resources Practices*. Thousand Oaks, CA: Sage.

16. Ibarra, H. 1992. Homophily and differential returns: Sex differences in network structure and access in an advertising firm. *Administrative Science Quarterly*. 37(3): 442–447; McPherson, M., & Smith-Lovin, L. 1987. Homophily in voluntary organizations: Status distance and the composition of face to face groups. *American Sociological Review*. 52: 370–379.

17. Janis, I. L. 1982. *Groupthink: Psychological Studies of Policy Decisions and Fiascoes (2nd ed)*. Boston: Houghton-Mifflin.

18. Aldrich, H. A. 1989. I heard it through the grapevine: Networking among women entrepreneurs. In O. Hagen, C. Rivchun, & D. Sexton (Eds.). *Women Owned Businesses*. New York: Praeger.

19. McPherson, M., Smith-Lovin, L., & Cook, J. 2001. Birds of a feather: Homophily in social networks. *Annual Review of Sociology.* 27: 335–361.

20. The term has a long and illustrative history. Robert Putnam in his groundbreaking book, *Bowling Alone,* traces its evolution from L. J. Hanifan's writing in 1916 to sociologist James S. Coleman's finally putting the term on the intellectual agenda in the late 1980s.

21. Fischer, C. S., & Oliker, S. J. 1983. A research note on friendship, gender, and the life cycle. *Social Forces.* 62: 124–133.

22. Aldrich, H. A., Reese, P. R., & Dubini, P. 1989. Women on the verge of a breakthrough: Networking among entrepreneurs in the United States and Italy. *Entrepreneurship & Regional Development*: 339–356; Renzulli, L. A., Aldrich, H. E., & Moody, J. 2000. Family matters: Gender, networks, and entrepreneurial outcomes. *Social Forces.* 79(2): 523–546.

23. Reese, P. R., & Aldrich, H. A. 1995. Entrepreneurial networks and business performance, in S. Birley & I. C. MacMillan (Eds.). *International Entrepreneurship.* London: Routledge; Aldrich, H. A., Reese, P. R., & Dubini, P. 1989. op. cit.

24. Aldrich, H. A., Reese, P. R., & Dubini, P. 1989. op. cit.; Cromie, S., & Birley, S. 1991. Networking by female business owners in Northern Ireland. *Journal of Business Venturing.* 8(3): 237–251.

25. Blau, J. R., & Alba, R. D. 1982. Empowering nets of participation. *Administrative Science Quarterly.* 27: 363–397.

26. Fischer, C. S., & Oliker, S. J. 1983. op. cit.; Marsden, P. 1987. Core discussion networks of Americans. *American Sociological Review.* 52: 122–131; Moore, G. 1990. Structural determinants of men's and women's personal networks. *American Sociological Review.* 55: 726–735.

27. Renzulli, L. A., Aldrich, H. E., & Moody, J. 2000. Family matters: Gender, networks, and entrepreneurial outcomes. *Social Forces.* 79(2): 523–546.

28. Aldrich, H. A. 1989. op. cit.

29. Renzulli, L. A., Aldrich, H. E., & Moody, J. 2000. op. cit.

30. Aldrich, H. A. 1989. op. cit.

31. Burt, R. S. 1992. *Structural Holes: The Social Structure of Competition.* Cambridge, MA: Harvard University Press.

32. Ibarra, H. 1993. Personal networks of women and minorities in management: A conceptual framework. *Academy of Management Review.* 18 (1): 50–87.

33. Aldrich, H. E. 1989. op. cit.

34. Aldrich, H. E., & Reese, P. R. 1997. Gender gap, gender myth: Does women's networking behavior differ significantly from men's? In S. Birley & I. MacMillan (Eds.). *Entrepreneurship in a Global Context: International Business & the World Economy.* London: Routledge.

9

WOMEN BUILDING MANAGEMENT TEAMS

There are five crucial jobs that need to be managed in any new venture; finance/money, marketing, operations/technology, people, and strategy/leadership. You need at least three people to do these jobs in the beginning, but as the business grows, you need each of these roles filled by competent individuals.

—Dr. Henry Morgan,
Dean Emeritus of Boston University and angel investor

Once your business passes the start-up hurdles and you've made the decision to grow, it's time to build your management team. Why do you need a team to grow your business? There are several reasons. In the first place, although you might be tempted to do it all yourself because you can control the details and you know your business best, there is strong evidence that businesses run by competent teams consistently perform better.[1] More important, however, if you want money for fast growth, investors require that key leadership roles be filled with qualified people. Generally these roles are marketing and sales, finance, operations, human resources, and strategic leadership. Your ability to bring together a management team signals to investors not only that the functional bases are covered, but also that you are savvy enough to persuade others to join in the development of your venture. Identifying people with top skills and capabilities, encouraging their commitment, and developing a culture to motivate them shows that you are qualified to lead your venture to growth.

In addition, there are many other benefits of teams. First, a competent team brings greater knowledge, experience, and skills to the business, which professionalizes the decision making, information flows, and day-to-day operations. Second, management teams extend the social network of the venture, and build its organizational capital, which facilitates growth.[2] Securing resources for growth often means working through personal contacts established through social networks.[3] The bigger the network reach of the team, the more likely this process is to be successful. Third, qualified teams help attract good personnel to the business.[4] People want to work with good managers, and they can be more easily engaged if the management team has a solid reputation and strong capabilities. Fourth, management teams provide insurance that the business will continue beyond the founders. Although you have developed the idea and launched the venture, to ensure it's continuance, it needs to become a viable organization, with systems and policies that support the delivery of the products or services. This means you need an executive team to coordinate and supervise these efforts.[5]

You're probably thinking this sounds good, and you can see the benefits, but how is a management team similar or different from the founding team? A founding team is usually comprised of two or more people who start a business in which they are at least partial owners. Not all owners are necessarily involved in management. Some founders might be involved during the pre-start-up phase and launch, but choose not to work in the business. The founding team might or might not be willing and able to stay on board for the growth of the venture assuming key roles on the management team. It's unusual for a founding team to have expertise in all five key roles, and so the core management team members are added during the venture's first year or two of existence.[6]

So how should you proceed? What challenges might you encounter? The rest of this chapter considers these issues. First, what do resource providers, and in particular, investors look for in a management team? There are generally five areas of consideration:

- Managerial knowledge across functional disciplines

- Technical expertise in the area critical to success of the business

- Complementary fit

- Strong business qualifications and experience

- Visionary CEO with a track record and leadership capabilities

At a basic level, the management team needs to have knowledge in marketing and sales, finance and accounting, and the operations of the venture. Of course, there is a need for someone to manage the people, or human resources, because as a venture grows it needs to develop systems and processes for recruiting, managing payroll, and handling benefits. Then, you need someone who has the technical expertise that links directly to the core of the business. Although you, as founder, might have either technical or functional expertise, chances are that your role will be the strategic leader moving the venture forward to meet its overall goals and vision, so you will need someone else to fill this role. Besides functional expertise, each team member should be able to cooperate and coordinate with the others. Everyone does not need to possess the same management style, but a complementary fit will ensure the venture can move quickly. It's also important that the qualifications, experience, and reputation of the management team are solid.

Now you would think that if you can put together a team that fits these criteria, it would be pretty easy to move forward. On the surface this is true, but, once again, we find that perceptions about women can get in the way. Consider the story of Hannah Wallace.

I cofounded our technology venture with my father 15 years ago, and have served as president for 8 years. By 1995, we had about 100 employees, several of whom had more than 10 years experience with us. Our open lunch-room, flex-time, and "family feeling" encouraged sharing of information across all levels and departments. We were quite profitable on about $30 million in sales, but decided that with new products in the pipeline, we could really grow the business with a new infusion of equity financing. Our present board, some of whom were investors, sug-gested it was time for me to move into a more "strategic" role and that a president (male) would be better suited to lead the company forward to the $100 million sales mark.

At the time, it seemed like a good idea to be more involved in strategic and future planning. So we recruited and hired a new president who had all the apparent qualities we needed: an MBA from a top business school, former VP of finance, and a reputation for swift decision making. Our board believed he was in the "right" networks to attract new funding and to create strategic partnerships. After 9 months, I knew it was a big mistake. Jim's preference for taking control and making decisions autocratically alien-ated many of the technical managers who had previously participated in the process. In the first year, he brought in a new VP of sales who doubled the marketing expense bud-get, and hired a new VP of operations at a big salary.

> At the same time, we were behind in our product launch and the sources of money and partnerships just did not pan out. I had to fire Jim, then come back to lead the business as we negotiated new sources of financing. I went to some of our customers, large technology firms, called colleagues in local CEO groups, and contacted other women executives. Through my network, we were able to secure investment financing through another large women-led firm, and one of our strategic partners.

In this story, even though Wallace had started and successfully managed the venture, her investors still felt she could not take her business to the next level, because she did not have strong connections in the financial networks. Where did these perceptions come from?

Perceptions about Women

Views that women are less capable of building a high-potential team are based on four different premises: first, the idea that women are more relationally than transactionally oriented; second, the comparatively small numbers of women in top decision-making positions of major companies; third, a female tradition of gaining work experience in staff rather than line positions; and fourth, the gendered composition of men's and women's networks. The perceptions are manifested in a variety of ways.

Women Don't Want to Share Ownership

Although nearly all entrepreneurs have a desire to control their venture at the outset, some believe that women have greater difficulty deciding to share ownership and control with partners. This idea comes from a couple of assumptions—first, that women are relational, rather than transactional, in working with employees, suppliers, and customers.[7] A relational approach binds women more closely to the venture and its organizational networks because of the depth of personal involvement. Second, some would say that women are more likely to create ventures that are an extension of themselves and their personal values than their male counterparts are. It is then only logical that it would be harder for women to give up control and delegate to a team, therefore, they can't build the best team.

Women Don't Recognize the Types of People Needed

This perception is based on expectations about the right way to do things. As we have noted in other chapters, so much of what we consider the standard for success is derived from examples of men. The "right" way to lead is to make tough decisions, be strong, and delegate well. Any variation from the "male" success model in strategic leadership might be viewed as a weakness. If a woman creates a flat organization, where information is widely shared and decisions are collaborative, she can be perceived as less capable of building the right kind of team or organization.

Women Are Outside the Networks

Then, there are networks. It is not unusual for entrepreneurs to bring together teams of people with whom they have previously worked. Entrepreneurs typically identify desirable team members based on who they know and who is recommended by their advisors. However, as we learned in the last chapter, women tend to have different networks than men. They might be unlikely to know or be linked to people with the right set of skills, values, and other resources to add value to the venture. If women are perceived as being outside the industry network, it might be difficult for them to identify or attract the best people for the job.

Women Just Don't Have What It Takes to Lead a Growth Venture

Can women make tough business decisions? As we noted earlier, women are less likely to serve as CEOs of major corporations. In fact, at this time, women lead less than 5% of the Fortune 500 companies. The small number of women at the top of the corporate world means that they are still viewed as the exception. At the next level of responsibility, there are very few women visible as either leaders or participants on executive teams. This means that very few men or women have the experience of working for a female boss, which only reinforces the belief that only men are qualified to lead large companies.

It is also true that women are more likely to have experience in staff rather than line positions. Staff positions are generally those that play supporting roles for line functions. Those holding line positions manage people and are held responsible for the performance of a division, unit, or product line. As a result of a concentration in staff positions, women are perceived as facilitators or helpers whereas men, gaining from their experience on the line, are pegged as leaders, and managers.[8]

Finally, perceptions about women's ability to put together a quality team become even more complicated when considering the gender of the teams. Women tap into their personal networks to find people complementary to their business, often choosing other women. When men surround themselves with men they have worked with, no one questions it. However, if a woman hires women, it might be questioned.[9] For instance, when Suzanne DePasse was hired to run Motown Records, she was highly criticized for bringing along her team of talented women to fill key jobs.[10]

There is an inherent tension in team selection. We know that heterogeneous teams (mixed in gender, experience, educational background, and other ways) are linked to higher growth potential for their firms. However, entrepreneurs prefer to work with and associate with those similar to themselves, and these similarities are usually based both on characteristics such as gender, race, and age, as well as internal states of values, beliefs, and norms.[11]

Fact and Fiction about Women and Teams

Are women really less willing to share ownership of their firms? If we look at ownership, women entrepreneurs worldwide are more likely than men to be sole owners of their businesses. For example, 85% of women-owned businesses in the United States are sole proprietorships.[12] However, according to the 1997 U.S. Census, 74% of all small businesses in the United States are operated as sole proprietorships. It's just the most common way of organizing a small business. When we consider separately the women owners of fast-growth companies, we find them more likely to share ownership than other women business owners (28% vs. 15%). There are, however, significant gender differences. Fast growing firms led by men have shared ownership in 50% of their businesses, while the same is true for only 28% of women-led businesses.[13]

It is difficult to tell just how much sharing of responsibility and leadership is taking place when a business is owned by spouses. In 1997, there were 3.6 million firms jointly owned by a husband and wife. These firms generated $943.9 billion worth of receipts.[14] What can't be deciphered from the numbers is the role that each partner played in the strategic decision-making activities of the firm. Often the wife is considered to be a means of access to corporate and government programs focused on women-owned businesses. Although these programs generally require a rigorous certification to ensure the women's strategic involvement, the perception often is that her role is more like a staff position in the corporate world, providing support for the husband and business.

If a woman is choosing a management partner other than her husband, who does she put on the team? A study of entrepreneurial teams, found that approximately three quarters of the teams that didn't include spousal partners were composed of members of just one sex, 16% being all women and about 60% including all men. In looking at the smaller teams, about 80% of two-person teams include people of the same sex.[15] It appears that both women and men have a preference for the creation of same-sex teams.

Why does this happen? First, the woman does it purposefully. She chooses others for the skills, educational backgrounds, or work experiences that would add value to the company. However, opportunity structures also come into play. These structures work as a context in limiting who the woman might invite. In other words, she can't invite someone she's never met, doesn't know how to reach, or might not even know exists.[16] Due to more limited professional networks, women are often searching in a smaller pool for their potential team members.[17]

There is additional evidence that people are more likely to recruit their management teams from among people who are most like them and from among people they know.[18] A national study of entrepreneurs in the process of starting a new venture showed that out of 816 respondents, representing 400 solo efforts and 416 entrepreneurial teams, almost 73% of all the team start-ups included only two people, 13% included teams of three, another 8% had teams of four, and only 6% included teams of five or more people.[19] The gender makeup of the teams represented some striking differences. Thirty-seven percent of the teams were made up of people that were all the same sex, 7% were all women and 30% were all men. The teams of two people were those most likely to be mixed (and most probably largely made up of spouses and partners). Teams of three or more were less likely to be mixed gender.

If we take out ties for familiarity (anyone who is a spouse or partner) we find that almost half of the teams with three or four people on them had at least two people on them who didn't know each other prior to joining the team and almost 75% of the larger teams contained a set of prior strangers. One potential explanation is that the larger teams were building more resource-intensive businesses.[20] Women are challenged in their efforts to identify and engage qualified strangers if they do not have strong professional network connections.

Then if we look at the most ambitious companies, those that went public, we can see that having women on the senior management team is a good indicator of strong performance. In fact, companies that go public have been found to have better performing stock if they have women on their top management team.[21] How likely is this scenario to occur? In 1988, Theresa Welbourne surveyed 136 companies that went public and found no women at all in upper echelon positions. By 1993, when she surveyed 535 IPO companies, she found that women were included on 27% of the companies' top management teams. Three years later she again examined companies that went public and found that women were in key executive positions at 41% of the companies.[22]

Despite the perceptions that women are less capable of putting together top teams, the evidence suggests women, like men, recruit teams from those they know, and that teams with women on them perform as well or better. With this in mind, how do you move forward? A good example of how to build a founding team is presented in the story of Flight Time, Inc.

Dara Zapata had the idea to start Flight Time when she found that tour groups, sports teams, and companies often needed to fly to destinations not served by scheduled airlines and that there was an available supply of underutilized aircraft. Even though she had extensive experience as a tour coordinator, airline operations manager, and aviation consultant, she knew that an aircraft charter brokerage business also needed expertise in two other areas: marketing and sales, and finance. The business required an individual who could market the business services and

negotiate sales for both sets of partners—the airlines, who supplied aircraft, and the customers who would travel on the airplanes (tour groups, corporate travelers, and sports teams).

Significant cash inflows and outflows and large information databases signaled the need for someone to manage information systems, and for an expert in finance and accounting. Dara approached Jane McBride because she had experience as a wholesale tour operator, was a licensed private pilot, and possessed extensive customer service experience in her previous job. Jane was ready to do something exciting and enthusiastically signed on with Dara. For three months, Dara and Jane met regularly to explore the feasibility of the concept. They called contacts in the travel business to see "if the idea of brokering airplanes was really off the wall or not."

But, they both agreed that the business still needed a numbers person. Jane remembered meeting Patti Zinkowski, who was now head of European accounting for Trans National Travel (TNT) the travel-related wholesale division of Trans National, a financial services company based in Boston. They located Patti in Europe and proposed that she join them. She came on board and within a month, Patti, Dara, and Jane officially incorporated Flight Time. Despite early challenges, within 5 years, the "three women from Boston" as they were called, created a unique database, and highly profitable enterprise.[23]

In this case, Zapata was very strategic about the roles and the individuals needed to start Flight Time before the business was even launched.

Building a High-Potential Team

Chances are you launched your venture on your own or with a team of people that included family members or people you already knew as coworkers in an earlier job.[24] Like most entrepreneurs, you used your social framework as a starting point. At the next stage of growth, you work within the networks you and your founding team know well and begin to reach beyond those boundaries.

How do you get started in identifying additional individuals who meet the criteria set forth by investors at the beginning of this chapter? One way to consider the pool for team members is to think of the possibilities of three concentric circles of candidates for teams: family, others you or other founders know personally (possibly through the industry), and strangers.[25] However, keep in mind that the relationship issues should be secondary to the functional issues.[26] In other words, although it might be an advantage to work with someone you already know and trust, it could become a disadvantage if there is not a good fit between the business and the candidate's skill sets. It won't matter how well the team gets along if everyone is a marketing expert and no one understands finance. Gender might then become an additional complicating factor in that women's education and work experiences are more similar to each other than to men's. Thus, there can be an increased likelihood of a functional gap appearing.

How important is it to have some kind of existing relationship with the members of your management team? Is your company more likely to succeed if you know the team members well? In many instances it has worked better for the firm if members of the top management team have worked together previously.[27] The social psychological benefits from existing or developing relationships among team members are important in that they help spread responsibility, share burdens, and increase confidence.[28] It's also easier to work together if the team has complementary (as opposed to overlapping) characteristics. In fact, the personal relationships, especially those that start as friendships, might serve as the glue that helps the team stay together and prompt the extra efforts needed during business challenges.[29]

Once you have identified potential candidates to join your team, you need to assess their potential contributions. The Colorado Capital Alliance, a not-for-profit angel capital network, suggests the following questions as a guide:[30]

- Is every key manager and professional staff member experienced?

- What management skills are needed to execute the plan?

- Are any functional areas of expertise missing in the team?

- What motivates the management team? Is there a fit among the motivations of all team members?

- Is this a family-run business? Will this always be a family-run business?

- What are the sales ability and the experience levels in the particular industry of the key players?

- How capable is this management team when compared to competitors?

Overall, the list addresses both individual and company-level questions to evaluate potential members of the team and how they might relate to the company and complement each other.

How do you then decide who fits your business and who doesn't? To a large degree this depends on the culture of your business and its fundamental values. The culture of your business is based on core assumptions about work, people, time, and the environment. Then there are norms, beliefs, and ways of doing things, some of which are formally articulated and some of which are implicit or tacit. For instance, what time can people come to work and leave? Is there a dress code? Are there informal norms for how people are to be greeted, treated, and responded to? An elite bicycle manufacturer in Massachusetts provided every employee with keys to the plant, complete financial information, and open access to production line scheduling. Employees made their own schedules and came and went as they pleased as long as they met production goals.

Sometimes culture is manifested in symbols; other times it is explicitly written in vision statements, pictures, and marketing materials. Georgia Berner, who owned a company manufacturing air curtains, had a large bell in the corporate offices that was attached to the manufacturing plant. Every time a salesperson landed a contract, he or she would ring the bell loud enough so that all 100-plus employees could hear it. Each salesperson had a distinct "ring" so everyone knew who to congratulate.

The culture of the business is the underpinning, the glue that will hold the business together as it rapidly expands. You need to assess what the founding culture is, and then think about how it might evolve. In bringing on new management team members, it's important to be able to articulate what the core values and culture are in order to gain their commitment to the venture and other management team members.

The care and feeding of teams is critical, especially in the early days. Too often the founder (or founding team) is so busy working on what she has determined to be the critical tasks that she doesn't realize that the culture of the company is being established with or without her guidance. The importance of cultural dimensions varies depending on the phase of development:[31]

- *Formation*—During this stage the focus of the founders needs to be on developing a sense of inclusion that honestly recognizes differing levels of power and influence and still promotes acceptance and intimacy, and helps each person identify his or her role in launching and growing the company.

- *Building*—The company is now launched and the focus needs to expand to include a plan for how the management team and other new members of the organization can function as a unit.

- *Working and mature functioning*—If the management team is in place for the long term, you must establish a culture that supports the mission, goals, and tasks of the company but also allows for differences in the management team to be valued.

Depending on the phase of your business, you should first identify what is critical so that you can measure and control it. Are you looking for outcomes of a team effort? Do you consider how people react to crises? Second, develop a habit of deliberate role modeling and coaching. The rest of the team will often follow your lead because they perceive that is how things are done in this company. If the connection is made between this type of behavior and the awarding of rewards and status, this behavior will be fostered in the firm. Finally, prepare specific criteria for selection, recruitment, promotion, and retirement or other types of exit.

Challenges in Team Formation

Although it might be easy to identify important steps in building a team, there are also challenges. For instance, there is the challenge of fitting new team members into an existing organization. The early decisions made by you and other team members "imprint" the organization with its systems, culture, and policies.[32] They create the foundation of the new organization. It is this set of values and norms that people will carry out in the work of the business. When new team members are brought in, founding members might not wish to change roles or relinquish responsibilities. Some members of the founding team might not want to see routines altered or relationships changed. If the team members are inappropriate for their roles, cannot work with each other, or lack commitment to the organization, the venture could fail. For example, a technology-based start-up in New Jersey functioned extremely well in the early stages with a four-person management team until three of the founders decided that they could not tolerate the perceived lower level of energy put into the venture by the fourth. The relationships were still too new to survive serious discord and one team member resigned, leaving not only a gaping hole in their marketing efforts but also a significant and unplanned debt incurred when they were forced to buy out the ownership of the departing member.

In another case, three entrepreneurs and friends founding a high-technology start-up venture decided they did not want to be subordinated to each other. They created an "office of the president" where each "shared" the president's decision-making role. Needless to say, the arrangement was confusing for customers, created internal dissent, and eventually damaged the business.

The challenge of sharing management roles brings with it many complex issues. First, when you allocate responsiblilities across multiple people, you create a new set of dynamics. Working in teams increases the opportunities for shirking, and incurs the need for monitoring systems, and a means of distributing incentives.[33] Failure to address these issues could limit your company's growth. A second possibility is that the more homogeneous or similar the team, the greater the potential for inferior decision making because of "groupthink" and insufficient airing of conflict.[34] Therefore if your team lacks a dynamic balance, your business growth and development will be hampered. Finally, there are identifiable links that exist between firm performance and dimensions of an entrepreneurial team such as speed, politics, and conflict.[35] Although conflict might sound undesirable, it can actually serve as a tool to help team members avoid complacency and mistakes.[36] Heterogeneity of the team can be a source of conflict, but conflict can be constructive if it allows different points of view to be considered.[37]

Summary

This chapter examined the ability of women to form management teams, which are crucial to venture development and growth. Although we associate successful ventures with a single entrepreneur, the fact is that most winning organizations are the product of a top-notch team working well together. Can women build management teams to grow successful ventures? There are perceptions that women prefer to maintain ownership and control, they are out of the network and therefore can't identify top talent, and they lack experience in their decision-making roles. We find that, indeed, a relatively few women have executive leadership experience, but their experience in staff functions, including human resources, can be an asset. We also find that women are growing their firms with team members they met through the process and not just those they knew prior to "going entrepreneurial." The value gained in growing a business with a team exceeds that of growing alone largely due to increased and enhanced capacities of those sharing ownership.

Notes

1. Lechler, 2001. "Social interaction: A determinant of entrepreneurial team venture success." *Small Business Economics*, 16:263–78.

2. Brush, C. G., Greene, P., Hart, M. M., Feb. 2001. "From Initial Idea to Unique Advantage: The Entrepreneurial Challenge of Constructing a Resource Base." *Academy of Management Executive*, 15(1): 195.

3. Roberts, E. 1991. *Entrepreneurs in High Technology*. New York: Oxford University Press.

4. Ruef, M., Aldrich, H., & Carter, N. M., April 2003. "The structure of founding teams: Homophily, strong ties, and isolations among U.S. entrepreneurs." *American Sociological Review*, 68(2): 195.

5. Aldrich, H. 1999. *Organizations Evolving*. Thousand Oaks, CA: Sage.

6. Eisenhardt, Kathleen M., & Schoonhoven, Claudia B., Sept. 1990. "Organizational Growth: Linking Founding Team, Strategy, Environment, and Growth Among U.S. Semiconductor Ventures," *Administrative Science Quarterly*, 35(3): 504.

7. Gilligan, C. 1982. *In a Different Voice*. Cambridge, MA: Harvard University Press.

8. Jones, D. January 27, 2003. Few women hold top executive jobs. *USA Today*.

9. Ibid.

10. Hill, L. & Elias, J. 1989. Suzanne DePasse at Motown Records. Harvard Business School video, 9-889-508.

11. Ruef, M., 2002. "A Structural Event Approach to the Analysis of Group Composition." *Social Networks*, 24: 135–60.

12. U.S. Economic census.

13. National Foundation for Women Business Owners. 2001. *Entrepreneurial Vision in Action: Exploring Growth Among Women- and Men-Owned Firms.*

14. Ibid.

15. Ruef. Aldrich, Carter, 2003. op. cit.

16. Ruef, M., 2002. op. cit.

17. Ruef, Aldrich, Carter, 2003. op. cit.

18. Ibid.

19. Ibid.

20. Ibid.

21. Welbourne, T. M., 1999. Wall Street likes its women: An examination of women in the top management teams of initial public offerings. *Center for Advanced Human Resource Studies. Working Paper Series.* Ithaca, New York: Cornell University.

22. Ibid.

23. Brush, C. G. and Bonacini, A., 1993. *Flight Time A—Start Up of an Air Charter Broker.* Boston University case; *CEO Plans to Fly to the Top,* 1999 Jan, Women's Business: 4–5.

24. Kamm, J. B., & Nurik, A. J., 1993. "The Stages of Team Venture Formation: A Decision-Making Model." *Entrepreneurship, Theory & Practice*, 17:17–21.

25. Aldrich, H., Elam, A., Reese, P. R., 1996. "Strong ties, weak ties and strangers: Do women business owners differ from men in their use of networking to obtain assistance?" in S. Birley & I. MacMillan (Eds.), *Entrepreneurship in a Global Context.* London: Routledge.

26. Ruef, Aldrich, Carter, 2003. op. cit.; Mosakowski, E., Dec. 1998. "Managerial prescriptions under the resource-based view of strategy: The example of motivational techniques." *Strategic Management Journal*, 19(12): 1169.

27. Roure, J B., Maidique, M. A., Fall 1986. "Linking Prefunding Factors and High-Technology Venture Success: An Exploratory Study." *Journal of Business Venturing*, 1(3): 295.

28. Bird, B. J. 1989. *Entrepreneurial Behavior.* Glenview, IL: Scott Foresman.

29. Francis & Sandeberg (2000:6)

30. Keeley, R. H., Cooper, J. M., & Bloomer, G. D. 1998. *Business Angels: A Guide to Private Investing.* Colorado Capital Alliance, Inc.

31. Schein, E. 1985. *Organizational Culture and Leadership,* San Francisco, CA: Jossey Bass.

32. Ibid.

33. Mosakowski, E. 1998. op. cit.

34. Janis, I,. 1982. *Victims of Groupthink.* Boston: Houghton Mifflin.

35. Eisenhardt, K. M., & Bourgeois, L. J., III, Dec. 1988. "Politics of Strategic Decision Making: Toward a Mid-Range Theory." *Academy of Management*

Journal; Eisendhardt, K. M., Sept. 1989. "Making Fast Strategic Decisions in High Velocity Environments," *Academy of Management Journal*.

36. Bourgeois, L. J., III & Eisenhartdt, K. M., 1988. "Strategic Decision Processes in High Velocity Environments: Four Cases in the Microcomputer Industry." *Management Science*.

37. Eisenhardt & Schoonhover, 1990. op. cit.; Tsui, A. S., & O'Reilly, C.,1989. "Beyond simple demographic effects: The importance of relational demography in superior-subordinate dyads." *Academy of Management*, 32:402.

10

NETWORKING FOR VENTURE CAPITAL

*Ask any venture capitalist. He will insist that he invests
in great deals and that gender does not play a part in the
decision making. Venture capital partners indicate that the
primary reason they don't invest in more women-led businesses
is that they just don't see many deals— viable or
otherwise—that are led by women.*

If venture capitalists are truly gender blind in their search for the best
deals, why is it that so few of their portfolio companies are led by
women entrepreneurs? Is the field of qualified women really so thin?
Or do women deliberately slow their companies' growth or look else-
where for alternative sources of capital? Do women have all the right
intentions, but lack the knowledge and connections to get their "plans"
into the right hands?

Or is the funding gap a function of the maleness of the venture
capital industry? Perhaps venture capitalists lack any direct connec-

tions to women entrepreneurs. Or they might see the deals, but underestimate their value because they have so little experience evaluating women entrepreneurs.

In this chapter, we address the hurdles women entrepreneurs with high-growth ventures must overcome to raise venture capital. We focus on the challenges of making the initial connections (network gaps) and of clinching a deal (overcoming male models of success). However, before we get into the details of those network disconnects and the model misfits, we offer some basic background information on the venture capital industry itself.

A Brief History of Venture Capital in the United States

Tracing the Roots of the Industry

American Research and Development (ARD), founded in Boston in 1946, is widely recognized as the pioneer of the modern American venture capital industry. Although there are many examples in history of wealthy individuals providing venture funding to underwrite high-risk enterprises (e.g., Queen Isabella of Spain was Christopher Columbus's venture partner), these transactions were individually negotiated agreements. They did not represent a systematic approach to bringing investors and entrepreneurs together to launch new ventures.

Shortly after the conclusion of World War II, Karl Compton (Massachusetts Institute of Technology), Georges Doriot (Harvard Business School), and several Massachusetts business leaders raised funds to support the commercialization of technologies developed during the war efforts. They organized ARD as a publicly traded corporation with a closed-end fund (fund with a specified ending date). Limited partnership funds (now the most popular form of venture organization) were introduced by Draper, Gaither, and Anderson in 1958, but did not become a widely accepted industry model until 20 years later.

In the early years of venture capital, there were relatively few funds and the pool of investors was small. Most investors were wealthy families or individuals (many of them successful entrepreneurs), insurance companies, banks, and corporations. For many years, the number of firms and the capital invested remained quite small. The industry pioneer, ARD raised less than $8 million in its first 10 years. (This is in sharp contrast to the more than $100 billion raised in the industry in a single year: 2000.)[1]

The Context of Growth

Legal changes in the late 1970s and early 1980s encouraged both individuals and institutions to raise their stakes in venture capital funds. Individual investors benefited from the Revenue Act of 1978, which reduced the tax burden on capital gains from 49.5% to 28% and the Economic Recovery Tax Act (1981), which further reduced capital gains taxes to 20%. The 1981 Incentive Stock Option Act provided another tax advantage for members of entrepreneurial teams who held stock options. (The act allowed holders of stock options to defer tax liability to the date of sale rather than the exercise date.)

In 1979, an amendment to the "prudent man" provision of the Employee Retirement Income Security Act (ERISA) opened up the possibility of private equity investment by large institutional investors. Pension fund managers, who were previously restricted in their rights to place funds in high-risk or alternative investments, found that the rule change gave them much more latitude to place a portion of their funds in venture capital.[2] In 1979, following the official change and further clarification by the Labor Department, the percentage of the total venture capital pool invested by pension funds shot up from 15% to 30%.[3] In subsequent years, the percentage of venture funding provided by pension fund managers continued to increase, averaging 40% to 50% of total funds raised annually and reaching a high of 60% in the early 1990s.

In 1990, venture capitalists raised 50 new funds at an average value of $53.6 million. The industry grew so rapidly during the next decade that, in 2000, 632 new funds were raised with an average size of $153.8 million, and several of the funds topped $1 billion. More than 50% of all capital raised came from public and private pension funds. Foundations, endowments, insurance companies, banks, and private individuals rounded out the list of limited partners. Most investments were made in closed-end funds that had a specified size (e.g., $100 million, $500 million), duration (7–10 years), industry focus, and, in some cases, a preference for a particular stage of growth (e.g., seed, growth, or later stage).

Understanding the Investment Process

Venture capitalists are best known for the financial resources they provide, but money represents only one of many assets that they afford to new enterprises. Each venture capital team brings a unique business network and specific knowledge of an industry, technology, or stage of organizational development. Individual members of a venture capital team are often seasoned entrepreneurs who have built substantial companies in a particular industry. Others are selected for their functional or financial expertise and all are expected to provide connections between the providers of venture capital (limited partners) and the consumers of venture capital (entrepreneurs). Once the team is formed, the general partners must aggressively market their skills and reputations for identifying and nurturing high-growth businesses to engage institutions and individuals as investors.

The general partners are responsible for structuring the "deals" with each entrepreneurial venture. Their goal is not only to maximize their returns while limiting their downside exposure, but also to create a deal that is perceived as fair to all parties and that provides substantial incentives and rewards to the founding team as well as to the investors. Many of the early-stage investments look more like debt than equity. For example, convertible preferred stock provides the investor a claim on the assets in the event of liquidation and the right to convert to equity in the event of success. Early-stage investments might also carry rights for the initial investors to participate in future rounds of financing at a pro rata share. Often, one venture partnership will provide the entrepreneur access to additional capital through the syndication of the financing round. Whether through direct contacts or through reputation, the lead venture capitalists can attract other investors in subsequent financings as well.

A general partner of the venture capital firm leading an investment will often take a seat on the board of directors of a portfolio firm. The board enables the venture investor an opportunity to provide management oversight, set performance benchmarks, and assist in the acquisition of additional resources. As the company develops, the venture capitalists assist in subsequent financing activities, including public and private sales. These efforts are intended to foster the growth of the entrepreneurial enterprises and to enhance the financial rewards at a later date.

Risks and Rewards of Venture Capital Financing

The stakes in the entrepreneurial investment process are high. Each of the parties (entrepreneurs and investors) bears some of the risk associated with the start-up of the new venture and each is well rewarded if the venture succeeds. Approximately one-third of the venture-funded enterprises are likely to succeed, but only a handful will ever be classified as blockbusters. Intel, Microsoft, and Home Depot are the exceptions, even among successful venture deals. Those venture-funded companies that do succeed provide substantial rewards not only for the entrepreneurs and their investors, but also for the many customers, employees, business partners, and communities associated with the enterprise. The oversight venture capitalists provide during the growth and development of a new enterprise makes the general partners value-added facilitators of the flow of capital between holders of wealth and entrepreneurs.

The venture capitalists are usually compensated in two ways. They are paid a fixed annual fee based on the funds under management (2–3% per annum). They also participate in the profits produced by the investments through their *carried interest*. Most venture partnerships first return all invested capital to the limited partners, then divide the profits in excess of the initial investment at a predetermined ratio. For example, with a 20% carry, profits in excess of the initial investment would be allocated to the limited and general partners on an 80:20 basis. The actual amount of the management fee and the carry are negotiable and are set at the time the fund is raised. (Although the terms can vary from one fund to the next, even within the same venture capital organization, individual partnership agreements are fixed for the duration of the funds.) The performance of a partnership's early funds plays a significant part in the venture capitalists' ability to raise follow-on funds and to negotiate their own compensation—including management fees and the carry.

At a fund's termination date, profits from the sale of companies (whether public or private) are distributed on a pro rata basis. In some cases, where there has been no sale, shares of the portfolio companies themselves are distributed. Limited partners are generally rewarded with above average returns (on average, 26% per annum over the most recent 10 years)[4] and the entrepreneurs benefit from the availability of financial and managerial resources and, ultimately, from the financial returns of a business with a greatly increased likelihood of success.

The Cultural Context for the U.S. Venture Capital Industry

The venture capital industry has flourished in the United States for many reasons. The Horatio Alger vision of great rewards for work well done persists. The national culture is one that encourages risk-taking and forgives failure. Job markets are fluid, making transition in and out of the employed workforce possible, and unemployment benefits provide a financial safety net. The legal system protects intellectual property and the financial markets provide liquidity for investors and entrepreneurs. Although other countries have tried to emulate the U.S. model of venture capital, they lag far behind, often because they lack one or more of these elements. In a cross-country comparison of early-stage venture capital investments made in 1995, United States-based venture investments of $3.4 billion were more than double the total investments ($1.5 billion) of the next 20 highest ranking countries.[5]

Venture Capital Cycles

The venture capital industry has consistently delivered superior long-term returns, but has suffered periodic downturns.[6] Throughout the decade of the 1990s, venture capital investments experienced record-breaking growth, fueled in large part by the commercialization of the Internet. Although Alan Greenspan raised the specter of "irrational exuberance" in the public markets in his January 1996 speech to the American Enterprise Institute for Public Policy Research, the NASDAQ continued to climb. The January 3, 2000 millennium edition of the *Wall Street Journal* included an article by columnist Thomas Petzinger entitled, "So Long, Supply and Demand: There's a New Economy Out There and It Looks Nothing Like the Old One." He commented:

> **The bottom line: Creativity is overtaking capital as the principal elixir of growth. And creativity, although precious, shares few of the constraints that limit the range and availability of capital and physical goods.... While creativity is everything today, capital is simply everywhere— cheap and abundant. Instead of financing technology innovation and development, the venture capital firms of Silicon Valley have become money factories for marketing campaigns. Going public, once a tool for financing growth, has instead become an exit strategy for investors.**[7]

Just three months later, on March 11, 2000, the NASDAQ reached its record high. The public markets then began to show signs of weakening and the IPO market slowed to a trickle as private companies realized that they would have to accept much lower valuations. Many scrapped their decision to go to the public markets in favor of second or third rounds of private financing.

However, as the financial markets continued to languish, many young ventures discovered that private funds were also hard to find. In 2001, venture capital partnerships raised only $40.7 billion in new funds and invested only $41.9 billion (down from a record $107 billion in 2000). There were only 88 IPOs in 2001.[8] In 2002, venture capital was still in the doldrums. Only $6.9 billion of new funds were raised and less than $25 billion were invested in approximately 3,000 deals. Because the returns on venture capital investment are so closely linked to the health of the public markets, the venture industry continues to be cautious, but there were signs of recovery in 2003.[9]

Building Partnerships, Professional Staffing

Venture partnerships like to describe themselves as experienced venture investors and industry professionals. A quick tour of the Web sites of some of the leading venture firms demonstrates the emphasis on "hands-on" industry experience as well as investing and management skills.

- Accel Partners is a venture capital firm dedicated to helping outstanding entrepreneurs build category-defining technology companies ... (we) meet this challenge with a "prepared mind"—a deep base of domain knowledge, relevant experience, and industry relationships.

- On average, our managing directors and partners have over 12 years of international investment experience. Many of our professionals also have significant operating experience, which gives us first-hand insight into the issues that affect growing businesses. (Advent International)

- Our success in attracting top early-stage opportunities results from our ability to provide unique value, focus, and counsel throughout the entire company-building process. As experienced board members and senior operating managers, we know firsthand the hard work and challenges of building lasting companies. (Greylock)

- We understand just how hard it is to start a business. Each of our partners has hands-on experience in operating and managing companies. We've all served as managers with accountability for profits and losses and had responsibility for bringing products to market. We've learned these lessons over 30 years of assisting new ventures and serving in top management positions at revolutionary technology companies. We know that success is rarely a straight line. (Kleiner, Perkins, Caulfield, and Byers.)

The Venture Capital Community Today

[The list of the top 100 venture capitalists] creates a snapshot of an industry, forever immortalizing it in print ... and this inevitably comes up—someone will ask us about the level of representation of some groups in the list, like women or African-Americans. I can assure you that the only criteria we used for the list were the number of deals a firm participated in and that we selected partners [to represent each firm] in cooperation with the individual firms.... That said, it is revealing to see how many of the most-active VCs are white males between the ages of 35 and 50 who got their MBAs from Harvard or Wharton and now live in Silicon Valley.[10]

—Jason Calacanis, Editor-in-Chief,
Venture Reporter, May/June 2002

Many of the principals in today's venture capital firms earned their stripes as successful entrepreneurs or senior managers with deep industry experience before becoming venture capitalists. They built substantial personal fortunes and established credible records as decision makers before joining a venture partnership. Although some firms hire young MBAs as associates and then train and promote them, the overwhelming majority of venture capitalists are experienced business leaders whose reputations and networks bring substantial benefits to the partnership.

This traditional, experience-based career path has meant that the venture capital ranks were largely closed to women during the first 25 years the industry was in operation. Furthermore, because women have only recently begun to attain high levels of responsibility in corporate America or to gain entrepreneurial experience in large-scale ventures, there have been relatively few who have followed the traditional path, transitioning from successful start-up experience to either general or venture partnership in the past 20 years.

The women who have joined the venture capital ranks since 1990 are likely to have MBAs and some industry experience, but few can match the depth of industry-specific knowledge or the entrepreneurial experience that their male counterparts have. Even more important than this experience–knowledge gap is the fact that most of these women lack the contacts that are so critical to engaging limited partners—the lifeblood of the firm's investment funds.

Women in the Venture Capital Industry

The Pioneers

Since the inception of the U.S. venture capital industry, there has been a significant gender gap in its management ranks. There are, of course, many illustrious venture capital women who have achieved considerable success—including industry veterans Pat Cloherty (Patricof); Jacqui Morby (TA Associates); Ann Winblad (a founder of Hummer, Winblad); and Kathryn Gould (a founder of Foundation Capital). In spite of the progress these women have made, there is no denying that men continue to represent the vast majority of the venture capital industry decision makers. As a result, both the composition of the venture capital network and the prevailing model of what a successful entrepreneur looks like are distinctly masculine.

In 1995, *Pratt's Guide to Venture Capital* listed 346 professional women in the venture capital industry, representing approximately 10% of management-track venture capitalists (including partners, principals, and associates).[11] The number of women decision makers increased to 510 between 1995 and 2000, but female representation in the industry actually remained almost flat at 9% of the total.

Furthermore, of the 346 women listed in the *Pratt's* 1995 volume, 64% did not appear in the 2000 guide. This high attrition rate compares unfavorably with a sample of men in the industry, only 30% of whom exited the industry in the same period. The facts that women comprise a very small minority of venture capital decision makers and that they leave the industry at a much higher rate than their male counterparts raise the question of "Why?" Institutional theory suggests that the industry's male-oriented norms might conflict with women's expectations and preferences. In addition, as long as there are so few women role models in the industry, it will remain difficult to attract and retain new, highly talented women to the venture capitalist ranks. Take, for example, Melanie Fisher:

Melanie Fisher considered herself one of the lucky ones. The job market for graduating MBAs had become very tight in the two years since she entered business school in Fall 2000. For the past few months, every conversation she had with her classmates seemed to focus on how hard it was to land interviews this year, let alone generate meaningful job offers. Melanie was elated when she was invited

to New York for second-round interviews with a midsize health care venture capital firm. Very few venture firms were planning to hire that year, but Melanie knew one of the managing directors very well and had impressed him with her energy, enthusiasm, and long-term commitment to the industry.

The interviews went smoothly and Melanie was feeling "on top of the world" when she checked in at the airport to catch a shuttle back to Boston. She decided to relax on her return flight rather than prepare for the next day's classes. She looked over the magazines available in the shuttle departure lounge and chose the May/June 2002 issue of *Venture Reporter*. She was pleased to find that the entire issue was devoted to the top 100 firms in the venture capital industry (based on the number of publicly announced deals each company had in the previous year). She was certain she would be familiar with many of the partnerships featured in the magazine and would enjoy learning more about both the firms and their superstars. Along with detailed descriptions of each of the top 100 companies, *Venture Reporter* included pictures and profiles of selected partners from these firms (two each from companies ranked 1–50 and one each from companies 51–100).

When Melanie heard the boarding call for her plane 20 minutes later, her spirits were considerably dampened. Of the 150 venture capital partners and managing directors profiled in the magazine, only 7 (4.7%) were women. For Melanie, that discovery was disheartening. The only silver lining she could find: though the total number of women in the venture capital industry was small, those who were in the game seemed to be doing well. The percentage of "top"

**players was reasonably good given women's under repre-
sentation in the venture capital decision-making ranks.**[12]

**The feature article left little doubt. Women simply were
not a significant force in the venture capital industry in
2002. Melanie wondered what her own chances for success
as a venture capitalist would be.**

Implications

There are several important consequences of the dearth of women decision makers in the venture capital industry. Although not intentionally
discriminatory, the overwhelming "male-ness" of the venture industry
creates significant entry barriers for women entrepreneurs. As we have
already noted, women entrepreneurs are likely to have fewer points of
entry to the network than do their male counterparts and, as we know
from our review of social capital and network theories, all-male venture capital firms will look primarily within their own (predominantly
male) networks when identifying potential investment opportunities.

For those women entrepreneurs who do get their noses (and their
business plans) inside the venture capital tent, most will find that who
and what they are represents a fundamental mismatch with the firm's
historically developed profiles of success. Because estimations of
future success are based on data gathered in the past, the criteria that
venture capitalists use for evaluating an entrepreneur's capabilities
look very male.

At the beginning of this chapter, we promised to look at two critical issues that affect women entrepreneurs' likelihood of securing a
venture capital investment. The first is their ability to tap into the venture capital community through network connections. The second is
the nature of the venture capital community itself—just who is and
who is not a part of the decision-making teams and what their models

of success look like. First, let's examine women's inclusion in or access to the right networks of financial providers.

Getting Access to Venture Capital Investors

Most venture capitalists have a tight and trusted circle of business colleagues who act as gatekeepers for high-potential deals and women have rarely been networked into this small inner circle.
—Trish Costello, Director of the Kauffman Fellows Program

When looking for expansion capital, entrepreneurs who are trying to create the next Fortune 1000 company are likely to seek out equity investors. In many cases, they do so because time is of the essence: They are in a race to claim the market space—or they need to establish patent control of a new technology. They cannot wait until revenues begin providing internally generated funds for growth. In fact, they might never even get into the marketplace without significant up-front capital investments.

Those entrepreneurs with enormous dreams and clear visions often need the most external resources to achieve their goals. They are the ones who write business plans, create elevator pitches, and develop short, pithy PowerPoint presentations. They are out pounding the pavements of Sand Hill Road in Menlo Park, California, and Route 128 in the Boston area, knocking on doors and trying to get the attention of the venture capital community.

However, few (if any) of the deals done originate from plans received over the transom. Just as for entrepreneurs, social networks are important for partners in venture capital firms. The venture firm's deal flow is its lifeblood, so partners are closely attuned to changes in an industry that show great promise. They are constantly seeking out individuals and teams that are in the best position to capitalize on those changes. This is not a "waiting game." Instead, they keep informed about who and what is "hot" through their personal reconnaissance and their extended networks of informal contacts.[13] A venture capital firm's success depends on whom, as much as what, the partners know.

Of course, venture capitalists reported receiving approximately 10 times as many proposals as could reasonably be reviewed each year and as many as 500 times as many as could reasonably be selected for investment. Most firms used a variety of screening mechanisms to winnow the number of business plans submitted to a manageable level. It was clear from our interviews that their network connections, selection criteria, and working models of success are tightly linked.

Each venture firm identifies particular industries, technologies, markets, geographic locations, or stage of business development as criteria for determining which deals to review and which to reject out of hand. Not one of the venture capitalists interviewed identified gender or ethnicity as relevant considerations in their selection process. Their primary concerns were industry, management team, business concept, and resources available.

A venture partner's prior knowledge of an entrepreneur's capabilities (usually based on a direct relationship) provided the most reliable way to gauge the quality and fit of the individual entrepreneur and the managerial team with the venture. A strong recommendation from a trusted colleague or advisor was considered the second most useful way to gauge quality. The preference for entrepreneurs already known to the venture capital decision makers (or to their close circle of advisors) makes network connections an important link in the process of securing resources—not only for getting introductions, but also for providing credible references.

A Connection or a Disconnect?

The overlap between the entrepreneurs' networks and those of the venture capitalists often determines who gets what deals.[14] Most venture capitalists invest in deals brought to them by people they know. In some cases, that might be the entrepreneur herself, but the introduction is more likely to be from another entrepreneur already engaged with the venture capital firm. It might also be a referral from another venture capital partnership that is looking for a coinvestor. Attorneys and accountants sometimes make valuable introductions. Whatever the source of the lead, it must be highly reputable and very selective in the recommendations it makes.

Based on the evidence that we have gathered in our studies of the Springboard applicants, even the most highly qualified women business owners have trouble securing equity capital for their businesses, primarily because they don't know the people and they don't know the ropes. Consider the case of Sherry Watkins, a talented, trained, and experienced woman entrepreneur.

Feeling butterflies dive and soar in the pit of her stomach, Sherry Watkins, founder of ERZ Health Systems, took a deep, steadying breath, as she stood behind the curtain waiting to go on stage at Regional Venture Forum. It had been a long hard haul getting this opportunity to tell the investors she heard shifting in their chairs on the other side of the curtain about ERZ, and she knew this might be her last chance. If she didn't get this investment, she'd have to close down the business.

For three years, Watkins and her team had worked 70- to 80-hour weeks to develop and test the software product they were convinced would change the way Medicare interfaced with health care facilities. The future of her

company hung on her ability to convince the investors in the audience to put up the $1.2 million she needed to keep the company going and get the software to market.

This wasn't the first presentation Sherry Watkins had made to investors. It seemed like she'd done little else over the past 18 months. Some presentations she'd made one-on-one to friends and family over coffee tables and others to angel investors over restaurant tables. But now she had a chance to present to an audience of qualified investors who had paid money to see a handful of companies present their investment opportunities. These people had their checkbooks with them, and if they could be convinced, were willing to strike a deal.

When she was finishing her MBA no one had told her raising money would be this hard. And she hadn't really given it a thought while she was working in the industry. She had worked eight years in software development before joining the top management team of this young start-up company. She'd paid her dues. Why was she having such a hard time getting access to the investors who could see the merit of her opportunity and fuel the next growth stage?

The moderator was beckoning. Watkins took a deep breath and walked to center stage.

There are very few women who are members of the business and social networks that could link them to the people best able to provide critical resources for a rapidly growing business. In spite of her education and experience, Watkins was not in direct contact with people in the investing community. She had worked diligently over the years to establish business competence and credibility. She had deliberately tried to expand what she thought were very useful network connections.

She had joined the local chapter of the National Association of Women Business Owners when she started ERZ three years earlier and became a member of the Rotary Club soon after that. She was active in her church and other civic groups. Contacts she'd made through these groups had helped her recruit several key people to her management team and had given her assistance in putting together an application for a bank loan. She had even used some of these network contacts to test her ideas and to provide feedback. However, none of her connections seemed to be very effective in getting Watkins and her plans before qualified venture capital investors.

Watkins had joined the local chapter of Young Entrepreneur's Organization (YEO) just six months earlier. It was at one of their meetings on raising growth capital where she learned of the Regional Venture Forum from Joe Cassidy, a local attorney and Forum organizer. When Cassidy heard the details about Watkins's company, he encouraged her to apply to the Forum. Although the Forum had only one other women-led company among its presenters over the past three years, he thought Watkins and ERZ stood a good chance. Members of her YEO roundtable echoed Cassidy's encouragement and volunteered to review her business plan and critique her practice presentation.

Until she joined YEO, Watkins had not known that Regional Venture Forums existed. She didn't know Joe Cassidy and certainly didn't know that a roundtable group could be so supportive and helpful. Although there were still no guarantees, it looked like her network connections had at least made inroads.

How unusual is Sherry Watkins's experience? Do other women who want to launch high-potential businesses with significant resource needs have similar experiences? What about the venture capitalists? Do they have women in their networks that have the potential to start high-growth enterprises or are they missing out entirely on this market? If they do meet up with talented women entrepreneurs, do they know how to value the business acumen and leadership currency the women bring to their enterprises?

Missing Links between Women Entrepreneurs and Venture Capitalists

Do You Know the Right People?

We have identified at least two important hurdles that women have to overcome before they can become actively engaged in those networks that include key financial resource providers. The first is a structural hurdle: The fact that women's networks are large and diverse, but made up primarily of family and social acquaintances rather than business contacts means few women are likely to have regular interaction with members of the investing community. The second is a more general selection issue: The gendered nature of industry employment frequently segregates women from the most powerful and effective business networks. These factors combine to present an overwhelming challenge for women entrepreneurs who want to build relationships with venture capital decision makers.

The Diana Project's research on Springboard women entrepreneurs who were seeking financial investments to grow their businesses indicates that these women did, in fact, have sizable networks. In addition, they had cultivated professional relationships with individuals who might be important gatekeepers. More than 70% of the high-growth women entrepreneurs surveyed reported that they had asked a business associate or attorney for advice and over 60% said they consulted accountants, other business owners, and family when they were looking for capital. Overall, they reported contacting up to 30 potential investors and making 12 formal presentations while seeking funding. However, very few reported direct connections to venture capitalists and none reported that they were working closely with entrepreneurs who had already secured venture funding—two of the most direct and productive links to venture capital partners. Table 10.1 summarizes the kind of contacts they used to gain access to the investor community.

TABLE 10.1   Networking Activities: Applicants for San Francisco and Mid-Atlantic Springboard 2000 Forums

Kinds of Advisors Contacted When Seeking Equity Investment	
Business associate	77%
Attorney	71%
Family or friends	69%
Other business owner	65%
Mentor who is fellow business owner	63%
Accountant	61%
Internet	61%
Mentor who doesn't own his or her own business	45%
Banker	39%
State or local business center	38%
General business consultant	36%
College assistance center	32%
Financial consultant	31%
Median number of hours per week talking to advisors	6
Median number of potential investors contacted	30
Median number of formal presentations made	12

Getting Connected

It is clear that entrepreneurs seeking venture capital have much better odds of success if they already know venture capitalists. If they don't have any direct links, they need to develop relationships with people who can open up the gates for them and help them get their deals presented to the right partnerships. The greater the overlap of the entrepreneur's networks and that of the venture capitalist, the more likely the entrepreneur will be able to get an audience, and then to tap into financing, which also provides access to critical knowledge and expertise.

Do They Know You?

Because the venture capital industry is overwhelmingly male and because men report that their networks are predominantly male, it is unlikely that women entrepreneurs' networks will have many points of overlap with those of equity investors. The result is that women will lack information about how to submit their business plans, who to contact, or how to gain attention for their deal. It also means that even if the plan makes its way into the right hands, the entrepreneur will still be an unknown quantity to the investor and thus a higher risk. This disconnect between women entrepreneurs and investors presents a huge challenge for women with high-growth aspirations, but it is also a challenge for the key decision makers in the venture capital network, because they won't "see" plans submitted by women. If they don't socialize and interact with women in a business context, they could be missing some very great opportunities.

Our findings suggest that men and women face many similar challenges in getting attention from potential investors, but in terms of possible network connections, women are severely handicapped. Their current networking activities rarely bring them into direct contact with the male-dominated networks in which they could interact with private equity investors.

Model Misfits

Getting to Yes

Does the gender composition of venture capital partnerships influence firm decision-making models? Yes, if all-male partnerships engender decision-making models and processes that favor men.

The venture capital industry is tightly interconnected and geographically concentrated; the decision makers have, historically, been overwhelmingly male.[15] Although each partnership is separate and distinct, the venture capital industry as a whole shares a set of beliefs and meanings that define membership and behavior. These become the rules of thumb that professionals use to make decisions. These institutional rules often exclude women from serious consideration because women simply don't fit the norm. Because women's capabilities might be more difficult for venture capitalists to estimate, the enterprises they lead are seen as being higher risk.

The combination of a perceived unacceptable risk/return relationship and investment discontinuities pose special problems for firms of varying types of ownership, many of which carry an extra burden of prejudgment with them as they approach the financial community. These include women-owned and minority-owned firms, and family businesses, franchises, and micro-businesses.[16]

Throughout the history of the U.S. venture industry, more than 95% of all investments have been made in ventures led by men. This heavy weighting toward male-led firms suggests that norms, behaviors, and collective beliefs about potential success are based on male models of competence and fit. (In general, men are socialized to be masterful, dominant, and competitive, whereas women are socialized to be nurturing and relational.[17]) If male tendencies are considered the norm for successful entrepreneurs, these views can, over time, become fixed and make it increasingly difficult for women to access venture capital.[18] Although institutional theory recognizes that perceptions and behaviors can evolve, the process occurs very gradually unless there are social upheavals, competitive discontinuities, technological changes, or other jolts.

Can Women Venture Capitalists Change the Equation?

Does the small but growing number of women decision makers in the venture capital industry make a difference to women entrepreneurs? Did the more than 500 women professionals in venture capital firms in 2000 increase the frequency and intensity of venture capital network connections with women entrepreneurs? Did having highly visible women decision makers in specific firms serve as a magnet, attracting more business proposals from women entrepreneurs to their firms, whether or not there was a personal network connection? Did the more senior venture capital women professionals influence institutional practices, particularly decision-making models, behaviors, and norms within their firms? It depends.

Two female pioneers in the venture capital industry were asked to be panelists at a business school conference in 2000. They met for dinner the night before the presentation to compare notes and plan their remarks. They laughed as they recalled their early years in the business. (One had joined her firm in the late 1960s and the other in the early 1980s.)

Each had chosen an assimilation strategy when joining her firm as a young associate. They recalled how important they had felt it was to minimize any differences (real or perceived) between themselves and their male partners. Like their male partners, they sought out only the most promising deals, those that combined innovative concepts and highly qualified entrepreneurs. Neither reported seeing many business plans presented by women, so gender had rarely been discussed in any of their partnership meetings. After some reflection, they decided that their firms might have received more plans from female entrepreneurs because of the fact that there was a female in the partner-

ship—but that didn't mean they were any more likely to make a deal with a female founder. Neither woman would ever have accepted anything less from a woman entrepreneur and, as they focused more intently on the issue, they realized that they probably demanded even more. Partly because there were so few successful female entrepreneurs to serve as models and partly because they did not want to be perceived as showing preferential treatment, the pioneers agreed that early in their careers they held the few women entrepreneurs they encountered to a higher standard.

The Diana Project research team conducted a survey of women partners in mixed-gender venture firms to gain an understanding of how their leadership affected the firms' ability to attract, engage, and invest in women-led ventures (as compared to the industry norms). The venture firms included in the study were chosen because they were early-stage investors, had women partners for a minimum of five years (1995–2000), and had at least $100 million under management. The questions focused on two specific issues:

- Do highly visible and experienced women venture capitalists increase the flow of women-led deals to their partnerships?

- Do highly visible and experienced women venture capitalists influence the decision-making models, processes, norms, and outcomes within their firms?

The Research Process

We identified women venture capitalists that had key decision-making roles and long-term relationships with their firms, using *Pratt's Guide to Venture Capital Sources* as the reference for industry membership at two specific points in time (1995 and 2000).[19] In 1995, *Pratt's Guide* listed 346 women in the professional ranks (associates, principals, and partners or managing directors). By 2000, the number had grown to 510 (see Table 10.2 for the full data set). We identified 118 firms with

TABLE 10.2 U.S. Venture Firms with Women Professionals, 1995 and 2000

| | 1995 Pratts | 2000 Pratts | | | 1995 Pratts | 2000 Pratts | % Increase |
	Firms Listed Only in 1995	Same 118 Companies Indexes Taken Each Year		Firms Listed Only in 2000	Total Number of Firms (601 with 118 Overlap)		
Firms in industry listing women principals	138	118 46%	118	227	256	345	35%
Average staff size listed	4.92	5.67	6.4	6.1	5.27	6.2	18%
Average number of women in firms	1.2	1.53	1.6	1.43	1.35	1.48	10%
Average % of women in listed firms	31%	35%	33%	29%	33%	30%	–9%
Firm reports multiple offices	47 34%	36 31%	33 28%	77 34%	83 32%	110 32%	33%
Average funds under management (000)	121	216	584	361	166	437	163%
Median funds under management (000)	53	100	200	125	67	135	101%
Year firm started (median)	1984	1983	1984	1989	1984	1987	0%
Geographic preference for investments							
U.S.					77 30%	96 28%	
East Coast including Mid-Atlantic					30 12%	27 8%	
West Coast					21 8%	26 8%	
Midwest					11 4%	6 2%	
Global					36 14%	60 17%	
U.S. & Canada					12 5%	26 8%	
No preference					61 24%	70 20%	
Firms with 1 woman listed	113 82%	76 64%	71 60%	163 72%	189 74%	234 68%	24%
Firms with 2 women listed	26 19%	25 21%	28 24%	51 22%	51 20%	79 23%	55%
Firms with 3 or more women listed	3 2%	13 11%	15 13%	13 6%	16 6%	28 8%	75%

TABLE 10.3 Women Professionals in U.S. Venture Firms, 1995 and 2000

	1995 Pratts	2000 Pratts		2000 Pratts	1995 Pratts	2000 Pratts	% Increase
	Firms Listed Only in 1995	Same 118 Companies Indexes Taken Each Year		Firms Listed Only in 2000	Total Number of Firms (601 with 118 Overlap)		
Number of managerial women in industry[a]	166	180	186	324	346	510	47%
Number of women at top decision level[b]	62	66	82	126	128	208	63%
Average number of women at top level	1.11	1.25	1.27	1.26	1.17	1.26	8%
% of women at top level	39%	40%	48%	45%	40%	46%	17%
Firms with at least one women at top decision level	56 41%	53 45%	63 53%	100 44%	109 43%	165 48%	51%
Firms with 1 woman at top decision level	50 36%	41 35%	50 42%	83 37%	91 36%	135 39%	48%
Firms with 2 women at top decision level	6 4%	11 9%	10 8%	15 7%	17 7%	25 7%	47%
Firms with 3–5 women at top decision level		1 1%	3 3%	0 0%	1 0%	3 1%	200%
Firms with 5 or more women at top decision level			0%	2 1%	1 0%	2 1%	
Number of women at mid decision level	53 31%	64 41%	66 38%	103 30%	117 36%	169 38%	44%
Average number of women at midlevel	1.13	1.25	1.25	1.1	1.19	1.15	–3%
% of women at midlevel	34%	39%	39%	37%	36%	38%	4%
Firms with at least one woman at mid decision level	47 34%	51 43%	52 44%	94 41%	98 38%	147 43%	50%
Firms with 1 woman at mid decision level	42 30%	43 36%	41 35%	86 38%	85 33%	128 37%	51%

Firms with 2 women at mid decision level	4	3%	5	4%	10	8%	7	3%	9	4%	17	5%
Firms with 3–5 women at mid decision level	1	1%	3	3%	1	1%	1	0%	4	2%	2	0%
Firms with 5 or more women at mid decision level												
Number of women at low level	43	25%	35	22%	23	13%	48	14%	78	24%	71	16%
Average number of women at low level	1.08		1.13		1.28		1.17		1.1		1.2	
% of women at low level	27%		21%		13%		17%		24%		16%	
Firms with at least one woman at low decision level	40	29%	31	26%	18	15%	41	18%	71	28%	59	17%
Firms with 1 woman at low decision level	37	27%	27	23%	14	12%	37	16%	64	25%	51	15%
Firms with 2 women at low decision level	3	2%	4	3%	3	3%	1	0%	7	3%	4	1%
Firms with 3–5 women at low decision level					1	1%	3	1%			4	1%
Firms with 5 or more women at low decision level												
Career Path												
Company migration[c]												
Number of women at same company '95 & '00	109				109				109	32%		
Women who changed firms between '95 & '00	11	7%			3	2%			14	4%		
Women who left industry after '95	155	93%			67	36%			222	64%		

(rightmost "% change" column: Firms with 2 women at mid = 89%; Firms with 3–5 women at mid = -50%; Number of women at low level = -9%; Average number of women at low level = 9%; % of women at low level = -34%; Firms with at least one woman at low decision level = -17%; Firms with 1 woman at low decision level = -20%; Firms with 2 women at low decision level = -43%)

a Number of women in industry based on count of first or middle name perceived as feminine.
b Women's decision-making hierarchy measures are based on job title. Because not all listings had titles, the number is less than the total number of women.
c Career migration calculated using women's names (not titles) to track 1995 to 2000.

at least one woman on the professional roster in both 1995 and 2000, although in several cases it was not the same woman (67 women left these firms between 1995 and 2000; 73 were added).

There were 109 women professionals who were not only in the industry, but also at the same firm in both 1995 and 2000. We narrowed the list to include only those women who met the criteria of senior rank (partner or managing director) with five or more years of experience in the same partnership and with funds of $100 million or more under management. The highly specified subset included only 34 women. These "high-profile" female venture capitalists who had been with the same firms for a minimum of five years were deemed visible to women entrepreneurs through the *Pratt's Guide to Venture Capital Sources* listings. We concluded that they had sufficient time to have had an impact on the firm's decision-making models and processes.

We interviewed many of these leading women venture capitalists to determine their interest or success in attracting more female-led deals to the firm. We also wanted to understand how these women partners and managing directors were shaping their firms' decision-making rules, processes, and behaviors (see Table 10.4). Our interviews concentrated on deal flow from women entrepreneurs, decision-making criteria within the firms, and views of the industry structure and norms.

None of these women participated in funds that specifically targeted female entrepreneurs and none expressed a preference for women-led ventures. All of the partnerships included male partners. Funds under management ranged from $100 million to more than $5 billion. The partnerships have been in operation from 14 to 34 years. The large funds tended to be more highly diversified in terms of industry focus and stage of investment.[20]

In their discussion of how their firms sourced new deals, the women venture capitalists indicated that their firms received unsolicited (over the transom) business plans, but were unlikely to invest in these. Preferred sources of deals included referrals from entrepreneurs in their networks and from other venture capitalists in the industry. All

TABLE 10.4   Interview Topics for Female Venture Capitalists

Individual demographics:	Name, firm, title, years with firm, career path at firm; previous experience in venture capital, in other industries, education, business responsibilities within the firm, special investment, and management focus within firm.
Firm demographics:	Age, funds under management, number of funds raised, size of firm, industry and stage preferences, primary source of deals.
Relationships with women entrepreneurs:	In own network, in over the transom deals, in general partnership deals; number presented, seriously reviewed by partners, invested in; current state of those investments; performance evaluation of those deals; performance relative to total portfolio of deals.
Open-ended discussion of:	Women entrepreneurs and their attractiveness to venture capitalists; women in venture capital — their careers, opportunities, rewards, and challenges; industry changes and expectations for the future.

of them indicated that they actively prospected for potential entrepreneurs in their preferred industry sectors and "positioned themselves in the mainstream of deal flows." A few of the women venture capitalists believed that they knew more entrepreneurial women than did their male colleagues and so had expanded the firm's network.

They were careful to point out that they did not have any preference for doing business with these women — at least not on the basis of gender. However, they believed that being connected through a professional network enabled them to know more about the talent and experience of the entrepreneurs and to make a more informed judgment about the entrepreneur's likelihood of success. A few indicated that male venture capitalists in their own firms or in other firms sometimes referred female entrepreneurs to them "because they might understand the deal better" or be more likely to "connect" with the entrepreneur, but they did not think that these were important considerations.

Just over 70% of the women venture capitalists were in partnerships that had made investments in female-led ventures. They reported multiple deals done, but believed that only a few of these investments (a cosmetics venture and a women's Web site) had any gender-related aspects. Although they could not report the total number of investments made by their partnerships in women-led ventures over time, the majority of the women indicated that their male partners had also brought in women-led ventures that were funded by the firm. Nine such deals were specified by name.

Performance Review

The women venture capitalists reported that the performance of the women-led ventures was on a par with overall portfolio performance. One reported that of her two investments, one was a big hit, selling at 14 times the investment, but the other was sold at a loss. Another reported that her two investments were sold—one in a private sale at a loss and the other at a substantial gain in a public offering. Another reported poor performance by one investment, but noted that the result was related to industry performance rather than the entrepreneur. Two of the women reported that they found it more difficult to manage portfolio companies with a woman CEO because women frequently associate business-related criticism with personal criticism and do not respond well in times of crisis.

The women investors were adamant that they did not invest in deals led by women because of any gender preference. They believed that the deal flow of women-led ventures to their firms was somewhat enhanced by their own network connections. However, to a woman, they insisted that they subjected every woman-led venture to the same high standards and scrutiny as any other deal. They noted the biggest problem in funding female entrepreneurs was the dearth of high-quality women-led businesses—a problem they traced back to the human capital issues of technical training and management experience. They observed that very few women were equipped to compete in the highest growth industries; they believed that women were making progress in the software arena.

The women venture capitalists reported that they held themselves and their deals to the same high standards as did their male partners, but several noted that they had influenced the decision-making process positively by bringing a new (more thoughtful and questioning) approach to the review process. One pointed out that the meetings were somewhat more formal because of her presence and, as a result, were likely to be more thorough.

They made several observations about being women partners in a predominantly male industry. Most said that the business was "gender blind" and that the partners made their choices of management partners and investments on the basis of objective quality standards. The women who had been in the industry the longest noted that there might have been unusual challenges to being female in their early years, but that those no longer existed. Several of the women observed that there is not a strong sense of collegiality or networking among the women professionals in the industry and some noted that women venture capitalists are more competitive with each other than are their male counterparts.

What Next?

The results of the interviews offer some promise, but also indicate that there is much work to be done. Women professionals in the venture capital industry have attracted more female-led ventures to their firms, even though they are not actively seeking out women-led ventures. The fact that women partners have apparently broadened the venture capitalist reach to include more women supports previous research findings that women have more women in their networks than men.[21] However, only a small number of the deals proposed are seriously considered and very few are accepted. Women entrepreneurs appear to continue to be disadvantaged in the broader referral system that provides venture capitalists with many of the most promising leads.

On the other hand, women venture capitalists perceive that the major barriers for women entrepreneurs are more closely related to human capital deficiencies rather than to social capital and network access. Because women do lag men in technical training, this observation might be a function of the fact that their venture firms specialize in technology. The data from the Springboard Forums does not appear consistent with these observations of inadequate human capital.[22]

The observation that the industry is gender blind and that investment choices are made based on objective standards seems to be a contradiction of sorts. Anecdotal and empirical evidence suggests that investment decisions are often more subjective, based on gut feeling rather than being truly objective. This raises the question of whether women in the venture capital industry are adopting the norms and beliefs of their male partners (rather than changing them) to succeed in their roles.

The women venture capitalists observed that their participation in the decision-making process has influenced discussions in new and positive ways, particularly in bringing new perspectives to the table. However, these changes have not resulted in substantial changes in the number or quality of investments in female-led businesses. There might be some institutional change taking place in the industry, but it is an extremely slow process. If and when there is a perceived benefit in accelerating change, it could come as a result of industry or policy mandate.

What Can You Do to Change Things?

Investigate Organizations That Provide Support

The Small Business Administration (SBA) has launched a Women's Network for Entrepreneurial Training (WNET). The mentoring program provides an opportunity for informal mentoring relationships between experienced women business owners and women whose businesses are ready to grow. Other resources include the following:

1. Online government-sponsored Web sites for women business owners. For example, *www.women-21.gov* is a joint effort of the Department of Labor and SBA to provide a one-stop federal resource for information, registration for online programs, and networking.

2. Mentoring "roundtables" throughout the country. See *http://ftp .sbaonline.sba.gov/womeninbusiness/wnet_roundtables.html*

In addition to using SBA resources, call colleges and universities in your area to determine what resources they can provide. Attend enterprise forums. Learn from other entrepreneurs and from professionals who support entrepreneurs.

Build Entrepreneurial Connections Now

Choose an influential entrepreneur from the community whose business is two stages further along than yours. Phone the person and say that you have been following the growth and development of their company through the media and others in the business community and that you're quite impressed with what they've been able to accomplish. Tell them that you have a business in a different industry sector, but one that is related via channel of distribution, production, and so forth. Let the entrepreneur know that you are trying to grow the company and would welcome her sage advice. Ask if you can buy this person lunch to learn more about how you can advance your own business.

Do Additional Venture Capital Research and Make Contact

Research the venture capital providers in your community. Try to identify a venture capital company that's right for you, based on industrial sector and stage of investment. Look at the companies they've funded and scour the list of senior managers at those portfolio companies. Try to find someone you went to school with or with whom you have something else in common. Call that person and ask for an informational meeting. If that goes well, ask for an introduction to his or her venture capital partners.

If you cannot locate an individual who can provide the connection, call a member of the venture capital team. Tell them that you are not looking for money at this time, but that you have a business in the early stage of development in a sector that is of particular interest to them. Briefly relate your success to date and suggest the potential you believe the business has. Ask for advice on what you can do to further develop it for that growth. Offer to buy this person breakfast or lunch.

In summary, take charge. Do your homework and then take the risk—get out there and meet people who can help. Tell them your story; begin to build their confidence in you and your business. Ask for the help they can provide and continue to pursue every lead.

Notes

1. National Venture Capital Association Web site, *www.nvca.org*.

2. Gompers, P., & Lerner, J. 1999. *The Venture Capital Cycle*. Cambridge, MA: The MIT Press.

3. Gompers, P., & Lerner, J. 1995. *The use of covenants: An empirical analysis of venture partnership agreements*. Working Paper 95-047, Division of Research, Harvard Business School.

4. DRI-WEFA, A Global Insight Company: Economic Impact of Venture Capital, 2002. Summary accessed July 21, 2003, at *www.nvca.org/nvca06_25_02.html*.

5. Gompers & Lerner.1999. op. cit.

6. Ibid.

7. Petzinger, T. 2000, January 3. So long supply and demand. *Wall Street Journal*, Millennium Edition.

8. National Venture Capital Association Web site, *www.nvca.org*.

9. Ibid.

10. *Venture Reporter*. 2002, May–June. Rising Tide Studios, New York. 8–94.

11. *Pratt's Guide to Venture Capital Sources*. 1995. Wellesley Hills, MA: Venture Economics, Inc.

12. *Venture Reporter*. 2002, May–June. Rising Tide Studios, New York. 8–94.

13. Bygrave, W. D. 1992. Venture capital returns in the 1980s, in D. L. Sexton & J. Kasarda (Eds.). *The State of the Art of Entrepreneurship*. Boston: PWS Kent: 438–462; Alimansky, B. 2000. Eight ways to ruin your chances of raising equity capital. *Journal of Private Equity*. Summer: 78–83.

14. Tybee, T. T., & Bruno, A. V. 1984. A model of venture capitalist investment activity. *Management Science*. 30: 1051–1076; Freear, J., Sohl, J., & Wetzel, W. E., Jr. 1992. The investment attitudes, behavior, and characteristics of high net worth individuals, in N. C. Churchill, S. Birley, W. D. Bygrave, D. F. Muzyka, C. Wahlbin, & W. E. Wetzel, Jr. (Eds.). *Frontiers of Entrepreneurship Research*. Wellesley, MA: Babson College: 374–387; Fiet, J. O. 1996. Fragmentation in the market for venture capital. *Entrepreneurship Theory & Practice*. 21: 5–20.

15. Bygrave, 1992. op. cit.; Timmons, J., & Sapienza, H. J., 1992. Venture capital: The decade ahead, in D. L. Sexton & J. D. Kasarda (Eds.). *The State of the Art of Entrepreneurship*. Boston: PWS Kent: 402–437; Brush, C. G., Carter, N. M., Gatewood, E. J., Greene, P. G., & Hart, M. M., 2001. Women business owners and equity capital: The myths dispelled. *Insight Report*. Kansas City, MO: Kauffman Center for Entrepreneurial Leadership.

16. Brophy, D., 1997. *Financing the Growth of Entrepreneurial Firms*. Chicago, IL: Upstart Publishing.

17. Gilligan, C., 1982. *In a different voice: Psychological theory and women's development*. Cambridge, MA: Harvard University Press; Aldrich, H., 1989. Networking among women entrepreneurs, in O. Hagan, C. Rivshun, D. Sexton (Eds.). *Women-owned businesses*. pp. 103–132. New York: Praeger.

18. Greenwood, R., Suddaby, R., & Hinings, C. R., 2002, February. Theorizing change: The role of professional associations in the transformation of institutional fields. *Academy of Management Journal*, 45(1): 58.

19. Although there are many directories of the industry, including the membership roster of the National Venture Capital Association and *Galante's Venture Capital and Private Equity Directory*, *Pratt's* is widely recognized as a comprehensive and consistent source of information. Every U.S. firm listing published in the 1995 and 2000 editions of the *Guides* was reviewed to identify females on the professional management track—associates, principals, partners, and managing directors. (In those cases in which the gender of a name was ambiguous, company Web sites were searched for information and, when gender was not verified, the entry was omitted.) Each individual entry was coded by year and job title. Firm characteristics included name, parent company (if any), location(s), age, size of funds, date of last fund raised, and investment preferences by industry and stage. The number and gender of other senior decision-making employees (partners or directors) and professionals (principals and associates) at the firm was also included.

20. For the most part, their primary industry concentration was in either software and software services or health care and medical devices. Approximately 40% of the women venture capitalists had technical undergraduate degrees (engineering, math, science) and more than 70% had MBA degrees. More than

50% had prior experience in the high-technology industry and 30% had been entrepreneurs.

21. Aldrich, 1989. op. cit.

22. Springboard Venture Forums were created to accelerate the process of women's access to equity capital. Events were held in six cities, including Boston, San Francisco, New York, and Washington, DC. The program was led by a consortium of business organizations and advocates including Oracle Corporation, Chase Manhattan, Harvard Business School, Northwestern University, Center for Women & Enterprise, Arch Ventures, and Silicon Valley Bank. These events showcased more than 200 women entrepreneurs at forums attended by more than 1,000 investors.

11

IN CONCLUSION

As promised, we have told you almost everything we know about the hurdles that women entrepreneurs must clear if they want their companies to be counted among the big winners. We have included many issues that all entrepreneurs must overcome, but we have also shown how these hurdles are higher for women.

We have provided you with a list of the major concerns that investors often express about women entrepreneurs, starting with their reservations about whether women have the right aspirations and ambitions to lead a high-growth venture. Many question if women set their sites high enough and can maintain the personal drive and commitment to see their enterprises through the many challenges that lie ahead.

We have also addressed the questions that trouble so many investors about women's capabilities to lead high-growth ventures. Because technology is so fundamental to most of today's most scalable ventures, women's education and experience is often seen as problematic. There continues to be some concern about women's understanding of numbers—particularly as they relate to finance—but we have presented substantial evidence that women are well trained in math and that an ever-growing number are also formally trained in business administration. The one remaining educational or experience barrier is technology. Relatively few women choose engineering, so they are unprepared—either by training or profession—to lead hardware, software, and semiconductor businesses. On the other hand, women are a very strong force in the life sciences and are gaining experience in the field. Many are poised to lead new businesses in the biotech field. Many women who are not technologists by training have brought tremendous organizational skills to lead high-technology companies. Meg Whitman (eBay) and Donna Dubinsky (Palm Computing and Handspring) are prime examples of such "nontechnical" high-tech entrepreneurs.

Of course, educational training and prior industry experience are directly linked to the strategic choices an entrepreneur makes, so most women choose industries that are not technology driven (retail and service sectors). Consequently, they often are excluded from the highest-growth industry sectors and their business concepts are less likely to be easily scaled up. Although not all high-potential businesses require software, hardware, or Internet expertise, but, in the industry sectors that most women choose, it is much harder to achieve the broad market coverage afforded by rapid rollout, or market dominance that comes with establishing a leading brand, or to realize the economies of scale that come with increasingly efficient manufacturing and distribution processes.

We have also pointed out how important relationships are in building any business—but particularly in building a large-scale business. All entrepreneurs are challenged to assemble a rich array of resources to get the business launched and to support it through its growth stages. Most entrepreneurs draw on their personal knowledge and reputations to gain access to the men and women who actually have the necessary resources. Although certainly not the only critical resource, money is fundamental. It provides the currency to acquire human, technical, and physical assets for the company. Financial capital can be drawn from personal reserves and can also be garnered from family and friends, but when these sources are tapped out, most entrepreneurs must turn to the institutional debt and equity markets.

Women entrepreneurs have achieved much greater access to personal and commercial debt. Although they do not draw on that source as often or as deeply as do male entrepreneurs, they have found the channels open and the money available, once they have established their businesses, acquired some bankable assets that serve as collateral, or established a predictable cash flow sufficient to support the debt.

What women entrepreneurs have not been very successful in doing is tapping into the private equity markets. They have received a very small share of the venture capital funds invested over the past 50 years and they continue to struggle for recognition and funding from that direction. We see the venture capital connection as one of the highest hurdles yet to be cleared by talented and ambitious women entrepreneurs. The fact that women are not in the equity funding networks and that they have very few points of overlap means that getting an audience is very difficult for women. For those who are able to run the gauntlet and get past the preliminary screenings, there is yet another hurdle to clear. More than 95% of successful venture capital deals have been led by men. Venture capitalists' models of what a winning entrepreneur looks like are very male—in style, presentation, education, experience, and social skills. Even the most talented woman will not fit the model, so she must overwhelm the past while she paints the picture of an extraordinary future.

We have shown you how women are often discounted on the basis of who they are, what businesses and industries they choose, and finally who they know and who knows them. We also explained where these perceptions come from—the historical expectations about women's roles in society, work, and family and the belief in the stereotypical heroic entrepreneur. Although there are variations on the degree to which these are believed or true, the reality is that the paradox exists.

We have provided some insights about these perceptions that you can use to enhance your own chances of success.

You are responsible for your own dreams and success. You need to think carefully about why you are becoming an entrepreneur. Are your dreams big enough to include others? Are you willing and able to share responsibility, ownership, control, and rewards to build a substantial and valuable business? If so, do you have the right tools? Does your package of education and experience qualify you to create and lead an enterprise of the size and type you have chosen? If not, are you willing to build your own repertoire of skills and capabilities or are you able to expand your company's capabilities by working with one or two founding partners whose skills, capabilities, and connections complement your own? If you are willing, are you able to sell your dream to people who can help you best? Can you build a blue ribbon management team that can get the necessary resources and execute the plan flawlessly?

As you think about your plan for a new venture, can you honestly say the industry itself is young, vital, growing, and potentially very rewarding? Will the rising tide of that industry be likely to sweep you and your business along toward success or will you be struggling just to stay afloat in a mature industry already crowded with well-established and well-resourced competitors?

If the industry is robust, do you have a concept that is unique, valuable, and somehow protectable? Is it potentially big? Will it be able to generate annual revenues of $100 million to $500 million within the next four to five years? What assurance can you provide that your business will not only be large and profitable, but will also be sustainable over a long period of time?

Will you be able to carve out exclusive territories or customer and supplier relationships? Will you be able to patent your technology and maintain a quality-service lead through that technology? If you cannot protect your business with the legal tools of patents, licenses, or franchise agreements, can you claim and hold the market through early mover advantage, tightly structured customer relationships, or loyalty-building techniques? The answers will depend on your strategic choices, your negotiating skills, and your resources.

Brilliant ideas are wonderful, but they are only dreams until an entrepreneur makes the personal commitment and marshals the resources necessary to execute those ideas. Getting resources is one of the most fundamental of entrepreneurial skills and it is very dependent on identifying, attracting, and engaging partners in your business. Educated identification is often based on prior experience. It is very important for an entrepreneur to know to whom to go to and to understand the pros and cons of working with specific individuals. Knowing enables an entrepreneur to identify the right partners and go after them with laser-like focus.

It is equally important in the resource game for the entrepreneur to be known—either personally or by reputation. It is only through personal or extended network connections that an entrepreneur can attract and engage resource partners. When she does, she must rely on their reputations and integrity to arrive at a deal that is equitable for all parties.

We know that women might think that they have men in their networks, so they might include some men from the predominantly male venture capital industry in their networks. However, men do not see it quite the same way. Very few of them reported having women in their business networks, so they are unlikely to be familiar with women entrepreneurs. We know that women can sometimes get access to the right decision makers by using intermediaries—other entrepreneurs, professionals in law and accounting. They then will have to rely on their intermediaries for social capital as well as introductions, because they will not have personal reserves of reputation and favors on which to trade. You can begin to make changes in your network connections by actively seeking out new avenues of exchange—by becoming involved in entrepreneurial forums and using the links provided by universities (e.g., MIT Enterprise Forum), professional groups (Commonwealth Institute, eMerging Women), agencies (Center for Women and Enterprise), and government-sponsored programs. Of course, attending meetings is only the first step. You will need to become actively engaged with other members of the groups, providing feed-back and support to them when possible and stating clearly your own interests and needs. These are long-term relationships, so it is best to get involved early and build the network connections gradually, but deliberately.

We don't expect women entrepreneurs to change the nature of the venture capital industry, but we are confident that there are many women working toward that goal. When the venture industry begins to include more women decision makers, women entrepreneurs will find it easier to make direct connections and to get into the screening process. If the men and women in the industry are good indicators of what will follow next, we can expect that women's business proposals will be held to the same high standards of performance and profitability as would any man's. For the foreseeable future, they will probably be held to an even higher standard because there are still so many unknowns associated with women as entrepreneurial leaders. Everything from what venture capitalists see as potential conflict between business and family demands to the different management and leadership styles that women bring to the table spells "risk" to investors unfamiliar with how these differences might impact firm performance.

We have provided recommendations for change—both large and small—throughout the book and we have every confidence that you can act on them. We are thrilled that you have the energy, ambition, vision, and commitment to lead the next generation of entrepreneurial blockbusters. We know that you will have to be entrepreneurial from beginning to end and that many of the challenges you will face are just part of the process. The need for vision, commitment, resources, and execution is universal. Your big challenge will be that many of the part-ners that you will need to make your visions a reality will have reserva-tions or concerns about your ability to succeed, at least in part because you are a woman. We encourage you not to let that deter you.

Remember that entrepreneurship is about change. It is both creative—in that it offers something new and improved—and it is destructive—in that what is new often displaces or replaces what already exists. This "creative destruction"[1] described by Schumpeter is exhilarating, but it is also difficult and sometimes frightening. If you accept the challenge to create something truly innovative, you can take a leadership role in changing the world.

Entrepreneurship is the instrument of social, political, technological, and economic change. It fosters creativity, provides individual rewards, and contributes to overall economic development. It provides an opportunity to solve business and social problems, to develop new jobs, and to create personal wealth. In a world where intellectual rather than physical strength is the basis of power, women are now gaining equal footing. There is no reason to believe that women should not have equal opportunity in the entrepreneurial arena. We hope this book has provided you with the tools to turn your biggest dreams into reality.

Note

1. Schumpeter, J. 1934. *The Theory of Economic Development*. Cambridge, MA: Harvard University Press.

INDEX

M

McBride, Jane, 201
Malcom, Marla, 68
Management team building,
    206–207
  areas of consideration, 193
  benefits, 192
  by women (perceptions about),
      195
    ability to make tough decision
        (questions about),
        197–198
    ownership-sharing questions,
        195–196, 198–199
    "right-way" ("male" success
        model) approach, 196
    women as network outsiders,
        196
  as challenge to growth, 27
  challenges to, 205–206
  vs. founding team, 192–193
  and perceptions about women
      (case example), 194–195
  reasons for, 191–192
  strategic considerations, 202
    cultural dimensions, 204–205
    functional vs. relationship
        issues, 202–203
    guideline questions for poten-
        tial candidates, 203–204
  see also Flight Time, Inc. man-
      agement team building case
      example
Marimba Software, 159
Marks, Valerie, 73
Mary Kay Cosmetics, 142
Mason, Linda, 168
Maui Goose of Hawaii, Ltd., 79
Mentors, 186–187
Microloan program, 118

Microsoft, 215
Mirant, 100
MIT Enterprise Forum, 55
Morby, Jacqui, 221
Motek, 104
Motives, 70–71
  and level of commitment, 71
  motivation for entrepreneurship,
      68, 72–74
    differences by gender, 74
    push or pull catalysts, 73
    self-analysis issues, 250
Motown Records, 197
Mrs. Field's Cookies, 142, 161–162
Mulcahy, Anne, 100
Museumshop.com, 155–156
MyPsych.com, case example,
    143–144

N

The National, 79
National Association of Women's
    Business Owners (NAWBO),
    78
NaturalLink, development case
    study, 103
Networks, 167
  benefits of, 174–175
    heterogeneity benefits,
        178–179
    homogeneity benefits,
        177–178
  boundaries/barriers, 175
    group behavior, 177
    personal identity issues, 175
    social identity issues, 176
  and challenges to growth, 27
  creation of (strategies for),
      187–188, 243, 251–252

ABOUT THE AUTHORS

Dr. Candida Brush is an Associate Professor of Strategy and Policy Director of the Council for Women's Entrepreneurship and Leadership (CWEL), and Research Director for the Entrepreneurial Management Institute at Boston University. She was a Research Affiliate to Jonkoping International Business School, Jonkoping, Sweden. She received her DBA from Boston University, an MBA from Boston College and a BA from the University of Colorado. She is the author of two books; *International Entrepreneurship: The Effect of Age on Motives for Internationalization*, and *The Woman Entrepreneur: Starting, Financing and Managing a Successful New Business* (Lexington Books, 1986), and has written sixteen book chapters, and more than 50 articles which are published in scholarly journals such as, *Journal of Business Venturing, Strategic Management Journal, Entrepreneurship Theory and Practice, Journal of Management, Venture Capital Journal, Academy of Management Executive, Journal of Small Business Management, and Journal of Business Research*. She has authored papers for the Organization for Economic Cooperation and Development (OECD) and International Labour Organization (ILO).

Brush is the 2001 recipient of the Entrepreneurship Mentor Award, given by the National Academy of Management Entrepreneurship Division and co-authored a paper receiving the SBIDA best conceptual paper for 2002. Dr. Brush was one of 18 researchers selected to participate in the 1995 *White House Conference Research Project: The Future of Small Business and Entrepreneurship into the Year 2010*, and was recognized by *Inc.* magazine in 1995 as one of the top 16 researchers in Entrepreneurship in the US. Dr. Brush served on the Executive Committee of the Entrepreneurship Division of the National Academy of Management, was an elected member of the Executive Committee for the Entrepreneurship Research Consortium (ERC), now referred to as the Panel Study of Entrepreneurial Dynamics (PSED), an international study of business start-ups. She served on the Defense Advisory Committee on Women in the Services (DACOWITS), an advisory committee to the Department of Defense, was a member of Fleet-Boston's Advisory Board, The Women Entrepreneur's Connection, and served on the Research Advisory Committee for the National Foundation of Women Business Owners. She is on the Board of Directors of Camp Starfish, a non-profit organization sponsoring a camp for emotionally handicapped children.

Professor Brush had early entrepreneurial experience in the airline industry, small business consulting and land development. Her current research investigates the ways women start and grow businesses, and resource acquisition strategies of in emerging ventures. Most recently with four other researchers, she was funded by the Kauffman Center for Entrepreneurial Leadership, U.S. Small Business Administration, the National Women's Business Council and ESBI (Sweden) to investigate women's access to equity capital, for research referred to as *the Diana Project*. A book, *Clearing the Hurdles: Women Building High-Growth Businesses* is forthcoming from Prentice Hall-Financial Times in May 2004.

Dr. Nancy M. Carter is the Richard M. Schulze Chair in Entrepreneurship and directed the John M. Morrison Center at the University of St. Thomas, Minneapolis, Minnesota. She is Leverhulme Visiting Professor at London Business School, London, England, and Scholar-in-Residence at the Entrepreneurship and Small Business Research Center (ESBRI), in Stockholm, Sweden. Prior to joining the faculty at St. Thomas, she was Coleman Foundation Chair in Entrepreneurship at Marquette University, Milwaukee, Wisconsin. Professor Carter  directs the MBA entrepreneurship program at St. Thomas. She has worked professionally in advertising and marketing research and works closely with government and private sector initiatives promoting entrepreneurship.

Dr. Carter serves on the International Board of Advisors, Jönköping International Business School, Sweden, and the Board of Directors of the Women's Business Research Center, Washington, D.C. She co-founded the Entrepreneurial Research Consortium, the organizing group for the Panel Study of Entrepreneurial Dynamics (PSED) and the *Diana Project*, a collaborative initiative between five universities to promote women-led growth companies. As part of her leadership directing centers of entrepreneurship at the University of St. Thomas and Marquette University she developed and implemented programs and curriculum for prospective and practicing entrepreneurs including a center for family business. She is closely involved with the U.S. Department of Commerce initiatives to extend entrepreneurship globally.

Her research focuses on the emerging growth businesses with a special emphasis on women- and minority-owned led ventures. She has published widely on organizations, strategy, and entrepreneurship. Her work has appeared in academic and trade publications including *American Sociological Review, Venture Capital Journal, Journal of Business Venturing, Academy of Management Journal, Strategic Management Journal, Entrepreneurship and Regional Development, Management International Review, Organization Studies, Journal of Management Studies, Journal of Management, Human Relations,* and *Journal of Managerial Issues.* She serves on the editorial review boards of *Entrepreneurship Theory and Practice, Journal of Small Business Management, Journal of Developmental Entrepreneurship,* and the editorial team of the *17th and 18th* editions of *Frontiers of Entrepreneurship Research.* Her research on women and minority entrepreneurs has been funded the National Science Foundation, the U.S. Small Business Administration, the National Business Women's Council, and the Ewing Marion Kauffman Foundation. She received her Ph.D. in Business Administration from the University of Nebraska, MA in Mass Communications from California State University, and BA in Journalism from the University of Nebraska.

Elizabeth J. Gatewood, Ph.D., is the Jack M. Gill Chair of Entrepreneurship and Director of The Johnson Center for Entrepreneurship & Innovation at Indiana University. Her work in entrepreneurial cognition received the National Foundation of Independent Business Award for best paper at the 2001 Babson-Kauffman Foundation Entrepreneurship Research Conference. She is a member of the "Diana" project, a research study of women business owners and equity capital access, funded by the Kauffman Center for Entrepreneurial Leader-

ship, the US Small Business Administration, and the National Women's Business Council. Her research has been published in the *Journal of Business Venturing*, the *Journal of Venture Capital, Entrepreneurship Theory & Practice, the Journal of Small Business Management*, and *Entrepreneurship and Regional Development*.

She is a past chair of the Entrepreneurship Division of the Academy of Management. She received the 1996 Advocate Award for outstanding contributions to the field of entrepreneurship from the Academy of Management. Dr. Gatewood was named the Texas Women in Business Advocate of the Year by the U.S. Small Business Administration. She serves on the National Advisory Board for Entrepreneurship Education of the Kauffman Foundation. She also serves on the Advisory Board for Spring Mill Ventures, a venture capital firm of the Village Ventures network.

Prior to her arrival at Indiana University in 1998, Dr. Gatewood was the Executive Director of the Gulf Coast Small Business Development Center Network, an organization providing training and consulting services to entrepreneurs and small business owners in the greater Houston region. Dr. Gatewood founded and served as director of the Center for Business and Economic Studies at the University of Georgia from 1983–1989. She taught at the Nijenrode Institute of Business in The Netherlands. She holds a BS in Psychology from Purdue University and an MBA in Finance and Ph.D. in Business Administration with a specialty in strategy from the University of Georgia.

Patricia G. Greene is the Dean of the Undergraduate School at Babson College, which holds the distinction of being ranked in the number one position for entrepreneurship education by *U.S. News and World Report*. She also holds the President's Endowed Chair in Entrepreneurship. Prior to this position she held the Ewing Marion Kauffman/Missouri Chair in Entrepreneurial Leadership at the University of Missouri–Kansas City (1998–2003) and the New Jersey Chair of Small Business and Entrepreneurship at Rutgers University  sity (1996–1998). Dr. Greene is a native of Hamburg, Pennsylvania. She earned a Ph.D. from the University of Texas at Austin, an MBA from the University of Nevada, Las Vegas, and a BS from the Pennsylvania State University. She was a founding member of the Rutgers Center for Entrepreneurial Management and the coordinator of the Rutgers Entrepreneurship Curriculum. At UMKC she helped to found KC SourceLink, the Entrepreneurial Growth Resource Center (EGRC), the iStrategy Studio, the Business and Information

Development Group (BRIDG), the UMKC Students in Free Enterprise Program (SIFE), the Kauffman Entrepreneurship Internship Program (KEIP), the Entrepreneurial Effect, the Network for Entrepreneurship Educators and Researchers (NEER), and the annual regional Business Plan Competition.

Dr. Greene's research focuses on the identification, acquisition, and combination of entrepreneurial resources, particularly by women and minority entrepreneurs. She is a founding member of the Diana Project, a research group focusing on women and the venture capital industry. Her work has been published in journals including *Journal of Business Venturing, Venture Capital, Entrepreneurship Theory and Practice, Journal of Business Research, Small Business Economics, Academy of Management Executive, Journal of Small Business Management* and *The National Journal of Sociology*.

Greene serves on the educational advisory board of the Center for Venture Education and the research advisory board of the Capital Formation Institute. She is co-chair of the Steering Committee for the Entrepreneurship Affinity Group of the AACSB. She has served on other advisory boards including those of the State of Missouri Small Business Development Centers, Kansas Women's Business Center, Growth Opportunity Connection, the Kansas City ATHENA*PowerLink*™ and the Helzberg Entrepreneurial Mentoring Program. Greene is a frequent speaker at national and international events. Prior to becoming a professor she worked primarily in the health care industry.

Myra Hart is the MBA Class of 1961 Chair of Management Practice at Harvard Business School. Her research and teaching focus on entrepreneurship—particularly the founding of high potential new ventures—and women in the professional world. She is a member of the Diana Project, a research team of five professors investigating women entrepreneurs' access to capital. Hart is the author or co-author of several books, book chapters, journal articles and more than 60 Harvard Business School cases and notes. She currently serves as the faculty director of the Marjorie Alfus/Committee of 200 Case Writing Initiative—a program created in 1998 to increase the availability of quality teaching materials featuring women as key decision makers and leads the new HBS Models of Success initiative. She has also served as co-chair of the entrepreneurship faculty unit.

Hart has created a variety of executive and MBA courses including *The Entrepreneur's Tool Kit*; *Women Leading Business: An Executive Forum*; *Starting New Ventures* (with Marco Iansiti); *Women Building Business* (with Lynda Applegate); and *Building Business in the Context of a Life* (with Leslie

Perlow). She also developed *Charting Your Course: Working Options*, a refresher course for HBS alumnae. Harvard Business School has recognized her contributions with the Apgar Award for innovation in teaching and the Greenhill Award for faculty leadership.

Her interest in entrepreneurship comes from personal experience. In 1985, Hart joined Staples, Inc. as one of four founding officers. She was the company's Vice President of Operations during the early years and, in 1987, took over as Group Vice President of Growth and Development with responsibility for the company's geographic and business expansion. Prior to joining Staples, Hart was Director of Marketing for Star Market Company. She was also general manager of a family-owned residential and commercial real estate firm, Hart, Shaw & Company for several years. She is a director of eCornell and Texada Software and serves as advisor to start-up businesses in retailing, food service, technology, and financial services.

Professor Hart is Chair of the Center for Women's Business Research and serves on the advisory boards of Springboard New England and eMerging Women of the Commonwealth Institute and is a member of the Committee of 200. She is a Trustee of Cornell University and a member of the President's Council of Cornell Women. She has served on Harvard University's Advisory Council on Shareholder Responsibility, the Harvard Children's Health Initiative, and the Executive Committee of the Entrepreneurship Division of the Academy of Management. She received a BA in Government from Cornell University and completed her MBA and DBA at Harvard University.

8 reasons why you should read the Financial Times for 4 weeks RISK-FREE!

To help you stay current with significant
developments in the world economy ...
and to assist you to make informed business
decisions — the Financial Times brings you:

1 Fast, meaningful overviews of international affairs ... plus daily
briefings on major world news.

2 Perceptive coverage of economic, business, financial and political
developments with special focus on emerging markets.

3 More international business news than any other publication.

4 Sophisticated financial analysis and commentary on world market
activity plus stock quotes from over 30 countries.

5 Reports on international companies and a section on global investing.

6 Specialized pages on management, marketing, advertising and
technological innovations from all parts of the world.

7 Highly valued single-topic special reports (over 200 annually)
on countries, industries, investment opportunities, technology and more.

8 The Saturday Weekend FT section — a globetrotter's guide to
leisure-time activities around the world: the arts, fine dining, travel,
sports and more.

FT FINANCIAL TIMES
World business newspaper

The *Financial Times* delivers a world of business news.

Use the Risk-Free Trial Voucher below!

To stay ahead in today's business world you need to be well-informed on a daily basis. And not just on the national level. You need a news source that closely monitors the entire world of business, and then delivers it in a concise, quick-read format.

With the *Financial Times* you get the major stories from every region of the world. Reports found nowhere else. You get business, management, politics, economics, technology and more.

Now you can try the *Financial Times* for 4 weeks, absolutely risk free. And better yet, if you wish to continue receiving the *Financial Times* you'll get great savings off the regular subscription rate. Just use the voucher below.